CICELY

A recent portrait

CICELY

★ ★ ★ ★ ★ ★ ★ ★

By

Cicely Courtneidge

With 56 Illustrations

HUTCHINSON
Stratford Place
London

Hutchinson & Co. (Publishers) Ltd.
London   New York   Toronto
Melbourne   Sydney   Cape Town

First published 1953

Printed in Great Britain
by The Anchor Press, Ltd.,
Tiptree, Essex

CONTENTS

LIST OF ILLUSTRATIONS

I

First Entrance

Most people start writing a book when they are twenty, then they fall in love, get married, and the great work is forgotten. Others wait until they retire, start gardening, and the great work is again forgotten. These two types of potential authors are lucky. They know they have something interesting to say and, as they never get round to saying it, who can argue with them? But you can argue with me because now I have begun to tell you about myself, and I realize two things:

(1) That I have led and am still leading a very full and interesting life.

(2) That in order to write about myself I have to know the person I am writing about. It was not until I began to think seriously about this book that I realized how little I knew about myself. So, in a way, this is a voyage of discovery for me, too.

I am a practical person and I decided to set to work in the traditional way. The following letter was sent to *The Times*:

15 *South Audley Street,*
London, W.1.

To The Editor,
The Times,
Printing House Square,
*London, E.C.*4.
Dear Sir,
        I am collecting material for a biography of Miss Cicely Courtneidge, the actress. I would be most grateful if anyone who has any

*letters or anecdotes or other data about Miss Cicely Courtneidge, the
actress, would send them to me at the address above.*

                                        I remain, sir,
                                Your obedient servant,
                                        Cicely Courtneidge.

The Editor read the above letter and acted as though it was
important news from his Chief Foreign Correspondent. It was
printed a week later. The result was as I expected: the members
of Whites, Boodles, and, of course, the Athenaeum and the Bath,
took not the slightest notice. Their attitude is what has made
the British Empire what it is today. But upon one member of the
Public the result was instantaneous: a reply was sent by hand.
Here it is:

Dear Miss Courtneidge,
            With reference to your letter in The Times *asking for
details about the life of Miss Cicely Courtneidge, the actress. You ought
to know all about her by now.*

                                I remain, Madame,
                                Your obedient servant,
                                        Jack Hulbert.

*15 South Audley Street,
London, W.1.*

My husband is a comedian and like most comedians he is
usually very serious. He thought I should know all about myself,
and perhaps he was right, so I looked at my reflection in the
mirror and I said, "How do you do?" "Not badly," I replied.
"It's a lovely Spring morning."

Wilson is wagging his tail and asking to be taken out for a
walk. The Spring flowers are splashing the edges of Hyde Park
with colour. What a day to be out and about. I can walk up
Piccadilly, along Shaftesbury Avenue, to Cambridge Circus, to
the Saville Theatre where there is a big sign outside: *CICELY
COURTNEIDGE in Ivor Novello's last Musical 'GAY'S THE
WORD.'*

There are pictures of me in the front of the House, dancing,
laughing, and singing. If I walk round to the back of the theatre,
where the bombs have left ugly gaps like an angry dentist, I can

go through a modest little opening marked Stage Door; click-clack up a flight of grey stone stairs to another door marked Drury Lane.

This is my dressing-room. It is more than that—it is a second home. Inside it is papered with telegrams, hundreds of them, wishing me well on my first night. On the right there is a couch set against the wall where I rest in between my calls. If I lie down I can get a better look at the room. There are signed photographs of Noel Coward, Ivor Novello, Charles Cochran, Frank Morgan, Dorothy Ward, and many others in my own profession. There are also some photographs of my family.

If I look at this room what does it tell me about myself? That I am a successful Star in the West End of London? Yes, it tells me that. But what else? "Oh, I know." You see that photograph over there—that one of a small girl in a frilly frock and a bow in her hair? That's me—at least it was when I was eight—playing Peaseblossom in *A Midsummer Night's Dream*. The photograph is a little faded and, if I remember, the subject was a little frightened. It was my first speaking part.

But that photograph does not take me back to the beginning of my story because I began, like most people, by being born. I am not going to give you the exact date because there are some secrets I am determined to keep. Any actress who was born in the same year will tell you she is younger than I am. This is sometimes so confusing I have to look at my birth certificate to make quite sure I was born in the year I won't tell you.

But I can tell you that I happened in Australia, and that at the time King Edward was proving to the French that an Englishman knew at least as much as they did about *l'amour*. That a pound was made of gold. That Radio had not been invented even by the Russians. That the Wright Brothers had still to hop off the ground. That there were Archdukes a-plenty—a Kaiser with an ambitious moustache—and a young man called Winston Churchill beginning to make his way in the world. Rudyard Kipling was in India, Cecil Rhodes was in Africa, the English were in England and most other parts of the world as well, and, fortunately for me, Mr. Robert Courtneidge and his wife were in Australia.

The place I chose for my first entrance was Sydney, New South Wales. The time I selected was late summer and the date, April 1st. The day was hot, dry, and dusty, but I was not to be

put off, although I could not have chosen a more inconvenient
time as my father, who was principal comedian in a comic opera
called *Esmeralda*, had a first night on the same day and he knew
that the farmers, wool merchants, and prospectors who came into
the theatre, filling the plain wooden benches and few red plush
seats, were going to be hard to please. My mother was naturally
worrying for him, and he for her.

Before he left for the theatre he gave instructions that the
minute the Baby arrived the news was to be conveyed to him
without delay—and so it was—though not in the manner he
imagined. It happened half-way through the third scene of
Esmeralda when Mrs. Asche, the mother of Oscar Asche, who ran
the hotel where my father and mother were staying, arrived
outside the theatre. By this time it was dark, but the theatre,
although small, was not difficult to find. There were gas-jets
flaring outside to attract the eye to gaudy posters and hand-
written play-bills, and Mrs. Asche, following my father's instructions, favoured the direct approach. She walked straight into the
theatre and found herself in the audience.

An attendant approached her. "Sorry. No seats. You'll have
to stand at the back."

"I must speak to Mr. Courtneidge," she said, excitedly.

"It'll have to wait," said the attendant, "and you can't speak
to him from here. You'll have to go round-back and ask for him
at the stage-door."

"I've got an important message for him," she persisted,
raising her voice.

"Shush," said the attendant.

"Shush," echoed one of the paying public.

"Don't you shush me," said Mrs. Asche, her voice growing
louder. "Don't you shush me when I've come to tell Mr. Robert
Courtneidge his wife has just borne him a daughter."

This last piece of information was delivered in a shout which
caught the attention of the audience and of the artistes on the
stage, including my father.

He took off his straw hat, mopped his brow, came down to
the footlights and said: "Ladies and Gentlemen. I must apologize
for this interruption but you have just heard the news. I understand I am the father of a daughter who has the good fortune
to be born in one of the finest cities—in one of the finest

countries—in the world." This announcement was greeted with boisterous applause mingled with cheers and stamping of feet.

I HAD STOPPED THE SHOW.

I not only stopped the show, I was named after it, but as a result of enquiries I have made since I do not think this was because I was born on the first night.

Knowing my father's preoccupation with the Theatre, I suspect it happened something like this:

Mother (thinking of me): "What shall we call it?"

Father (thinking of the show): "It's been named already—Esmeralda."

Thanks to my mother I received a second name, Cicely, after my maternal grandmother, who sang in Grand Opera at Covent Garden.

My father thought after the first-night reception of *Esmeralda* that he was in for a long and successful Australian tour, but as the tour progressed he discovered he was wrong. The news of my arrival, which had won the sympathy of a first-night audience, was a bit of business which an astute comedian like my father should have repeated at every performance. *Esmeralda* did not do well enough to keep him in Australia, and so one day, when I was only a few months old, he decided to return to England and try his fortune there.

I do not remember anything about my first sea voyage, and I put this down to the method of packing sea-going babies in those days. It was done like this. They took one baby (in this instance—me), wrapped it in yards of flannel and, if they found this tiring, they took a rest—because there was more to come. The flannel was followed by yards of muslin. Despite the flannel and the muslin the baby was often still able to breathe. The baby-packers then completed the job by placing a thick veil over the baby's face. This was supposed to stop the baby from breathing in dust. In my case it nearly stopped the baby.

My first home in England was in Chorlton-cum-Hardy, a suburb of Manchester, where we had a tiny house which reflected the not so successful Australian tour of the comic opera *Esmeralda*. I realize now that a less successful tour might have meant theatrical lodgings off the Oxford Road. Don't think I am complaining about my start in life. It is true I did not like being called Esmeralda, but I had had the good sense to pick the right parents and this made up for Esmeralda.

My father had all the vitality, driving force, and imagination of the Northern Scot. He also had my mother. He ran the Theatre and she ran him. I always felt there was a perfect understanding between them. In the Theatre he could be fierce and seemingly intolerant because only the best was good enough. At home he knew that he got the best from my mother who, for all her gentle ways, had a good business head and great judgment in the Theatre; quite half of my father's success was due to her intuition. He was wrapped up in the Theatre. She was wrapped up in him. She ran his wardrobe, looked after his accounts, and the family. They were a good partnership.

When you are a child there is something safe, sure, and precise about your assessment of the people around you. It is as though you are equipped with an emotional radar. You cannot say, for example, why you feel security, but you know when it is there. I felt secure. I did not feel very close to my father because it was the way of a father, at the turn of the century, to maintain a relationship with his children which was a mixture of warmth and extreme dignity. He was there and he was the axis of my life. But how I wish he could have understood children better! Like all Victorian and Edwardian fathers, he was full of *clichés* about children. *I* must be seen and not heard, obedient, polite, respect my elders, sit up straight, eat what I was given, ask no questions, hear no lies, occupy my mind, and above all understand that Father knew best. But there were times when I found his best very hard to understand.

The first instance of this I can recall was shortly after we moved from our tiny house to a new one which had twin-stone lions guarding the front door. It was called Beech House and apart from the twin lions it had another sign that the Courtneidge family were on the up-and-up: a huge playroom which ran the entire length of the top storey, and here I played by myself until my father and mother had the good sense to provide me with a brother. His name was Charles. And by the time he arrived my name was Cicely.

It is an amazing thing to me how, when you peer into the past, something quite unexpected comes into sharp focus. I see, for instance, my mother dressing for the theatre and myself looking over the edge of the drawer to see which brooch she would choose from her jewel-case. I can hear Charles saying, proudly and loyally, to my father, when I was reported for being hopeless at arithmetic, that he was just as good. But my outstanding memory of Beech House is the day I nearly lost Father Christmas.

It was a cold, grey, and damp Christmas that year in Manchester at the end of the Gay 'Nineties, but Charles and I did not care about the weather. Christmas was a week of gas-lights, mountains of geese and turkeys hanging from the shop fronts, misty windows of toys and sweets, the shouts of the poultryman, be he inside a shop or out on a street stall. It was all noise, buying, bustling, secrets, paper rustling, and the smell of cooking in the house. We lived in a world of Christmas and if you had asked Charles or me where we were at that time we would probably have told you—instead of Manchester—"Christmas". We had a feeling of being on tip-toe with life all day long. We had done our shopping, tied our parcels, hidden them in cupboards, taken them out, fingered and re-written—re-tied and hidden—them again. It was a wonderful world to live in until one of my friends, who was a few years older, asked me a question:

"Do you believe in Father Christmas?"

"Of course I do."

"Why?"

"Don't you?"

"No, of course not. It's your father."

"Who told you?"

"I caught my father at it."

"Not really?"

"Cross my heart. You don't really think that one man could go to every house in the world in one night, delivering toys, unless it was Fathers."

I thought this over and I must say that I wavered, and then, with more heart crossings, I was convinced. It was all a trick. There was no Father Christmas. I was angry and sad. I told Charles and he was even sadder. I told my father and if I had only known it at the time he was the saddest one of all.

He said: "So we don't believe in Father Christmas any more? Well, let me tell you, Father Christmas doesn't call on people who don't believe in him."

Charles and I were shocked. It was one thing saying we did

not believe in Father Christmas but another being proved right. We decided, without discussion, that we had gone too far. It was only two days before Christmas and during this time Charles and I prayed more insistently than any two children have ever prayed before, and when we came to "God Bless Father," and "God Bless Mother," we added in a loud voice, "AND GOD BLESS FATHER CHRISTMAS." This was said so that it could be heard all over the house.

Christmas Eve arrived. Up in the big bedroom my brother and I had our hip-bath in front of the coal fire. Outside we could hear the clop-clop of the horses on the stone-paved streets, the clang of trams, the shouts of the still busy shopkeepers. We lay for a long time in the darkness, whispering to each other, hoping and wondering whether all was well. At last we slept, only to wake as first light peeped through the open Venetian blinds.

We crawled to the bottom of the bed where two woollen stockings hung, tied over the brass rail. *They Were Empty*. Not even an orange.

We shivered, our bare feet on the green linoleum.

"There's nothing," I choked. *"He hasn't come."*

"Perhaps it's too early. Perhaps it's not morning yet," said Charles.

But we both knew it was morning. I do not know how long we cried, or whether we fell asleep again. I do know that for us the star of the year had fallen.

At breakfast my father sat in his usual place at the head of the table as though nothing had happened. Indeed this was only too true. Mother had hardly a word to say. She kept looking at us and then at my father and I sensed that something had made her sad too. After the meal we went to church and I told Charles, who, with his fair curls, looked as white as a ghost, that I thought we had nothing to lose by having another shot at praying. We prayed so hard and so loudly that my father and mother were embarrassed, and the rest of the congregation intrigued that the Lord's Prayer had become an appeal to Father Christmas.

On our return home it was my mother who came to the rescue.

Quite unexpectedly, she said, "Sometimes Father Christmas calls to see children on his way back from giving presents—if they have been very good all day."

An early photograph

The young lady on the extreme left is Peaseblossom

A family portrait. (LEFT TO RIGHT) Self,
Mother, Charles, and Rosaline

And bang on the cue, with a promptness which was unrealistic, came a mighty off-stage rattle of fire-irons and coal-scuttle.

"That must be HIM on the roof," said my mother.

We raced for the stairs, but before we could reach the drawing-room door our Christmas presents came tumbling down into the grate.

Charles and I ought to have cheered but the situation had been held too long. We had been punished for doubting the existence of Father Christmas and nothing anyone could do would make up for it—even if Father knew best. We gathered up our presents and said: "Thank you. Thank you for being so good," and ran to our room and cried. They were my first bitter tears. I had to blame someone other than myself, so I blamed my father. Charles blamed me.

I did not know Father had followed us into the room until I heard his voice.

He said, "Why are you crying?"

"I don't know."

"Oh yes you do. You have destroyed something without having anything to put in its place."

"But I do believe in Father Christmas. I promise I do."

"So do I," he said, patted me on the hand, brushed his lips against my hair, and left. Perhaps he wanted to say he was sorry. But he did not know how.

For years I had nightmares about that Christmas. Why had Father done it? Would he do it again? Why hadn't he understood how important it was to have stockings filled? Why did it matter whether we believed in Father Christmas or not?

I am afraid I never quite forgave Father for that particular punishment though I know he thought it was a good and fitting one. I was to experience many other instances of my father's determination to do what he thought was right. In the Theatre I was to discover he had good reason for thinking he knew how to handle people. After all, he became the most successful theatrical manager of his generation and possibly in the history of the British Theatre. He believed he owed a great deal of this success to the discipline he maintained in the Theatre. This may have been true, but at home he should have been guided by Mother.

B

II

Manchester

I CLAIM I was as bad at school as Winston Churchill. I know this is a very bold claim, but I'll go further: my record was even worse than his and I was consistent. My father was not the type to give up easily, and he sent me to many different schools but right up until the time I left, when I was sixteen, my record was always the same: as a scholar I was nowhere. Nothing inspired me to do this. Like Winston Churchill's absorbing interest in English. My bad scholarships seemed to come naturally. Just as some children have a tremendous capacity for learning, so I had apparently an equal capacity for taking nothing in. I think that this was so highly developed in me I fascinated my teachers so that when my lessons were over and they retired to the Common Room they would vie with one another to see who could produce the best story of the hopeless case of Esmeralda Courtneidge.

I can vouch for, at least, one of the stories they probably told in the Common Room. It happened during a history class with a mistress who was not only new to the school but was having her first experience of me. She started off on what must have seemed a reasonable proposition. How much did her class know? She had only to ask to find out. She asked me. I knew nothing. She had obviously not been warned and imagined I was not in earnest. She addressed the entire class, but in reality she knew, they knew, and I knew, that she was speaking to one person.

"Young ladies," she said, "your papas send you to school to learn, and it is my task—nay, more than that—it is my duty, to see that you acquire some knowledge. It is possible, of course, that some of you, through greater diligence, are more forward than others. But it is not possible, however backward you may be, to have no knowledge whatsoever. I repeat—it is not possible to be completely without knowledge."

Here she looked at me, and I looked at the girl sitting behind.

"It is now nearly time for break," she went on, "but I would be failing in my duty if I permitted you to break until you have *all* answered *one* simple question correctly."

Once again she looked at me, and once again I looked at the girl behind.

The mistress now turned to the blackboard and there she wrote a number of dates. Nothing complicated, mind you, just dates in history giving the comings and goings of kings and the battles they fought. Then she gave each one of us a date to memorize, wiped the blackboard clean, and said: "Now you know the answer to the question I am going to ask, so all you have to do, as a class, is to give me your answer and then you may *all* go. If anyone fails to answer correctly then the *entire* class stays behind. Is that understood?"

We nodded, silently, and she proceeded.

One by one she asked her questions and one by one the answers came back pat. I was near to the end, just after 1066. She paused when she came to me. Victory was in her grasp. "Now tell me," she said, gently, "tell me, Esmeralda, what is the next date after 1066?" She looked at me, waiting.

I looked right back at her. "1067," I said.

There was a hush and something very near to a moan escaped her lips as her pointer clattered to the floor. "Class dismiss," she muttered. She was defeated.

I wish I could have told my father why I failed him at school, but even if I had I do not think he would have understood. He believed in regimentation and I hated it. I hated the drab uniforms with the endless rows of buttons, the ugly lace-up boots, but most of all being poured into a mould. Mind you, I am talking of over forty years ago when it would have been an amazing proposition to suggest that children were individuals and that they should be treated as such.

Those were the good old days, when children of eight were sent to work in the mills, down the mines, in the factories, for a few shillings a week. I should have considered myself one of the lucky ones. I may not have liked the rigidness of schooling in those days, but at least my father was trying to give me what he had missed. He was self-taught. His mother, who was left penniless with two children, had to go out to work for three shillings and sixpence a week. She could not afford to furnish a room or even provide a bed. They slept on straw which covered an earthen floor. When you consider this background it was not unreasonable for him to be perplexed, as he made his way in the world, that his daughter failed to take advantage of the opportunity he was giving her.

He might not have felt so badly if I had been able to offset my poor scholarship with good sportsmanship. Oh yes, even in those days young ladies played games, with decorum, mind you, but games, nevertheless. Only too well I recall those spiffing games of hockey.

I remember how we used to go to the playing fields well dressed for the fray—thick woollen stockings, the ever faithful lace-up boots, knee-length tunics, and velour hats jammed down over our eyes. The captain of my team was a jolly good sort. She knew, bless her, where the weakness of the team lay. It lay with me. She used to say, hopeful, enthusiastic, optimistic, hearty back-slapper that she was: "Now for heaven's sake, old girl, play up today. Remember, keep calm. Don't make a mess of it. All you have to do is to keep your head."

All I had to do? What fiddle-faddle! As if I wanted to lose my head. It was the others who were so wanton in their recklessness. At one moment they were a collection of quite nice young girls until they were transformed, when a whistle blew, and some soppy date yelled, "Up the School!"

Prior to all this, a foolish games mistress had armed these normally inoffensive girls with large sticks which they seemed to use for the purpose of hitting one another. It is true that in those days, as in these, hockey was played with a ball. But this did not help when they hit the ball, which was very hard, and nearly always hit me. And even if they missed the ball they still hit me. I had a reasonable instinct for self-preservation and I spent my time trying to keep out of the way. Unfortunately, I was not as successful in this as I would have liked and they often caught up with me.

Once the captain said, in exasperation, "Really, Cicely, what sort of a game do you think you are playing?"

I retreated out of range of her hockey stick, and I said firmly,

"I will crack the next person on the shins who comes near me."
I must have looked very determined even as a twelve-year-old.
I was dropped from the team. And a jolly good thing, too.

I suppose by this time you are saying to yourself I was such
a hopeless case at school you would not have paid my fees. No
good at learning. No good at sport. Was there anything the girl
could do well? There was. I was the best day-dreamer of my school,
and long before Mr. Thurber recorded *The Secret Life of Walter
Mitty* there was the secret life of Esmeralda Cicely Courtneidge.
Of course, some of my dreams were as you would expect, about
myself in the Theatre. These dreams always had the same ending.
An enormous basket of flowers was handed to me on the stage by
my leading man, who was invariably played by my brother Charles.
I always asked him the same question. "Who are they from?"

And he always gave me the same answer. "Look at the card."
I did so and it read, *'From your greatest admirer—Father.'*

My daydreams at school seemed, at the time, so ridiculous
I kept them to myself in case anyone should think I was not only
a stupid child but also quite mad. You see, my dream school
was light and sunny, with walls of egg-shell blue, enormous
windows through which the sun could beam and you could see
the trees and the flowers outside. The classroom was bright with
the colours of the different dresses we were wearing, and a pretty
young school-mistress was talking to me as though she was
interested in what I was thinking. And sometimes I would be the
only girl in the class, but I did not feel lonely because there was
the school-mistress, smiling at me, and saying as though she really
meant it, "Tell me, Cicely—what would you like to do?"

My dream was no more detailed than that, just an impression,
as dreams often are, but a definite impression of a School World
that was light, happy, and free. Above all, a place where I *wanted*
to be. Usually a rap on the knuckles from a ruler brought me back
to reality, and there I was, with my fellow-sufferers, ruling
margins, listening to endless and unexplained facts, writing them
down, walking along silent corridors, plaiting my long curls,
sitting in straight rows, listening to the interminable orders in
a grey, unhappy, confined world, where I *never wanted* to be.

Another part of the Secret Life of Esmeralda Cicely Courtneidge
I used to enjoy concerned my life at home and this dream was
equally improbable. I would imagine myself arriving home from

school determined to see my father, to tell him, once and for all, what was on my mind. Of course, he was not there. He was at the theatre. But this did not deter me, and I would tell my mother that *I had* to see him, run outside, hail a hansom, and say to the driver, "Take me to Mr. Robert Courtneidge." Never the name of the theatre, mark you, but just "Take me to Mr. Robert Courtneidge."

When I arrived at the theatre I was always told my father was busy, but I would insist, "Tell him his daughter wishes to see him." My father would then appear and I would begin: "Father, you know I am going to be an actress. Well, I think it would help if I spent as much time in the theatre as possible."

At first he would say, as he did in real life: "Cicely, you are only a child, and childhood is not for amusement. You must work, *work*, WORK."

I would reply, "I'll work a great deal harder if you let me do more of what I want to do."

He would say, as he so often did, "You can only be successful if your life is properly regulated, my child."

And I would reply, boldly, as I never did, "Father, my life is so regulated, from the minute I open my eyes in the morning until I close them at night, I feel I am in some sort of prison"— and before he could reply I would add, quickly: "May I have some money, please?"

"But, Cicely," he would say, "you've had your pocket money for this week."

"I know, Father, but twopence doesn't go far and I've got a hansom waiting."

He would be astonished at my extravagance, and then roar with laughter, give me a florin, and say: "You've certainly got a mind of your own. You are a real daughter of your father. I've been so busy making a success of things in the Theatre, what with all the pantomimes I'm putting on, that I have not realized you were unhappy. In future, I promise, I am going to see you have some time to yourself, and so long as you work well you may do what you like, even come to the theatre."

Then I would kiss him and take the hansom back to Mother, where I would announce, "Father and I have just had a talk and he quite understands my point of view."

My mother would say: "I knew he would, Cicely. You only had to talk to him."

And thereabouts the dream would be over because in reality I would not have dared to approach him in this way and even if I had I am quite sure the result would have been different.

If anyone spared the rod and spoilt the child it was not Robert Courtneidge, and no whim of mine was allowed to interfere with the railway-like time-table which governed my life. When I reached home from afternoon school there were hours of dancing, elocution, and singing. The spirit in my case was strong, but the flesh was weak. I was anaemic, a disability I seemed to share with many of my contemporaries, and on reflection I think that one of the major achievements of my youth is that I survived the treatment for anaemia popular at the time.

Father was so concerned with my paleness and refusal to put on weight that he also added some treatment of his own. "Physical exercises . . . that's what the child needs . . . healthy physical exercises first thing in the morning . . . soon build her up . . . look at me." And so they began. Though a small, slight man, my father was wholeheartedly in favour of the craze for cold water and early morning exercises. To this end he engaged an instructor to come and put him through it each morning. And now I was to be added to his self-inflicted torture. "A fit mind in a fit body" was my father's slogan at the time. He couldn't do much for my mind but he was now determined to do something for my body.

Every morning he rose at seven-thirty. First a cold splash, breaking the ice in the jug when necessary, and then it was the turn of the instructor, who opened the windows, and through the walls I could hear: "One, Two, Three, Four, Five, Six, Seven, Eight . . . Inhale . . . Exhale . . . bend forward . . . bend sideways . . . bend back. One, Two, Three, Four. . . ." For half an hour this would continue and then it was my turn. First a cold splash, then dressed in long black woollen stockings, a liberty bodice, gym bloomers, and blouse, I was ready for my torturer.

Unfortunately the instructor was also ready for me. "Cum on, Cicely," he used to say, in broad Lancashire. "Head-up . . . shoulders down . . . chest out . . . stomach in . . . inhale . . . exhale." After a minute or so of this he would stop and look at me, curiously. "Are you breathing?" he would enquire.

"Oh yes!" I replied. "I'm breathing very hard."

"It doesn't notice," he said.

"Doesn't it?" I said.

"No," he affirmed.

I was encouraged. "Do you mean to say I can breathe and that you really can't tell?"

"Apart from the fact that you are alive, no one would know you were breathing."

I thought this was very clever on my part and I went up in my own estimation, but the instructor did not share my view. Deep breathing, or in my case, shallow, was usually followed by stretching and bending exercises until my back ached and my arms and my legs felt limp. Then, my instructor would exclaim, "For Heaven's sake, put tha' hand straight and bend down proper-like—tha' can bend down, can't tha'?"

"No," I would pant, "I can't bend down. I'm too tired."

Sometimes my father would visit us on a tour of inspection, and as the door opened my chest would go up, my shoulders down, and my stomach in. I might try to take things easily with the instructor, but not with Father. He would soon put a stop to it—or, far worse, order another half-hour. Why, when Father was present the instructor could even see me breathing.

Father's physical training cure for my anaemia so appalled me I used to put my heart and soul into the part of acting the bonny girl. I tried to overcome my paleness with five minutes of pinching and slapping my cheeks outside the dining-room so that I could make an entrance with a scarlet face to say a hearty "Good morning." My thinness I could not disguise. I just hoped it would go unnoticed; but it never did. Suddenly, in the middle of a meal, Father would say: "Come here, child . . . stand up and let me look at you . . . you're as thin as a whistle . . . what are we going to do with you? . . . We must get some colour into those cheeks of yours . . . Mother, give her a second helping of rice pudding at once." As pale as I was, I blanched at this suggestion, and can you blame me? Before the meal my anaemia had already been treated with two glasses of milk, boiled eggs, and doses of iron medicine sucked through a straw. This was reinforced at meal-times with all the food I most disliked: hunks of underdone meat, soggy vegetables, milk puddings, prunes, and more eggs. I do not mean to be disrespectful to chickens. I know they try very hard to please, but they never pleased me. I hated their eggs more than anything else. And my mother discovered that eggs, poached, boiled, fried, scrambled, or otherwise disguised, still tasted and looked like eggs to me. It is for this reason that even today I can never really feel friendly to chickens.

Neither the food, eggs included, nor the exercises improved my health. The real trouble was I was working too hard and growing too fast, and quite apart from my school and stage training, Father had organized a nightly appearance for me in the first act of his musical *Tom Jones*, an adaptation of Fielding's novel, which he had written with A. M. Thompson, with music by Sir Edward German. And for this I was taken to the theatre, where I appeared in the chorus, spoke three lines, and was then rushed home to bed long before the show was over.

It was round about this period that something very wonderful happened. My mother gave birth to a daughter who was named Rosaline, and from the first I loved my sister very much. Somehow the new arrival broke into the routine of our household and for me there was an added interest in life. I already had my brother Charles to boss and now I could fuss and pet over my sister; and I was grateful for this because I had very few friends and little opportunity for making any.

During the next two years Mother noticed the change Rosaline's arrival had made in me and remarked upon it to Father. She said, "I think Cicely's health is beginning to improve."

"Do you?" said my father. "I cannot subscribe to that opinion. But don't worry—I have some plans for her."

I wondered if this was going to mean a change in school, diet, or physical training instructor.

"My plans for Cicely," continued my father, "concern Switzerland. Now what do you think of that? I have arranged to send her to school there, in Lausanne. There she will have mountain air, walks round the lakes, good food, and a well-disciplined life that will make all the difference to her health. Tell me, Cicely, what more could you want?"

I could have told him that I wanted to stay at home with Charles and my baby sister, but the words would not come. I tried to remember what I had learnt about Switzerland and wished I had been better at geography because I could not picture where it was, only that it was somewhere far away.

Suddenly, I felt lonely.

And that is something you can feel very deeply, particularly at fourteen.

III

"The Arcadians"

★

At fifteen, after two years in Switzerland, apart from the holidays, my schooldays were over and I came home for good. The relief and joy at my astonishing good luck made me laugh from Lausanne to Victoria Station. "Now," I thought "no more rules, lessons, or do's and don'ts. Here I come, the great actress, to enchant you all." And when I said "Great Actress" I meant exactly that. I had no ambition to be a comedienne. I really believed I was grown-up, free, and the world was mine.

How wrong I was. How utterly and completely wrong. The world was by no means mine, and, more important, neither was I free in any way at all. The world was my father's and everything I did, thought, or said, from now on, was still to be organized by him. He was no longer the struggling actor. He was more than up and coming. He had taken over the management of the Royal and Prince's Theatres, Manchester, and the reputation he had already won with his Shakespearian productions had brought him offers to join the two great actor-managers of the day, Sir Herbert Tree and Sir George Alexander. Father determined to remain his own master and launch out on his own in London, where he was already living when I arrived home from Lausanne.

At first he wanted to continue in London with his Shakespearian productions, but as the opportunity did not present itself he turned to musical plays. The first production of his own in London was *The Blue Moon*, by Harold Ellis and A. M. Thompson, with a score by Howard Talbot and Paul Rubens. It was very successful and the cast included Billie Burke, who was later to marry the great Flo Ziegfeld and become an international film star. He followed this at the Apollo Theatre with another musical play, *The Dairymaids*. He collaborated on the book with A. M. Thompson, and he had another success. In the case of *The Dairymaids* there were two very beautiful young girls. How I envied and admired them; Phyllis Dare, who was so modest and unassuming, and still is, and Dorothy Ward, who played a small part with tremendous vivacity, and who is still playing leading parts with the same vivacity.

The great theatrical figure at this time, during the early part of the century, was the fabulous George Edwardes. He was a big, handsome man, with most charming manners, and when I heard Mother say one evening that he was coming to dinner I waited, at the top of the stairs, in my nightgown, and rushed to the banisters to see him arrive. As the maid took his hat and coat he caught sight of me, and I blushed and was about to retreat when he said, "If you'd like to come down and introduce yourself, young lady, I'm quite prepared to lend you my coat."

I ran for my life in case Father overheard.

Evidently he and Father got on very well that evening because they went into partnership at the Adelphi Theatre, and afterwards they produced *The Duchess of Danzig*, a play, rather curiously called *The Devil*, and a pantomime, *Cinderella*. Everything that George Edwardes did was warm and lavish. I hoped that he and Father would form a permanent partnership, but after the three shows I have mentioned Father decided on the greatest gamble of his life, and he decided to gamble alone. He took a lease of the Shaftesbury Theatre, which no longer exists, as it received a direct hit during the first year of the last war, and spent £12,000, a great deal of money even in those days, upon reconstructing the auditorium. He opened at the Shaftesbury with a musical comedy, of which he was part-author, called *The Arcadians*. This was against the advice of most of his friends and all the members of the cast. The reason for this was that *The Arcadians* was based on fantasy and there was a strong prejudice, in the musical comedy world, against this type of plot.

I remember Father coming home one day during the early stages of rehearsal and saying to Mother: "I've lost Alfred Lester. He's walked out on me."

This was disaster. Alfred Lester had been engaged to play the part of Peter Doody, the jockey, and was the leading comedian.

I remember my mother saying, hopelessly, "Have you looked

everywhere?" as though Alfred was hiding in a cupboard or under a bed. In fact, Father found him hiding in Devonshire, and he had to reason with him until three o'clock one morning before he grudgingly consented to return to rehearsals.

The whole family went to the first night. Mother, Charles, Rosaline, and I sat in Father's box, breathless and silent, keeping our eyes only for the stage. We felt the importance of every single moment of that first night, and I sensed exactly what Father and Mother were feeling. They had no need to worry. *The Arcadians* was an immediate and huge success.

I still have a copy of *Play Pictorial*. B. W. Findon tells the story of *The Arcadians* far better than I can under the heading of 'A Feast of Melody and Mirth'. He says:

"Mr. Courtneidge is without a superior. The scenery, the grouping, and the general stage effects are pictures of delight for the eye, and do full justice to the entertaining book provided by Messrs. Mark Ambient and A. M. Thompson and the charming and consistently melodious music composed by Messrs. Lionel Monckton and Howard Talbot, who have been well fitted with lyrics by Mr. Arthur Wimperis. A more exquisite and amusing entertainment than *The Arcadians* has not been seen since the days when genuine comic opera was the vogue; and the Shaftesbury Theatre, the interior of which has been reconstructed and redecorated out of all recognition, should be crowded nightly for many a month to come.

The central motive is Gilbertian in its whimsicality and the adroitness with which it is developed. In the first act a romantic glade in Arcadia, an exquisite sylvan scene, we see the sudden appearance of Mr. Joseph Smith, a prosaic restaurant proprietor with a passion for aeroplanes. He exhibits no less surprise than the bewitching Arcadians and in the course of mutual explanations he tells a lie, whereupon he is immersed in the Well of Truth, from which he emerges in the scanty costume of Arcadia, with a luxuriant head of hair and minus the mutton-chop whiskers which previously adorned his face.

It is then decided by the beautiful and enthusiastic Sombra that he, now christened Simplicitas, shall in company with her and the pretty Chrysea, descend to earth to 'set up the truth in England for evermore, and banish the lie'. They begin their crusade at Askwood races, where naturally they cause considerable curiosity, being still clothed in the costumes of Arcady. Here Simplicitas meets his wife, who, not recognizing her husband, proceeds to fall in love with the young stranger, which gives rise to much comic business between Mr. Dan Rolyat and Miss Ada Blanche.

Then comes the opportunity for Simplicitas to distinguish himself. The jockey who was to have ridden The Deuce has been savaged by that ill-tempered animal and Sombra arranges that Simplicitas shall take his mount. The Arcadians have the gift of speech with animals, and at the approach of Simplicitas the brute becomes as gentle as a lamb. An exciting and extremely well managed description of the race follows, and Simplicitas with his arms around the horse's neck rides in a winner to the great satisfaction of its owner, Jack Meadows, who has staked his all on the event, including the hand and heart of Eileen Cavanagh, who has for her representative Miss Phyllis Dare, with a most piquant Irish brogue and captivating manner.

In the next act we are taken to the Arcadian restaurant, which has become the rage of London, and where the diet is that of the simple life, which is more than can be said of Simplicitas, who is having, as he says, 'the time of his life', but in endeavouring to explain the reason of an all night absence tells a lie, and he is again immersed, and reappears as Mr. Smith, with his bald head and shaggy whiskers, to the astonishment and somewhat to the confusion of his wife. Such, briefly, is the outline of a story which gives capital opportunities to all concerned.

The daintiest performance in the piece is the Sombra of Miss Florence Smithson, who bears herself like a Peri and sings like an angel. A sweeter and more unforced voice has never been heard on the musical comedy stage. Her success was immense. Another excellent vocalist is Mr. Harry Welchman, who may be described as the love hero of the plot. There are two master comedians in the company. Mr. Dan Rolyat sings and plays in his own inimitable manner as Smith and keeps the audience in roars of laughter, while Mr. Alfred Lester, as the saddest-hearted jockey who has never won a

race, is equally amusing. His song, 'I've gotter motter—always
merry and bright' is one of the funniest things in the piece,
which is brimming over with humorous entertainment. Miss
Ada Blanche is very diverting as Mrs. Smith. There is not
a weak spot in the cast."

I also felt there was not a weak spot in the cast but this did
not prevent me from making a vow that I would get into *The
Arcadians* somehow. I had to be part of that music and wonder
and magic.

The Arcadians proved to be my father's greatest money-
spinner, and to this day it is still earning vast royalties throughout
the world.

Nearly twelve months after the first night I heard that someone
had fallen out of the show through illness, and there was a
vacancy in the chorus. I thought this was a good opportunity
to speak to my father. On the morning in question I dressed
quickly and ran downstairs, hoping to catch him before he left
the house for the theatre. But he had risen earlier than usual and
was already on his way down to the office at the Shaftesbury.
I asked Mother if he would be back for lunch and she said: "I
don't expect so. He has a very busy day ahead and he probably
won't be back until after the show tonight."

There was only one thing to do, and that was to see him at the
office.

Before I set out I rehearsed, in front of his study chair, what
I would say. I played both parts.

Me (gaily and without a care in the word): "Good morning,
      Father. I'm so pleased that you're having such a won-
      derful success."

Me (gruffly): "Sit down, my dear Cicely. I've been wanting to
      have a quiet chat with you ever since we opened, but I
      just haven't had the time."

Me (eyelashes fluttering): "Oh, I quite understand, Father.
      First nights and settling down and all that. I don't think
      there can be any doubt that you're in for a long run. But
      what I've really come to see you about is myself. After
      all, I *have* left school, and I'm just as old as some of the
      girls in the show, and I'm sure I've had more training.

So, please, Father, now that someone has dropped out—
please—give me a chance."

ME (gruffly—but leaping at the opportunity of engaging *Me*):
"Why, of course, my child. As a matter of fact if you
had not brought up the subject I would have done so.
You must start rehearsals straightaway."

ME (graciously): "Oh, thank you, Father! You have made me
the happiest girl in the world."

I was running through my idea of how I wanted the interview
to go when my mother, who had overheard my voice, and then
my imitation of Father, walked in to find me alone, speaking to
an empty chair. "I'm going to ask Father for a job," I explained,
hurriedly.

Mother smiled. "Why not wait until he comes home, or,
better still, leave it to me to tell him what's in your mind?"

But when I insisted there was not a moment to lose she let
me go. I did not waver in my purpose until I was actually in the
corridor outside his office.

This was my first experience of a theatrical manager's office
during the run of a major success. There was a hungry crowd of
people already waiting to see my father—although it was still
early in the morning. Telephones were going, and there was a
constant coming and going of people, an excited undertone to
their conversation. And as the office door opened and closed
I could hear the sound of my father's voice and, "Yes, Guv'nor";
"No, Guv'nor"; "Straightaway, Guv'nor."

I waited, unnoticed, for about a quarter of an hour, my
resolution ebbing with the minutes. I was just about to go when
my father came to the door, saw me, and said: "Oh, Cicely! What
are you doing here?"

"I've come to see you?" I said, weakly.

"I'm afraid I'm very busy," he began.

"But it's terribly important," I said.

"You had better come in," he replied.

If he was surprised to see me he did not betray himself. I
hardly waited for the office door to close behind us before I
blurted out the purpose of my visit.

"Father, please give me a job in *The Arcadians*. I know I won't
fail you."

There was a silence. He looked down at his desk and then at me. I tried to smile. And still he did not speak.

"I heard there was a vacancy in the chorus," I said.

"So that's what you've come about," he said, flatly. "I'm afraid that at present you're wasting your time and mine. One day, Cicely, I will be able to say that you are ready to take your place on the professional stage, but in my humble opinion that day has not yet arrived. I assure you, my dear child, that when it does I will be the first person to tell you so, but until then there is only one course open to you, and that is to go on working and learning, making yourself proficient in every department of your chosen profession."

"But, Father," I protested, "I've been training since I was six. How much longer do I have to wait?"

"That I cannot say," he replied. "It is entirely a matter of what progress you make, and that depends, as you should know, upon self-discipline and application. Now remember the advice I have given you and on your way out tell my secretary I want to see him. Good morning, Cicely."

I took a penny horse-bus along Regent Street, got off at Baker Street, and walked the rest of the way home to St. John's Wood. It would be an understatement to say that I was frustrated. If you had seen a long-faced, slender, delicate-looking girl, with far too many curls, walking past Lord's Cricket Ground in the year 1910 and remarked that she looked as though she was crying, then you would have been right. I was in tears and I could not stop them. They were tears not of self-pity, but of anger, salted with desperation. Training! Self-discipline! Application! I had never known anything else from the age of six and I saw visions of all the training to which I had been submitted.

There was Edward Royce, my first dancing teacher, who had made dancing seem all aches and pains. He 'broke-me-in' and 'turned-me-out', limbering with legs well over the shoulder, and if they didn't go naturally then Teddy would force them up, higher and higher. My early years of training were often agony. I always had plenty of vitality but I was never strong, and dancing had been only a small part of my training; there were deportment, elocution, singing and music lessons, and this had gone on—an unrelenting programme of discipline and application—for eleven years. And all my father had to say

In the chorus of *Tom Jones*

As I appeared in
Princess Caprice

Sometimes I find
time to go riding

A young
undergraduate I had
yet to meet

to me when I asked him for a job was in effect that "I was not ready".

All right. I told myself I would go on training. I, too, could be stubborn. If he did not think I was sufficiently trained at the age of sixteen, then I would go on training until I was an old woman. Then he might be sorry that he had left it too late. Too late? What a terrible thought! But I consoled myself that if he did not notice me in time someone else surely would. I was not going to be one of those flowers which are 'born to blush unseen'. If I was going to blush, then I wanted an audience.

By the time I reached home I was filled with a fanatical determination to show my father what I could do. I think my mother and sister Rosaline were puzzled to see a rather fixed smile on my face. "Everything's all right," I said; "it's just a matter of waiting a little longer." And then I went straight into the music-room. There was, after all, no time to be lost. I sat down at the piano.

I must explain here that although I had practised the piano at least an hour a day for years, I was not accurate. I went at the piano with gusto, banging down the wrong notes, stamping down the pedals, but to me the noise was wonderful. My singing was better than my playing, but the combination must have sounded dreadful because after a few minutes Mother came into the room, followed by Rosaline.

She waited until I had finished, and then she said, "Are you sure everything is quite all right, Cicely?"

"Of course it is," I affirmed.

"Then what are you doing?" she asked.

"I'm just following Father's advice," I replied.

From then on the only moments of my life which were not given up to a rigid schedule of training were the moments of eating and sleeping. I had not lost sight of *The Arcadians* and I had seen it as many times as I could persuade my father to allow me. Just after my sixteenth birthday I asked Harry Gratton, who was a friend of the family, and also a well-known producer, to give me an opinion of my work. I sang for him, and he did more than give me an opinion. He sent for my mother, and I had to sing the number again. It was a catchy tune out of *The Arcadians* called 'I like London. I like Town'.

Mother was astounded at the progress I had made. She went

off to find Father. I sang it again and again for him. He did not openly share the enthusiasm of Mother and Harry Gratton, but at least he did say: "Cicely, though there is plenty of room for improvement, I may be able to find a job for you. I will see you in my office."

When I went to see him at the theatre I thought it was to begin in the chorus. I did not know that one of the cast had left the Company to get married and Father had been struggling for some time to improve a dull understudy. I sat waiting for my call while he was losing patience rehearsing her. Suddenly he caught sight of a familiar face looking eagerly at him, and he walked over to me and said, "Do you think you could do it?"

"I'll try, Father," I said.

In four days I was ready, and made my first appearance on the London stage. The number I sang was, 'I like London. I like Town', and I was, naturally, elated when it was encored, so I believe was Father, because he said, "That is the first time there's been an encore for the number since the show opened." That was praise indeed. Naturally, in my first real part with my first successful song, I felt on top of the world. My salary was £5 a week. But I was not allowed to handle this. Father gave me £2, and the rest went on Academy fees, savings bank, and insurance. Out of my £2 I had to buy all my clothes, pay my tips at the theatre, my bus fares home, and any extras such as meals, cups of tea, and so on. The biggest item was clothes. I not only had to dress smartly, as an actress, but as the daughter of an important theatrical producer.

The fact that I was earning my own living did not bring any measure of independence. Life was still organized by Father. Up at 8 a.m.; physical jerks 8–8.30 a.m.; breakfast at 9 a. m. Then a bus to the Royal Academy of Music, and then on to Espinosa for dancing, home to lunch and an hour's rest in the afternoon. In the evening there was the theatre and at night there was bed. And in the morning, – – – – – Oh yes! You know about that. And so it went on. I have not mentioned picnics, supper parties, or any other form of relaxation, for the very good reason there was none. But all work and no play did not make for a dull life. I was far too happy now that I was in the theatre.

I soon realized that if I had thought Father a martinet at home, it was nothing to the discipline he imposed in the theatre.

Punctuality was one of the tenets of his life and there was no such thing as an excuse for being late, no matter how valid. He expected everyone to be on the stage five minutes before a call so that as soon as he walked into the theatre rehearsals could start. Once he called us at ten o'clock, on a morning when there was a real old-fashioned pea-souper fog. The sort you seldom see these days except in Hollywood thrillers set in London. On that day it was useless to call a hansom or board a bus, as the horses could not see in front of their nosebags. I set out early and fumbled my way from St. John's Wood to the Shaftesbury, but despite my efforts I was late; but not as late as the rest of the cast. I was the first to arrive. Not quite the first, for there was my father in the auditorium, waving his watch at the stage manager.

"Here I am, my boy," he shouted, angrily, "sword in hand" —and then he waved towards the empty stage—"and no bloody army."

After I had been in the show for a few months I was given the part of understudy to Phyllis Dare, who was playing the lead. It was shortly after this that Phyllis, who had not missed a performance for twelve months, asked Father for a holiday. He agreed, but asked her to await the arrival in England of an Australian girl. Father had not seen the girl himself, but had had very good reports of her, and thought she might prove a great discovery. When he met this unlucky girl, who arrived, complete with an escort of a mother and two aunts, he at once told her that she did not walk, or speak, or dress the way he wanted. But her voice was not too bad. She was a willing girl and ready to learn.

Out came the hoops.

And for the next few weeks she had a taste of the routine I had known for so many years. From eight in the morning, physical jerks, and then elocution, deportment, singing, dancing, until it was time for bed. She was wonderful. She was blessed with a fine physique which now stood her in good stead. The time was fast approaching for Phyllis's holiday when, one morning at rehearsal, Father said to Miss Australia, "Smile." She smiled. He said, "Once more." She smiled again. "Come closer," he demanded, and he peered at her mouth like a horse-doctor. "Just as I thought," he affirmed. "You have large gaps between your teeth. This really won't do. You must go to my dentist at once and have them fixed."

She went to the dentist. He fixed the gaps all right. He removed four of her front teeth and gave her a plate. Then Father decided there was something more fundamentally wrong with her. Something the dentist could not fix even if he removed all her teeth. She just wasn't right for the part.

She went back to Australia with memories of a free trip to England, and a very trying experience, four false teeth, and I am sure a determination to get married, settle down, and have nothing more to do with the stage for the rest of her life.

It may be amusing to look back on this incident now, but at the time I felt very sorry for that little Australian girl. But her misfortune was my opportunity, because I took over the part from Phyllis Dare.

I sang and played with all my heart and tried to remember the hundred-and-one instructions Father had given me. The result? Well, it was mixed. Some of the critics were kind enough to talk about my freshness and vitality. But others had a different story to tell: "This raw, inexperienced child . . . This unpolished schoolgirl . . . She has been given the part because of her father's position . . ."

But I was in Arcady, where everyone is happy, and I had too much joy in the part to become despondent about their criticisms. The audience liked me, and one day I hoped the critics would, too.

So, I went on working. Just a bit harder, that's all.

IV

Love at First Sight

(Tom—Dick—and—Harry)

I HAVE been happily married for many years, and as the result of my experience I want to give you a little advice: never tell your husband about your early love affairs. It is bound to make him jealous. The only reason I am breaking this rule now is because it is quite impossible, to my mind, for any woman to write the story of her life without admitting she has been in love, or been loved, more than once. First of all, no one will believe her; and secondly she would have to be very unattractive to have gone through life with only one man falling in love with her. But despite the fact that I feel forced in honesty to make these confessions, I am sticking to the rule of no names, no pack-drill.

If Jack Hulbert, or anyone else for that matter, thinks he can identify the men I am going to tell you about, then it is no good asking me for confirmation, because I won't tell. There is another reason for the 'no names' rule. The three young men with whom I fell in love before I met Jack are still alive. One of them, and this is to whet Jack's curiosity, is a Major-General who has recently retired with a double D.S.O. I know the double D.S.O. narrows down the field so I am not going to say any more about him. My second was the son of a millionaire; today he is a millionaire. My third was a small-part actor when I met him, and I am sorry to say he is still a small-part actor, although he is playing bigger small-parts.

I did not fall in love until quite late in life. I think I was about eight and he was the same age. The reason I fell in love, to the best of my memory, was because he was a boy and I liked boys. This romance also taught me a lesson about men and love. A lesson I did not forget. A woman should never put herself on a pedestal, because a man is liable to leave her there. It was the fault of my brother Charles that I stepped on to the pedestal in the first place; but once there it was difficult to step down, and even when I did my admirer did not approve.

He first set eyes upon me when I was one of the four fairies skipping on and off the stage in *A Midsummer Night's Dream* at the Prince's Theatre, Manchester. He had taken his parents to the theatre because of his passion, at that time, for fairies. He also went to school with my brother, and the morning after the visit to the theatre he approached Charles, to discuss fairies in general, but me in particular. Charles was naturally flattered that someone, a year his senior, should consult him about anything.

"Tell me," said the Fairy Lover, whose name, incidentally, was Tom, "are the fairies real?"

"Which one?" said Charles, playing for time and airing his knowledge. "Mustard Seed, Cobweb, Moth, or Peaseblossom?"

"Oh, all of them!" said Tom.

"Yes," confirmed Charles, "they are all real."

"How do you know?"

"I've met them."

"Not really," said Tom, incredulously.

"Bet you I have," insisted Charles.

"Bet you three marbles you haven't," said Tom.

"Bet you four," said Charles, who knew when he was on to a good thing.

Tom considered the proposition seriously for a moment. Charles was asking a lot of marbles.

"Are they real live fairies?" Tom said, cautiously. And this is where Charles wrecked my first romance before it had really got under way. He overplayed his hand and said:

"Of course they are live."

"Prove it," challenged Tom.

"On my word of honour," said Charles. But he was not going to be allowed to win so easily.

"If I meet a live one, then I'll give you four marbles," said Tom, who was obviously destined not to buy any Brooklyn Bridges in his life.

"But you have seen them with your very eyes," said Charles, cunningly.

"Ah! But I haven't touched them," replied Tom.

This was *touché*, and Charles knew he had to work fast to win those marbles. "You can meet a live one and touch her if you like," Charles offered.

"Any one?" said Tom.

"Yes," said Charles, throwing caution to the wind.

Tom became specific. "I want to touch the one who said 'Here am I'."

Charles was in luck. This was a simple introduction to effect. "You want to meet Peaseblossom," Charles said, triumphantly.

"I'll know if that's the one when I see her," said Tom, who was now already beginning to regret the four marbles.

Charles flew home that day from school and told me exactly what had happened. "All you have to do, Cicely, is to be a fairy at home as well as on the stage; and I'll get Mummy to let me have Tom to tea."

I agreed at once to this proposition. I would do anything for Charles. And anyway, I had never felt the part of Peaseblossom, as written by Shakespeare, gave me enough scope to prove my histrionic ability. At home I could add some touches of my own. Many actors and actresses feel the same way about authors.

When the day arrived for Tom to visit us my tea was brought to me in the playroom upstairs. I arranged this because I thought it would spoil the illusion if a fairy was first introduced at the tea-table, drinking tea and eating cakes, just like any other mortal.

Charles and I often used to put on shows in the playroom for visitors, or members of the family; and Mother quite understood that the audience, even if it consisted of only one, should not be introduced to the cast before the show.

We had fitted up a small stage in the playroom, complete with old sheets for curtains. I waited behind these for Charles and his friend to appear. I had borrowed some ear-rings, brooches, bracelets, and a necklace or two from Mother's trinket-box, and I was garnished with them all, together with some paper wings.

Charles made Tom sit on the floor, two or three feet away from the stage, and then he made the following announcement: "Ladies and Gentlemen. I wish to introduce to you the one and only live fairy that people can touch." Then he pulled aside the sheets to reveal me standing on an improvised pedestal made of boxes, and here is where I think I improved on Shakespeare.

I smiled at Tom, and then my mouth began to move, but no words came.

Tom exclaimed, quite understandably, "I can't hear what she is saying."

"Of course you can't," said Charles, brightly. "Only people who believe in fairies can hear them."

Tom was obviously impressed. We had him in a spot, and his four marbles were as good as in Charles's pocket.

"You can touch her," invited Charles, and this Tom proceeded to do, rather nervously, one finger lightly on my right wing.

"She's the same one I saw on the stage," he concluded, "and she's real. I believe in her."

This was my cue to speak and I did so while Charles collected his marbles. "Here am I," I said. "Here am I. Here am I." I wanted to say all the wonderful words I had thought up for the occasion, but I could not think of them. I had fallen in love with Tom at first sight. Don't ask me why. It just happened.

I am not quite sure the exact moment when it happened, it was either just before or just after he touched my wing, or it may have been when he actually touched my wing. The point was that I could not take my eyes off him. Here was a dilemma. I wanted to come down from my pedestal. I wanted to become engaged to Tom, but there was Charles to think of, and what Tom would say when he knew he had been duped.

I did the only thing a woman could do under the circumstances. I got right down from my pedestal and tried to make the best of two worlds. "You can be friends with me now," I said to Tom, and stretched out an inviting hand, but he backed away. "Don't be frightened," I said. "Now that you believe in fairies you have nothing to fear. I will make you my Prince Charming." My book of words was becoming a little mixed, but it sounded pretty good to me, but Tom still backed away, fear in his eyes, and then he suddenly turned, ran out of the door, downstairs, and out into the street.

I ran after him but he was too quick for me, and I baulked at running through the streets of Manchester, my paper wings flapping behind.

Charles was overjoyed at my performance. He had never seen anyone so frightened by a fairy in his young life and probably never would again. And I had a feeling, at the time, that I had done my job too well. You can fall in love just as sincerely at eight as any other time in life, and I wanted to see the object of my affections again. But as each day, which seemed like a year, passed and Tom refused countless invitations to come to tea, I realized that all was completely lost. I decided that I would never get over my lost love. And I was not far wrong, because it took me at least a month. That is a long, long time when you are eight.

Dear Tom,

If you happen to read this, please forgive me for frightening you. I have forgiven you for running away.

Cicely.

Well, that disposes of the Major-General.

Apart from making eyes at boys when I went for walks during my two years' schooling in Switzerland, nothing romantic happened to me until I had left school and was appearing in *The Arcadians*. And on this occasion I did not take the initiative. My admirer was gay, crazy, and altogether quite unusual. Dick could afford to be all of these things.

One night in the stalls I noticed a handsome-looking young man. The next night I noticed him again, applauding vigorously, and enjoying himself immensely. The third night he was there again, and just before the curtain rose baskets of flowers appeared in my dressing-room. There was no card with them, but I guessed he had sent them. About a week later the flowers included a note introducing him, and so we met and the romance had begun. It was an exciting romance from the start, as Dick was an incurable practical joker. Usually, I do not like practical jokers; the sort of people who give you an electric shock when you shake hands, pull the chair away when you are about to sit down, or squirt water in your face when you admire the flower in their button-hole. I suppose my reason for not liking this type of humour is that the laugh is always gained through the physical discomfort of someone else. For example, although I was very fond of George Graves, the greatest box-office draw of his time, I never really enjoyed his practical jokes. I remember one show I was in with him when he used to nail a bucket to the stage, just before the small-part actor, whose job it was to remove the bucket, came on.

The poor man would, in full view of the audience, tug hopelessly
at the bucket, while George Graves would stand aside and roar
with laughter. I was not amused.

Dick's type of practical joke was kindly, often against himself,
and always had a happy ending. One night, for instance, he would
arrive in the stalls with a false beard and a false laugh, and before
long the whole theatre would be laughing with him. But the
important thing was that he did not make the audience laugh in
the wrong place. The next night he would arrive, having taken
the whole front row of the stalls for his friends, who were all
instructed to applaud and encore me. I, naturally, forgave him
for this.

Even his gifts had a laugh attached to them. One night a
single forget-me-not would arrive on an enormous cushion.
The next night a tiny bunch of flowers, and from then on the
size of the bouquet would grow bigger, working up to a grand
finale of a basket of flowers so huge that the call-boy could not
get them through the door and I had to go outside to receive
them. On another night a crate was wheeled along the corridors
and arrived on a trolley outside my dressing-room. I signed for
it and one of the stage hands split it open with a crowbar. Inside
was packing, and still more packing, until my dressing-room was
filled with packing. At last came the gift. Eight delicate, silver
vases, each containing a sweetly scented model flower. A rose,
a lily, a violet, jasmine, carnation, gardenia, lilac, and a sweet-pea.
They were the most fragile little things I have ever seen and the
perfume of the flowers did not fade.

That is what I meant when I said that Dick's practical jokes
always had a happy ending. But our romance did not. The
trouble was that Dick insisted upon thinking of me as a child.
He was right, which made it even more aggravating. He would
court me, openly, and I adored him; but whenever I tried to get
the conversation going my way, and any woman knows what
way that was, he would say: "When you are grown-up I am going
to ask you a very important question. There is plenty of time to
be serious later on."

I would insist that I knew all about life, but of course I did
not. My life in the theatre was watched over by my father, and
at home by both my parents. As a matter of fact I don't think
I would have been allowed to speak to Dick for one moment if

he hadn't been the son of a millionaire. You'd be surprised how much that can help a man in life. No. You probably wouldn't.

Just when it seemed that our romance was at its height, Dick's father wrote and recalled him to the country where the gold came from—Africa. Of course we promised never to forget each other.

Dear Dick,

If you happen to read this you have proof that I have not forgotten you. But if you care to read on you will discover why I stopped writing.

Cicely.

That disposes of my millionaire, apart from the reading he has to do.

Of course I knew when I came to my next romance that the others had not been the real thing I imagined them to be. This is what happens to all old romances when they are succeeded by a new one. I have now, as you have probably guessed, come to Harry. Our love was secret and hopelessly out of this world. He was a young actor and in the same show. I thought him handsome, thrilling, and he thought I was beautiful and thrilling. This is how people look to each other in all romances. If they didn't there wouldn't be any.

Harry was not given to many words, but those he had were the right ones. He used to say, "Cicely, you're wonderful."

I used to nod my head and close my eyes in ecstatic agreement, and say the same to him because I thought he deserved it. I believe in reciprocal entertaining. Every day he put flowers in my dressing-room, together with passionate notes protesting his love. I also sent him notes protesting my love. I did not send him flowers. Remember, women were still without the vote.

It is very easy for me to joke about my love for Harry now, but then it was real, and so intense that it became almost frightening. My mother wondered what was the matter with me, and well she might. When I was not with Harry I spent my day sighing, looking right through people as if to find him. And I went so off my food—I was never much on it—that Mother began to think I was going into a decline. This proves that you cannot judge by looks. I was feeling on top of the world. Harry and I had wonderful bus rides to and from the theatre and the Royal Academy of Music. We spoke that peculiar language of young love which is part sign language; you know, nudges, shoulder touching, and a complete A to Z with the eyes. This was backed up with spoken language which is quite incomprehensible to anyone else but the lovers.

This consisted of, "Oh, Harry . . . !"

Harry would consider this statement and say, "Oh, Cicely . . . !"

We would then go back to sign language and take up a new thread of conversation later on. We said the same words, "Oh, Harry . . . !" and "Oh, Cicely . . . !" but they meant something entirely different. I hope you understand this because if you don't I haven't got time to explain.

Harry stole his first kiss from me in the dim half-light outside the Royal Box at the theatre. And when I say 'stole', I am right only if you can say 'stole' when something is freely given. In this sense of the word Harry was the Raffles of his day. Discovery came, after a few weeks of pledging our everlasting love, in between rehearsal calls. My mother saw us together, not once on the bus, but several times. Innocently, she told my father, and I was summoned, that's the only word for it, to his study.

"Sit down, Cicely," he said. "I have something to ask you. I understand you have been seeing a lot of Harry?"

"Yes, Father."

"I gather, too, he has been buying you flowers and chocolates?"

I agreed that this was so.

"And where, may I ask, have you been meeting him?"

"On the bus, Father."

"I am astounded that a daughter of mine should meet a young man behind my back, travel about in broad daylight as bold as brass, and accept gifts from him, without even your own mother being told. Do you realize how badly you have behaved? The deceit of it all! The impropriety of it all! An actor in my own cast! Aren't you ashamed of yourself?"

"No, Father."

This was not a diplomatic answer and it brought further charges of deceit, unladylike behaviour, lowering myself, and so on. Finally he asked me the sixty-four dollar question.

"Has this young man kissed you?"

I nodded.

"Where?"

"Behind the Royal Box, Father."

"In full public gaze?"

"Oh no, Father! There were never very many people about."
And then, thinking it was time to take the offensive, I added
firmly, "I love him."

"Love? What do you know of love? At your age? What are
you thinking of? An actor, a small-part actor in my own show!
And you the daughter of the Producer."

The tirade went on and on. I was everything that was bad and
mad and improper. Finally, he turned and stood in front of me.
"You are never to see this man again. I forbid it. Do you understand? I forbid it entirely."

I stormed. I argued. I wept. Father stormed, argued, but did
not weep. "Give me your promise," he repeated.

I refused. The tirade continued. Still I refused. Until, at last,
exhausted but stubborn, I went up to my room.

Social convention is very strong. It is now the convention
for children to disobey their parents. Anything else would be
unthinkable and frowned on by Society in general. But when
I was nineteen it was still the convention for children to obey
their parents, and however much I argued with Father I knew
that unless I could get him to change his mind my romance with
Harry was over. So I did not dare to meet my love on the bus
any more. But I did convey to him that something dreadful had
happened and that I could not meet him behind the Royal Box.
I consoled myself that I had only to obey Father for two years
and I would be of age and able to marry Harry and live happily
ever after.

And then one day Harry disappeared, without a word. Father
had sent him on tour in the Provinces.

It seemed a dreadful break. I cried and longed to see Harry
for months. Mother did her best to help me over my heartbreak.
She was gentle, and asked young people home, a thing Father
had never encouraged. My heart was broken and I was quite sure
it would never mend and I would be a spinster for the rest of my
life. I became very single-minded about being a spinster. I
decided that one of the best qualifications for my new role was

to become a Sunday School teacher. I was quite wrong, because when you have to deal with a lot of children you begin to think it would be easier to have a family of your own.

But I had to do some penance for my lost love, and as Father would not hear of my becoming a missionary in China, I settled for Sunday School teaching, where I found there was always a ready supply of young heathens.

Every Sunday I set out, Bible story-book in hand, and trotted along to the church in St. John's Wood, where a large class of rather grubby children were awaiting me. They were quite young and not too well behaved. By this I mean that they sometimes paid no attention whatsoever. There was so much shouting, talking, and a general air of confusion, and no one listening but just speaking to hear the sound of their own voices, that an onlooker might have concluded they were preparing to be politicians. Still, these were in my early days as a Sunday School teacher, and whenever I despaired of controlling my unruly mob of 'little dears' I would say to myself, "Harry, I am doing this for you." It was not long before they got my measure and I got theirs. My measure was that I would stand no nonsense. And theirs?—that they understood this.

First I read a Bible story, and then I tried to get the right answers to my questions. That over, I got them, more or less, into a neat line and marched them into church, arranged them in a pew and sat down at the end to keep order during the Children's Service.

Dear Harry,

        If you happen to read this, you have proof that I did not forget you easily. But how could you have married after only four weeks on that tour? Still, I'm very glad it turned out so well.

                                          Cicely.

I really thought I would never get over Harry and was quite resigned upon the career of a spinster.

How was I to know I was about to meet a young man called Jack Hulbert?

V

Love at Second Sight

★

BEFORE I tell you how I stumbled in love with Jack Hulbert I must tell you about an argument I had with Ivor Novello. It was when we were discussing love. I told Ivor that the one thing he had missed out of all his plays was the sort of love most people experience—love at second sight. Of course he disagreed with me. He said, "Darling, everyone longs for that wonderful moment when they meet the person of their dreams, fall madly in love at first sight, and the story ends happily ever after." I said: "That is the fault of you people who write romantic plays. You have created a legend that the only real love is love at first sight, but it just isn't true." Ivor was not impressed and dismissed my argument with a wave of his elegant cigarette-holder. I did not have a cigarette-holder with which to talk back so I could not pursue my point. I am going to do so now, and I need your help.

If you are a man then I ask you to be frank with yourself and answer the following questions. And if you think I am being personal then you are right, but there is no other way of finding out about people.

FIRST QUESTION: "Was your wife the woman of your dreams?" If she is standing behind you and looking over your shoulder then I do not mind if you nod your head, or say, "Of course she *was*." If you are alone I want the truth. Aren't I a mixer? SECOND QUESTION: "Did you fall in love with her at first sight?" To save time, I am going to suggest to you that with the little woman out of the room your answers should read as follows: "My wife was not the woman of my dreams but she has become so." This not only constitutes an answer to both my questions, but proves you are diplomatic enough to be Foreign Secretary of Great Britain.

This is flattering you, but I am sure you will forgive me. You have told me the truth without hurting anyone.

It is now the turn of your wife and I want her to answer the same two questions: "Was your husband the man of your dreams?" "Did you fall in love with him at first sight?" Please stop smiling like the Mona Lisa. I see. That smile is there to stay. Well, there is no point in my persisting with my questions, so both of you sit comfortably side by side, because I am going to tell you what I believe to be the truth.

First of all, next time you go out, take a look at the people. What do you see? Mostly men and women. Let's take the men first. What are they like? They are young and old, tall and short, ugly and handsome. You notice that very few are young, tall and handsome. But a young, tall, handsome man is the star of your dreams. (And mine.) Try and find him when you're awake.

Now for the women. Despite beauty parlours, there is no escaping the fact that women come in all shapes and sizes, just like men. The reason for this is that they are born that way and it is very hard to alter them. The point I am trying to make is that very few men and women have the obvious sort of physical attraction necessary to make the opposite sex fall in love at first sight. How, then, do they fall in love? I don't think they do fall. They stumble. And in doing so they have more time to discover many qualities in each other, more obvious than physical attraction, some of their own imagining. This leads them to a declaration of their love. And a declaration of love usually leads to a lie, a nice lie, a pretty one, that we must keep on telling. It is—"I loved you the moment I first set eyes upon you." What else can you say? "I did not notice you at first." "After all, you take some getting used to." You can't say that because it may be the truth, and you can't risk the truth when you're in love.

For example, someone once said, "You can admire a beautiful woman for her intelligence and an intelligent woman for her beauty." This technique is obviously very successful, but very boring. On the other hand you can't do it the other way round because if you want to be successful in love you have to fit the pattern authors and poets have laid down. They insist that the only real love is of the First Sight variety. If it isn't—it isn't love. How wrong they are! Have they never heard of love at Second Sight?

Our engagement picture

Before the ceremony with my
father, and after the ceremony
with my husband

This sort of love can be just as lasting as any other. More lasting; with love at second sight you even get to know the person you love before you tell them so. This has obvious advantages. You may think I am stressing the importance of love at second sight because I am basing my views on personal experience. I fell in love with Jack at second sight and that is how Jack fell in love with me. If you find this difficult to understand, because we are such glamorous creatures, then I can only tell you that the glamour has come with the years. When we first saw each other we were quite different.

We first met when the German Army had two more years' training to do before they began the First World War and everyone in prosperous, powerful England, that is everyone in the know, was quite certain that the only reason the Germans were building up the most powerful war machine the world had ever known was to protect themselves from a powerful aggressor, like the Belgians. We were still living in the days of a British Empire upon which the sun never sets. It was true that some people said this was only because God would not trust us in the dark, but nobody listened to them.

It was against this settled background of life, which was obviously going to continue on its own sweet way for ever, that Father was planning a new show. He badly needed a success. Since his good fortune with *The Arcadians* he seemed to have lost his touch, but not his confidence. During the run of *The Arcadians* Father had spent two years laying the foundations of a play called *The Mousmé*. It was based on a trip he had made to Japan and was meant to be a beautiful picture of Eastern life. It was beautiful, but it was not funny. Father had relied upon the verbal promise of a leading comedian to play a part he had specially written for him. He even persuaded Sir Oswald Stoll to release the comedian from a previous contract, only to learn when rehearsals started that the comedian had gone into another show. As a result Father lost £20,000 and some of his faith in human nature. £20,000 contains a lot of faith, and it took Father many years to recover from this blow. He put on *Oh! Oh! Delphine*, with Harry Welchman, Reginald Owen, Iris Hoey, and Cicely Debenham, but this was only a moderate success.

During its first few months' run I went on a sea voyage to South Africa with Mother, who for some time past had been

D

looking fragile and tired. There were dark shadows under her eyes and the slightest exertion seemed too much for her. Father thought a sea voyage would help to restore her health and I realized that Mother needed me more than the Theatre.

While we were outward bound it became increasingly clear to me that Mother was not getting any better. The reason for this was obvious as soon as we reached Cape Town. Suddenly, or so it seemed, though it must have been inevitable to older eyes, Mother collapsed, and for the first time I admitted to myself something I had long understood—Mother was seriously ill. Fortunately, nursing, air, sun, and food were nowhere better than in South Africa and Mother's health improved sufficiently for us to journey home. If we carried too much luggage, it was labelled 'Too Much Hope'.

Back in London, Father welcomed us. He gave one look at Mother and for the first time in my life I saw that he was frightened. And from then on he spent a great deal more of his time with her away from the theatre. I was surprised to see Father so affected. He had always seemed to me an emotional Gibraltar. Somehow Mother's illness gave us all—Father, Charles, Rosaline, and myself—a common denominator we had never had before. We should have been depressed but we were not! I think for the reason that when someone you love dearly is ill, you convince yourself, as we did, that they must be getting better because you need them. Mother realized this too and acted her part to convince us.

A short time after we came home, Father said to me: "I have a new show for you. You are to play in *The Pearl Girl* with Alfred Lester and Lauri de Frece."

I was naturally very pleased.

"Who is going to play opposite me?" I asked.

"A young undergraduate down from Cambridge," Father replied.

I was astonished, but before I could say so, he added, "I am taking you down to Brighton tomorrow and you will be able to meet him."

I thought this was absurd. Father was obviously joking. How could he possibly ask a young fellow in a cap and gown to play opposite an experienced actress? I had never found it easy to question a decision of Father's and it took me a little time. At the first attempt I said:

"Father, will you please tell me something?"

He nodded so gravely that he put me off. So I asked him again as our train left Victoria Station for Brighton to meet the young undergraduate.

I said, "How long is this journey going to take?"

He told me, and I was annoyed with myself for being a coward. I had received an answer to the question I was asking, instead of thinking. This is aggravating to any woman.

After a while I tried again, "Father, there is something I really must know."

He glanced up irritably from his newspaper. "What is it this time?" he asked.

"How much longer is this train journey going to take?" I said, weakly.

"Five minutes less than the last time I told you," he said, and went back to his paper.

"Really, Father," I protested, "it is too bad."

"This is a very good train service," he said. "I don't know what is the matter with you."

"How would you like to play opposite a schoolboy?" I said. There, I had told him at last!

Father laughed. "So that's what's troubling you?"

"As a matter of fact, it is," I said.

Father reassured me. "Then you have no need to worry. The young man you are about to meet is, in my humble opinion—and I base this upon the little experience I have had in theatrical management—a person with a great deal of promise. Indeed, he not only shows talent as an actor but as a writer."

"How can you say that," I said, "when you told me yourself that he is only just out of school?"

Father looked as though he would pull the communication cord.

"I said nothing of the sort," he insisted. "You know very well I told you he was an undergraduate."

"I don't see what difference that makes," I replied.

"It makes a great deal of difference," he said. "Undergraduates are schoolboys grown up."

"Even if he is grown up," I persisted, "I don't see how he can have had any experience."

"He may not have had much experience," replied my father, "but what he has been able to accomplish already without experience makes me confident of his future. I think you ought to know," he went on, "that while you and Mother were away I went to the Globe Theatre to see a performance of a revue, *Cheero Cambridge*, which this young man had written for The Footlights Dramatic Club. It was well enough written and he, also, showed sufficient promise in the leading part to convince me that he had a future. I engaged him for *The Pearl Girl* on the spot. Is there anything else you want to know?"

"Yes, Father," I said, meekly, but feeling much brighter, "how much longer is this journey going to take?"

He did not answer, but went back to his newspaper and left me to my own thoughts.

These were of Father's brilliant young discovery who now looked very different to me. Previously I had, in my mind's eye, clothed him in a mortar-board and gown, with a studious expression which peered at me from behind glasses. At best I had seen him without a mortar-board and gown, but with a straw hat and a studious expression which peered at me from behind glasses. But I reasoned that if my father, who employed the most glamorous people of his time, had fallen for a young man on sight, then every turn of the wheels, every puff of the engine, every toot of the whistle, was taking me nearer a young man as amusing as George Graves, as debonair as Joseph Coyne, as handsome as Basil Hallam. Altogether a Prince Charming. It seemed too good to be true. Was there such a man?

I looked at Father. He sat opposite, perched on the edge of his seat, like a confident blackbird, with his dark hair, dark eyes, dark suit, and an overall air of confidence as though he was the first bird to catch the first early worm. Looking at him, I was convinced that I was a very lucky girl, who should have realized that there were times when Father, indeed, knew best. After all, only a young man who combined the wit of George Graves, the charm of Joseph Coyne, and the looks of Basil Hallam could have persuaded that wise-looking blackbird to take him under his wing. Here was an occasion, I told myself, when it was well worth being the daughter of a theatrical manager. It wasn't every day a young actress had the chance to play opposite a young man, who was not only witty, charming, and good-looking, but was so forceful a personality that he had impressed himself on everyone who saw him, even Father.

I made up my mind there and then that the young man was probably spoilt. Obviously, every girl he met fell for his wit, charm, and looks. But I was going to be different. Life might have been a series of successes for him up to date. That was fine for the type of girls he had met. They had fallen over themselves to be noticed by him. I would not be so easy a conquest. He could be as witty as he liked, but he would have to try very hard before he heard from me the laughter that had greeted his epigrams from a naïve Cambridge audience. And he could charm the Spring buds down from the trees before I fluttered an eyelash; and as for his looks—well—I would look the other way. Of course, this was only the beginning. Later on I would be gracious and show him that I, too, could unbend. I was unbending when the train stopped at Brighton.

We took a growler, a four-wheeled horse cab, to the Theatre Royal, where they were presenting a touring company of Father's show, *Oh! Oh! Delphine*. Father was usually careful about expenses, and would often walk to save a penny bus, but when it came to appearances—the London Manager arriving at the local theatre—then it had to be in style.

The curtain had not yet risen when we were shown into our box. I looked around for the witty, charming, and good-looking young man. He was not there; and Father told me he was watching the show from another part of the House. I remember nothing of the first half, as I spent most of my time trying to pick the young man out of the audience. At last a handsome young man, with dark good looks, caught my glance and flashed a smile at me. I turned my head, primly, towards the stage, mentally congratulating Father for having chosen so well. At the first interval there came a tap on the door of the box. I heard the door open, and Father say, "Come in," and then to me: "Oh, Cicely, this is Mr. Jack Hulbert! . . . my daughter Cicely, Mr. Hulbert."

I took my first sight.

He stood there, straw hat in hand, thin, fairish, studious blue eyes peering at me from behind glasses. What a let down! I thought: "Oh no! Even Father can't do this to me!"

Jack thought, and I know this, because he confessed it in a weak moment years later: "Oh no! Even Mr. Courtneidge can't do this to me." You see, Jack had imagined the Manager's daughter a sophisticated beauty, and he saw instead a thin, pale girl, who looked at him with disappointed eyes. That was the one thing we had in common at the moment of our first meeting —complete and utter disappointment. I made my "How-d'you-do" sound as convincing as possible and watched the show. Jack sat at the back of the box. For him, the World of the Theatre seemed suddenly less attractive than it had been.

Our disappointment with each other did not communicate itself to Father. He was not concerned with what we thought of each other, but only if we were right for his new show.

Jack and I began rehearsing for *The Pearl Girl* the following week. We were cast as two young lovers. It did not take me long to make up my mind that although my opposite number had an extraordinary face, a chin a mile long—this is an exaggeration, but I am sure it must feel like a mile to any fly—he also had enough confidence to take all the knocks and still come up for more. As for me, Jack was beginning to think: "She might be plain. She might be skinny. But what fun she is to work with!" And how we worked! Not only at rehearsals, but away from rehearsals, at every moment and in every corner we could find. The more we worked the more we began to respect each other.

At first, Jack's kisses were only stage ones. Brief and uninteresting, but quite efficient-looking from the front of the House. On the stage Jack was bursting with vitality. He obviously believed the world was his and that soon the West End of London would confirm the high opinion he had of himself. It was this confidence which sustained him when Father was critical, as he often was. I knew success was not as easily won as Jack imagined, but his optimism was catching. If hard work at rehearsals was a guarantee of success Jack had nothing to worry about. Sometimes we would work until two o'clock in the morning. But even at this early hour, when human resistance is supposed to be at its lowest, we were still Miss Courtneidge and Mr. Hulbert to each other.

Every week-end I used to go down to Bournemouth to see Mother, who was not making the recovery for which we had all hoped. One week-end she said, "Tell me, darling, about this Jack, who takes up so much of your letters?" "He's the young man in the show," I replied. "Do you like him very much?" she asked. "He's a lot of fun," I replied, evasively. Mother smiled, and came direct to the point, as mothers often do. "I'm glad you're happy," she said. "I want you to be happy and I want you to marry someone who makes you happy." How absurd Mother's remark seemed to me, then. But not as absurd as I pretended to myself. At the back of my mind that curious person who is our real self kept hinting to me that rehearsing with Jack was becoming more pleasant than the ordinary run of rehearsals should be.

After Mother's words, I certainly looked at Jack more seriously. I began to assess him and I saw beneath his gaiety a reliable person. What intrigued me most about him was the apparent ease with which he took to his first venture into the professional Theatre. He had come straight out of another world. His father was a doctor. Jack had been educated at Westminster and Cambridge, where he had read History and Psychology. He was a B.A.—I know that in these days we have Rectors of Universities in the Theatre, but in those days even a B.A. was a curiosity.

When Jack turned to playacting at Cambridge, Dr. Hulbert did not, as many fathers would have done, disown him. For he loved the Theatre himself. For years, father and son had seen every new show in London together from the gallery. If he was disappointed, or anxious, that his son should choose a profession that was so uncertain, he did not show it. Instead he showed his faith in Jack's ability, and when the Footlights show was put on at the Globe Theatre, for one performance, Dr. Hulbert made certain that every London Manager was there, and for once sat in the stalls, instead of the gallery. He regarded it as quite fitting, and not in the least surprising, that Mr. Robert Courtneidge should sign up his son there and then. *My!* What confidence those Hulberts had—and still have.

You remember me telling you that I was not quite sure when I fell in love with a little boy, whether it was just before, during, or just after the moment he touched my fairy wing. Well, it was like that with Jack. Neither of us can say with certainty whether it was at the beginning, the middle, or towards the end of our rehearsals that we fell in love. When we were finally aware of it, everyone in the theatre swore they had known all along. The first inkling that Father had was pretty vivid, and he tells the story is his book, *I Was an Actor, Once*:

"During these rehearsals, busy in my own work, I had

not perceived the trend of events till one day when all the Company were rehearsing at the Helvetia Club Room, in the street adjoining the Shaftesbury. There was a little stage at the end of the room, in front of which was a curtain raised and lowered by a cord at the side. Stopping for a moment, I looked round and asked for Cicely and Hulbert. There was no answer for a moment, and I was about to repeat the question when some wag, catching hold of the cord, slowly pulled up the curtain disclosing the two truants, seated, oblivious, in each other's arms."

We were so oblivious of everyone else that we did not know Father had seen us until Fay Compton told me, and I told Jack. By this time he had already proposed and I had accepted. But there was a reservation—Father. Jack said: "Well, if that's all you're worrying about, I'll ask him. Nothing simpler." I said, "You don't know Father." And I told Jack about Harry and how Father had sent him on a tour of the Provinces. This made Jack think again. "But he wouldn't do that with me," he said. "Why not?" I replied. Jack rubbed his chin. "Yes, I see what you mean," he said. "Better leave it until the show opens," I suggested; "since Harry went out on tour he's never been heard of since." Jack laughed.

I suspected his laugh was forced. And when he agreed that it was safer to wait until after the opening of *The Pearl Girl,* I knew it was.

The Pearl Girl was a success, and it also proved that not only was Father's confidence in Jack justified, but so was Jack's confidence in Jack. There was no hesitancy on Father's part when Jack and I told him we wanted to get engaged, but he stipulated that we should not get married until the time was right. This was not as much as we had hoped. But, on the other hand, nothing is as much as lovers' hope. And we were lovers. We waited. We could afford to wait. We were certain of being in each other's arms every night when the curtain went up.

The run of *The Pearl Girl* went on, and then, like all happy things, came to an end.

Well over a year after our engagement was announced, when Father was preparing *The Cinema Star* to follow *The Pearl Girl,* Jack made up his mind that we had waited long enough. He went to see Father and told him so. Father said, "In the ordinary way I would agree with you, my boy, but you obviously haven't heard the news." "What news?" asked Jack. Father took him to the window. "Look," he said, "can you hear them?"

Jack looked and he saw what Father meant. The newspaper boys were running along the streets, carrying placards—*Germany Invades Belgium*. And above the sound of the traffic he could hear their voices. One word, sounding harsher and clearer than others— WAR! WAR! WAR!

"I thought this might happen," Jack said, "and I suppose you want us to wait until it's all over?" "Yes," Father agreed, and he looked at a calendar on his desk.

"August 4th. You shouldn't have to wait long. Not more than a matter of a few weeks—months at the most."

When Jack told me of Father's decision I tried not to show him my disappointment.

"We can wait," I said, firmly.

"Of course we can," said Jack, who smiled and kissed me. We knew we could because we believed our love was real and would endure. It may not have been love at first sight, but it was the love most people have, and it seemed very good to us.

It has proved so, and that is what I was trying to tell Ivor Novello about—Love at Second Sight.

It does endure.

VI

Marriage

I WOULD have been appalled if I could have foreseen my future during the early part of the First World War. Perhaps I would not have been surprised if I had known that my mother was going to die. She had been ill for so long it was not entirely unexpected. But I would not have believed that my father would lose so much money in the Theatre, that within a few months of the outbreak of war he would owe £7,000 to his friends, and would have to sell the lease of his house, his motor-car, furniture, and even his books; that my brother Charles, who had always seemed a baby to me, would join the Army, be seconded to the Royal Flying Corps, and be shot down over Flanders; that Jack would try, time and time again, to join the Army, but as often as he tried, be turned down as medically unfit. And to signify this he would have to wear an arm-band, for his own protection, until he found a doctor who remembered what Nelson did, and turned a blind eye.

And as for me—I was to experience failure. Not only the failure of a show but a more personal one. I was to be out of work for two years, and—here comes the rub; not because times were difficult in the Theatre, but because nobody thought I was worth employing.

Fortunately, I could not see the future. I could see only the present, and, despite the war, the present seemed a good place to be. When Father told Jack that he thought the war would be over in a matter of months, he was being canny compared with other people who honestly thought we would be in Berlin within a few weeks. Our optimism was such, and our illusions were so unbroken, we went to war with the bands playing, the colours flying, proud and confident. We did not want to lose them but we thought they ought to go. We knew that war was bad, but it was fought out of sight and sound to keep the Home Fires Burning. And we had plenty of coal to burn and plenty of food to cook.

My brother Charles volunteered twenty-four hours after the declaration of war. He was still in his teens. I remember he came into the drawing-room of our house in St. John's Wood and said, his face lighting up with a smile: "I have some news for Father. Where is he?" "You must tell me first," I said curiously, "or I won't tell you where Father is." "I've joined up," he said quietly. "You're pulling my leg," I replied. "No," said Charles, "it's a fact. Honest Injun." "But you're far too young," I protested. "I know," he said, "I'll just have to learn to be old."

And he learned, as thousands like him learned, to be very old while they were still very young; a paradox which lends itself to war. At first, Father was surprised—Charles had acted without consulting him, but he was so proud that his son was one of the first to volunteer that surprise easily gave way to pride.

Mother was so ill that we dare not tell her Charles had gone. We tried to cover up his absence from her bedside, as we thought the shock might be too much for her, but it was not long before it became obvious that if we did not tell her so she would never know. When, at last, we did tell her she was sinking fast, and I really don't think, at least I pray, that she was able to feel absences any more. At the end of August Mother died.

When your mother dies, part of you dies too. At least, that is how I felt. Grief was my world until I said to myself: "You've got to pull yourself together. Mother would not approve of this. There are other people in the world besides you. Father needs you now if he has never done before. And what about your young sister, Rosaline? She needs you. Pull yourself together. Run the house, look after the family. Help Father in the Theatre." That is how I spoke to myself and that is how I tried to behave, as I believed Mother had brought me up to behave.

Despite my efforts, Father would not be comforted, and my task was made more difficult when he had to withstand a series of setbacks in the Theatre at the same time. The cause of the first setback had its origin when, a few months before the war, George Edwardes transferred to him the rights of a German play with music. Jack was part-author of the English version, called

The Cinema Star, and this was the first professional show when he was associated with the book. It was produced at the Shaftesbury Theatre. We had a wonderful first night and looked set for a long run. I was in the cast, together with Dorothy Ward, Lauri de Frece, Harry Welchman, Jack, and Fay Compton. Fay was one of the loveliest girls I have ever seen, and being blessed with the most wonderful sense of humour we became great friends. We shared a dressing-room together and laughed our way through the entire evening. Indeed, our lack of control on the stage incurred the displeasure of my father, but long before he could implement his threat to dismiss us immediately should such a disgraceful thing ever occur again, war intervened, and the German origin of the play proved fatal to the London run. After struggling vainly for a time to keep the show going, Father had to close the theatre. He also thought seriously of disbanding the cast and cutting his losses. But I suggested to him that we might have better luck with *The Cinema Star* on tour. I knew he had a great deal of money invested in the show and the only hope of getting some of this back was in the Provinces. I was proved right.

The fact that *The Cinema Star* was originally a German show was little known away from London and we played to very good business. We certainly did not lose and we more than paid our way. But not enough to make up for the losses on the London production. Running expenses, including salaries, were kept as low as possible and Jack and I could not afford to stay in hotels. We lived in lodgings. They were usually cheap, clean, but not always comfortable. They would also have been lonely if Jack had not sometimes called at my rooms to keep me company and talk about our plans for the future; top priority being, since Jack and I had been engaged for two years, when would Father agree to our being married? These discussions were so innocent that we were both incensed, and surprised, to receive a curt note one day from Father, which said, and I will give you an extract from mine: *Under no circumstances is Jack to visit you in your rooms. And under no circumstances must you call upon Jack.*

Father's note to Jack was quite different. It said: *Under no circumstances are you allowed to visit Cicely in her rooms. And under no circumstances is Cicely allowed to call upon you.* As we were forbidden to meet in our rooms, we had to meet outside. This meant too much walking, so we spent our day going for tram rides. We would have preferred to have gone by bus, but there were practically no buses in the Provinces in 1915.

We became experienced tram riders. By this, I mean that we became accustomed to the sickening, swaying, jolting movement of trams. We also became used to the hard wooden seats, the backs of which had been designed by an obscure sadist, who was obviously determined to make his mark in the world. He made his mark on us. Our conversation on the tram rides followed the theme of those we used to have, in greater comfort, in our rooms; when would Father allow us to marry? Was he trying to make us break the record for the longest engaged couple in the world? We decided he was.

Once when the tram rides were getting too much for us we took up golf—but as I never succeeded in hitting a ball and only succeeded in breaking my clubs—we went back to the tram rides. Then Jack thought of a bold plan. He said, "I believe in action, don't you?" "Nothing less," I said, remembering my golf clubs. "Let's put up the banns," he said. "But what will Father say?" I replied. "That's the whole point," said Jack enthusiastically, "when we have put up the banns, we'll know." And we did. Father still said, "Wait," as firmly as he had ever done. He was certainly keen on our breaking that record. So back to the trams we went; and within a few months we were almost beginning to feel at home in their functional ugliness.

One day, not long after the tour of *The Cinema Star* had ended, and we were in a new show, *The Light Blues*, Father said, "Don't you think it is time you two got married?" Jack and I agreed that this was a very interesting proposition. We did not want to appear over-enthusiastic in case he changed his mind. I think I went a little too far and made it appear that I, for one, had to be argued into it. Father said, thinking he sensed reluctance on my part: "I think perhaps you had better wait another few weeks. What do you say, Jack, my boy?" His boy did not say anything, but Father saw something in the set of Jack's chin, and the light of his eyes, which said a lot. Enough for Father to say quickly, "I think after all you should get married straightaway."

So, at last, we were married, at St. Paul's Church, St. John's Wood. The same little church where I had once struggled to be a Sunday School teacher. At the time of the wedding we were playing at Hull. There was a good deal of publicity given to the wedding by the management of the theatre and I had to travel down to London on the Sunday to be ready for the ceremony on the Monday. It was a white wedding. Jack looked taller than ever in a topper and morning coat. And I hope I looked my best for him in all the frills, cream satin, and a long veil.

Jack and I waited, impatiently, throughout the ceremony for the parson to say, "I now pronounce you man and wife." Then we sailed out to Mendelssohn's "Wedding March," and signed the register. And then, believe it or not, we had to take the train back to Hull for the evening show. We had tried our best to persuade the management to let us off for a short honeymoon, if only for a few days. Jack tried first, but the management would not listen, so I had a go. "You can't ask us to play on our wedding night," I told them. They thought they could but they promised to think it over.

All Sunday I pleaded with Father to help us and he did so. He wired them: *Please give permission my daughter and Hulbert have one day at least for honeymoon. (Signed) Robert Courtneidge.* I was quite sure they would say "Yes" because I still believed Father was all-powerful in the Theatre.

We drove from the church to the Langham Hotel for our wedding breakfast. There were speeches, congratulations, toasts to the happy bride and groom, and then we were handed some telegrams. "Let's open one or two," I suggested. "Not now," said Jack, "let's leave them until tomorrow." But I opened one and it was from Hull. The management's reply to Father's telegram. It read: *Certainly not. You must appear tonight. (Signed) Morton.* I still have that wire. It hangs in a frame on the wall of my dressing-room, a valuable exhibit of the Courtneidge Collection.

I was heartbroken. But there was nothing more to be done, so Jack and I returned to Hull, played that night, and we had no honeymoon. Three months later we had a holiday, but it was not the same. I am traditional enough to believe that the moment for honeymoons is immediately after the wedding, and for us the moment had been missed for ever.

When we returned to London Jack and I found a small flat in Great Portland Street to set up home. Father gave us the furniture. *The Light Blues* was due to open in Town within a few weeks.

It had done well during the seven months' tour of the Provinces and we had great expectations. Jack was again part-author and we had a good cast which included Dorothy Ward, Shaun Glenville, that fine character actor Edmund Gwenn, who played my stage father, and a young, thin, pale-faced youth, who seemed to know everything and infuriated me because he was always right, called Noel Coward. During rehearsals he consistently aired his views, although he was never asked, and if he did not agree with the way a scene was being developed, even though he was playing the smallest part, he would say so. This made him difficult to understand, particularly when my father repeatedly said, "That young man is going to make a name for himself one day"; and more so when Father never once said anything like that to me, or Jack. Noel played the part of Mr. Pyecroft, and in one scene in which he appeared he had to peel a banana which he offered to the leading lady, Dorothy Ward. I have never seen anyone, either before or since, peel a banana with such engaging skill. Neither, for that matter, have I ever seen anyone offer a banana with such professional urbanity.

Noel has never forgotten those early days. One of the funniest things I have ever seen is his imitation of me singing, as Popsy Velour, a young and sprightly *ingénue*:

"Don't you go a-counting of your chickens,
   Wait till they're all hatched out,
   For you never, never know what's going to happen next,
      And you may be vexed
      Or a little bit perplexed,
   So don't you go a-counting of your chickens,
   Wait till they're all hatched out."

One of the discoveries I have made through the years is that nothing is dearer to a woman than the life-long friendship of her men friends. They are always extremely kind, charmingly tactful, and, on the whole, blessed with agreeable understanding. And since I learned to understand Noel, which I did long before the provincial tour of *The Light Blues* had finished, there has always been a warm bond of affection between us, and today he is one of my best friends. Noel has a great heart and only those who are close to him are able to penetrate the barrier. When failure has come my way he has always made a point of being near at hand, and whether in London or New York he has always been the first to come and see me. I have a tremendous admiration for Noel, not only for his work, where he stands alone—because Noel is supreme—but for the man himself. If anyone thinks Noel is indifferent, cynical, and supercilious, let them remember *Cavalcade* and *Bitter Sweet, Brief Encounter* and *In Which We Serve*. Where could you find greater humanity or humility than in either of these two plays or two films which Noel has written? I would gladly forego all my comedy to play a part in a play which Noel had written for me. And if it should happen that, in the not too far distant future, I should find myself with Noel playing a part like Jane Marryot in *Cavalcade*, then one of my dearest wishes will have come true.

For the London opening of *The Light Blues* we lost Dorothy Ward and Edmund Gwenn. Dorothy, owing to a previous contract, had to go into a new revue at the Empire, and Teddy Gwenn, owing to the war, had to go into the Royal Army Service Corps. (Number 827461, Driver Gwenn to you.) They were replaced by Cicely Debenham and Albert Chevalier, but the West End first night of *The Light Blues* proved to us that, although we liked London, London did not like us. We came off after three weeks!

Of course, there were lots of excuses. There always are when you have a failure; and this is as good a time as any to list them for you for your future reference. When there is a war, then it is the war, despite the fact that lots of shows are successful during war. When a show fails in peace-time, then it is because there is not much money about. This, despite the fact that lots of shows are successful during peace. When it is warm, then it is too hot for people to go to the theatre, despite the fact that some shows still manage to put up HOUSE FULL boards. When it is cold the weather keeps people at home, despite the fact that some shows still manage to put up HOUSE FULL boards.

There you have war and peace, weather and money, excuses for failure; although there are some other excuses nearer home. The cast is not right. The cast is right but the book is wrong. And the cast and the book are right, but the music is wrong. Last of all we have the cast, the book, and the music, all of them right, but the theatre is wrong. Of all the straws which are clutched during a flop then 'The theatre is wrong' is surely the

Pam's christening—the two gentlemen on Jack's RIGHT are P. G. H. Fender, then captain of Surrey C.C.C., and brother Claude, while Nannie Kennedy holds the baby

My first male impersonation

A schoolboy impersonation in *Review*

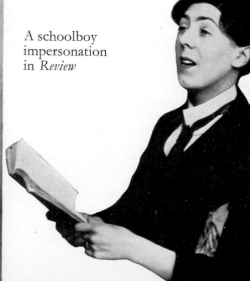

Noel Coward watching me scribble a note on the convenient back of
Edward Lewis in a scene from *The Light Blues*

The Pearl Girl. Myself with Alfred Lester and Jack

best. Bricks and mortar cannot answer back. You notice, by the way, that there is never a suggestion that the show may be wrong and the audience right.

I am not saying that the last suggestion applied to *The Light Blues*. I am honestly not certain what caused the audience to stay away, except every excuse that I have listed for you. Take your pick. I do know that the effect of *The Light Blues* being withdrawn was to throw us all out of work.

Since *The Mousme*, Father had had a series of failures. It is true the tour of *The Cinema Star* was a successful one, but it could not make enough money on tour to make up for the £20,000 he had lost on *The Mousme*, followed by his loss on the London production of *The Cinema Star*, and, to cap it all, the failure of *The Light Blues*. His capital was gone. He was in debt. He could not get another show and he had to close the theatre.

For the first time in my life I had to go out and look for a job outside my father's management. I was not deterred by this prospect but excited at the thought of working for someone else. I was young. I had a good record in my father's shows, and the confidence which stems from years of training and practical work. I was not unduly worried for Father, for despite the loss of his fortune, accumulated through many years of work, I was confident that he would be able to hit back. When you are brought up in the Theatre you think like that. Success and failure are very close together and neither of them last for ever. I was sure that he would make a come-back, and I was equally sure that I would have no difficulty in earning a good living. Jack was very soon at work again in *See-saw*, an André Charlot revue.

I thought that it was only a matter of days before the telephone would ring in our flat with a request from one of the London managements for the services of Miss Cicely Courtneidge. It did not ring! This was incredible to me, and I tested the instrument to see whether it was working. It was. I thought that meant they had not got my telephone number. I put this right with informal notes to the managements, telling them that I was free, and where I could be contacted. Once again I waited for the 'phone to ring. It did not ring. And once again I tested the instrument to see whether it was working. It was. This forced me to the conclusion that there was only one thing to do. I had to 'phone them. They were polite. They were interested, and they would let me know.

E

And so they did—with complete silence. I dropped pins to check up so I should know.

Was it possible, I questioned myself, that they did not want me? Of course not. How utterly absurd, I thought. Not want *Me*! I know why it's taking so long for a job to come my way. I am a featured player, and featured parts don't grow on trees, I told myself. It was just a matter of time. I had to be patient. So I was.

I sat at home, looking at the clock, the telephone, writing letters reminding people I was available, looking at the clock, the telephone, writing letters, looking at the clock—tick-tock, tick-tock—until I could wait no longer. I had to get out. If work wouldn't come to me, then I would go and get it. There was nothing like personal contact, I decided.

I put on my best hobble skirt and picture hat and, using my parasol with a flourish worthy of a wand of office, I went to see all the dear friends in management who not only knew me, but my father as well. They were polite, interested, and they would let me know. I began to wonder what was the matter with them.

It was at this time that Jack came home with some news that made him very happy. I knew what it was before he could tell me. He had taken off the arm-band which signified he was medically unfit for War Service. He was a young man and he hated the thought that people might think he was not prepared to do his bit. At last he had found a doctor prepared to pass anyone who was breathing. This meant it was even more urgent for me to get a job, as we had practically no savings and Jack's pay from henceforth would be the proverbial shilling a day.

I was left alone in our flat with the telephone, the clock, and a writing-pad. The telephone did not come to my assistance, and letters which first brought polite but evasive replies went unanswered. People who at first used to see me were now engaged or out. I settled down to a daily routine of the rounds of the agents; Charing Cross Road in the morning, and Shaftesbury Avenue and Piccadilly Circus in the afternoon. As the months went past I became used to waiting in their offices. It was now increasingly clear to me that I was not wanted. There were shows going on, people dropping out, tours being planned, contracts being signed, but not for me.

I was faced with the dilemma which confronts all theatre folk at some time in their careers—should I go on waiting and slowly starve (Oh yes, it was becoming as bad as that), or should I take a job outside the Theatre to earn my daily bread? If I waited I might indeed starve. If I took a job, then I might never be able to get back. If I waited long enough perhaps Father would be back on his feet. But what sort of a person would that make me? I pondered. One not meant for the Theatre, because the only person who considered me employable was my father. Perhaps this was true, but despite these disquieting thoughts I refused to give up.

Apart from my own determination, I was sustained by letters from Jack which always had the same encouraging theme:

"Don't lose faith in yourself. Stick it. Just as you are down, so one day you will be on top. From being slanged and insulted by agents, one day you will have fans by the mile, queueing up for your signature. I know you are going to be a great star and in your heart you must believe that too."

When Jack wrote about my being slanged and insulted by agents, he was right. The longer I looked for work the more rude and outspoken they became. Their general trend was to say: "Miss Courtneidge, you're a damned nuisance. We have nothing for you. You should know that by now. The only reason you have had work before is because of your father. No one else will employ you, so please don't worry us. We are far too busy." That sort of talk was not easy to take.

And after eighteen months without my having landed a job, even Jack's letters lost some of their confidence: "Never mind, darling. The War will soon be over and we'll be together again and then everything will come all right—just you see." All I could see was that if I waited for Jack to come home and look after me it would be confirmation of my failure.

I had to do something. I had tried everything, or so I thought, until one day, in 1917, a poster caught my eye. It was a Music Hall bill. Music Halls were flourishing at the time with great artistes like Marie Lloyd, Little Tich, Vesta Tilley, George Formby, Fred Barnes, Florrie Forde, and George Lashwood, all playing to packed houses night after night.

It gave me an idea.

VII

Out of Work

I NEVER intended to be a comedienne. I wanted to be a glamorous singing star of Musical Comedy. The idea of going into Music Hall was forced upon me after I had explored all other avenues, as they say in Parliament, and discovered that the avenues, at least in my case, were *cul-de-sacs*. I did not even turn to Music Hall in the belief that I was right for it. I did so simply because I thought it represented a last throw of the Theatrical dice; and anyway, I had to try and earn some money to pay the rent, buy the groceries, and keep the home together until the war ended and Jack was demobbed.

During my search for work I had become so used to rebuffs that as soon as the idea of going on the Halls occurred to me I approached some Variety agents. I did not expect them to welcome me as a new darling of the Music Halls. Their reaction to my suggestion was down to my expectations. They were not rude, as other agents had been, they were just disinterested. One of them did go so far as to enquire about my act, and I said, "I can sing and dance." And I reeled off the names of the shows in which I had appeared.

"So your last show was nearly two years ago," he observed pointedly.

"I'm afraid it was," I agreed.

"I can't book you," he said, "not on that type of stuff."

But I was not going to be beaten as easily as that. I went to Father and he advised:

"First of all you must work up an act, and then go back to the agents and ask them for a show date. They should give it to you, and if you have what they want, they might book you."

Laurie de Frece, Harry Welchman, Dorothy Ward, Jack, Fay Compton and myself in a finale from *The Cinema Star*

Another scene from *The Cinema Star* with Laurie
de Frece, the principal comedian, centre stage

The Nine O'clock Review with Harold French on
my right and Bobby Howes on my left

This was not wildly encouraging. But it was a chance. I scraped together a few pounds and went to see Harold Simpson, who was one of the best lyric writers of his day. Harold had been working with Jack. I explained my predicament to him and asked him to write some numbers for me. Within a few days he had turned out one called, 'Oh! What a Naughty Old Gentleman Father Must Have Been', and I worked on a dance routine with a parasol to go with it. Meanwhile, he also wrote two character numbers for me, one being 'The Knut in the R.A.F.' I rehearsed for a month, and at the end of that time I felt well enough armed for another go at the agents.

The information that I had a new act brought from them some vague promises, but nothing more definite. I again turned to Father and he suggested that the only hope was for me to take out a Bill on my own. I asked him what, exactly, he meant and he explained:

"If you can get together enough money to engage other artistes, pay all the expenses of the week at the theatre, you may be able to get a booking at one of the smaller Variety halls in the Provinces."

I asked him to go into details and he did so.

"First of all you need to raise about £100," he said.

"But I haven't a penny," I exclaimed.

"Nor have I," he replied. "I'm just giving you the details you asked for."

"All right," I said with forced gaiety, "let's pretend I have £100. What then?"

"You begin by getting a Bill together. This means you have to engage at least six acts. None of the acts must be doing your type of work. I know this sounds obvious, but you wouldn't think so, if you had seen some of the Bills I have seen. I think your best policy would be to get in touch with a trustworthy agent. You'd better go to Hartley Milburn. He's a friend of mine and I know he'll do his best to guide you. Leave the booking of the acts to him. He will make sure that they will form a well-balanced Bill: an instrumentalist, illusionist, male vocalist, speciality act, cross-talk act, and a comic, or something along those lines. The acts will cost you about £60."

"That's fine," I said. "I go to Mr. Milburn and he spends £60 of my imaginary £100. That leaves £40 for me. I don't know why I haven't done this before."

Father smiled knowingly and continued. "Oh no, it doesn't!"

he said. "You have to pay for your printing, that means throw-aways, double-crown posters, twelve and eighteen sheets, and possibly two or three forty-eight sheets. You also have to pay your share of the heating and lighting of the theatre."

"How much will that cost?" I enquired.

"About £25," he estimated.

"That leaves me with only £15 out of my £100," I said.

"Not so fast. I haven't finished yet," Father remonstrated. "Hartley Milburn doesn't work for nothing. You have his commissions to pay, so you had better earmark about £10 for that. And don't think you still have £5 left because you haven't. There are your own fares and living expenses for a week, the transport of your scenery to and from the theatre and, oh yes!— I nearly forgot—a few pounds for band parts, orchestrations, tips, and there may be one or two other items I've missed out."

"But, Father," I exclaimed, "if what you say is right, and I am sure it is, then £100 won't be enough."

I sounded so depressed that Father sensed he had to be more encouraging unless he wanted to put me off the project altogether. "I may have over-estimated an expense here and there," he said. "I probably have. I wanted you to know all the pitfalls. On reflection, I am sure £100 will cover your expenses, but you certainly won't have anything to spare."

"So that means I get nothing for myself," I said.

"Quite possibly," he agreed. "When you take over a Bill, you have to pay all the expenses I have enumerated. There is, however, the other side I have not yet mentioned. In return for taking over the Bill you receive a share of the takings. If business is good you will make a few pounds. But if it is not, and your share of the takings comes to, say, only £50, then you will have lost half your capital. Do you understand?"

I said, "Oh yes," although I still couldn't quite see how I was going to earn any money. But I reassured myself that Father would not have made the suggestion if I stood no chance at all of winning through. I spent the next few days borrowing money, and to my surprise I was able to raise £100, and Father, broke as he was, lent me £25 of this.

With the £100 in my hot hand I went to see Mr. Hartley Milburn, who had offices in Leicester Square where the Odeon Cinema is now. He was a portly man, with thinning dark hair, softly spoken, deliberate in manner, and a twinkle in his eyes. I liked him for the twinkle. I had not spoken to him for long before I realized Father had briefed him well on my behalf. He set to work at once to get a Bill together, an opening date, and agreed to take care of all the details.

A fortnight later he rang me up and told me to be ready to start. I felt so elated at the thought of working again that I forgot to ask him where I was booked to appear. I poured thanks upon him, with a torrent of words, so that he forgot to tell me where I was opening, and he had to ring back to say:

"Oh, by the way, you're opening at Colchester. It isn't one of the best dates, even on the 'Number Two's', but it is a start and the reports from there will decide your future. If they are encouraging we may be offered better dates. We may even be able to get you a 'Number One' where you can really play to some money. Meanwhile, I've been trying for Norwich and Peterborough, and they've promised to let me know after you've opened."

For someone like myself, who had played in three West End shows, two of them successes, this wasn't exactly setting the Provinces on fire. My £100 investment was already beginning to seem a threadbare gamble, but I had made my bet. So, with a song in my heart, a muted song, but a song nevertheless, I took the train to Colchester. By the time I reached Colchester the song had given way to trepidation and I began to doubt the wisdom of what I was doing, and wished Father and Jack had discouraged me. I began to see clearly for the first time all the points against the project. I was gambling with borrowed money. I had never before appeared in front of a Music Hall audience, and though I might be able to wring some tears from them, I had no reason whatever for believing I could make them laugh. Jack thought I could and had written and told me so, but he was biased.

That is how I thought, and that is how I was thinking on the side of the stage when I saw my number go up in the frame, and someone said to me, "You're on, Miss Courtneidge." I think I only went on because it required less courage than running away.

I went on, with two years of utter failure behind me, and an unknown audience in front. My first cameo was a song, and then a dance with a parasol. Thank heaven Laddie Cliff's number had a catchy tune. They applauded; not with great enthusiasm, but they applauded. I rushed off to make my change and came back for my second cameo. This was pathos, which suited the mood of the time. It was called, 'And Sister turned away'. The scene was an Army hospital. A soldier is dying but does not realize it. The Hospital Sister (me) does. But 'just in case' he hands the Sister a souvenir to send to his wife. He gives a cheery message as he cannot write, and explains the souvenir to the Sister. Finally, he tells her to say soon he'll be coming back to Blighty and what a grand time they will have together on his return. And the Sister, stern Army Nurse though she is, just turns away, holding the souvenir and not daring to let the soldier see her face, for Army Sisters don't cry or upset their patients, you know.

At the end of this cameo there was silence, and I wondered which way the cat was going to jump. And then it came—applause—good, solid applause. This time I walked more confidently back to my quick-change room on the side of the stage.

I strutted back for my last number. Yes, strutted, that's what confidence does for you. My final cameo was 'The Knut in the R.A.F.' I was in uniform. A man's uniform. I had never done male impersonation before, but I swaggered, and sang, and burlesqued. The audience loved it and I knew they did. I could feel they were with me. They stamped their feet, whistled, and laughed. Yes, they laughed. And I knew then that I had found my place in the Theatre. Not just the Music Hall, but laughter, making people laugh. I was so happy when I went off to really big applause. I was right. Jack was right. Father was right; and what was even more exciting, my £100, I mean my friends' £100, was safe.

I had made the Music Halls.

And how quickly the world changed for me! Next morning, telephone calls from the agents, telegrams and Press notices. Before that first week was out I had been booked, not for Norwich and Peterborough, but for the Victoria Palace, London; and by the time I left Colchester there were contracts for the next three and five years, with options for ten.

I 'phoned Jack to tell him I was on the first rung of the ladder. A slightly different ladder to the one I had started on. I asked him, "What should I do in the future?"—by that I meant, "Should I change my act for London?" and he replied: "Do in the future? Why, do what you've been doing in Colchester. Make them laugh."

I have never stopped trying.

VIII

Music Hall

★

Almost everything happened to me in Music Hall. I was booed and applauded. I was banned by a Watch Committee. I had a manager who lost himself and a good deal of my money. I had two assistants, one who was fast and could not be heard, and one who could be heard but was slower than a Russian saying "Yes." I met most of the famous personalities of the time and played some of the biggest dates in the country and, without doubt, all of the smallest; but I enjoyed the life. This was probably because of the ups and downs of music halls, not despite of them.

If you want experience of your fellow men at their kindest and cruellest go and stand alone on a music-hall stage on a Saturday night in some provincial town and try to amuse them. I have done so and won their acclaim. But in my early days I also experienced shouts, mutterings, boos, and even had pennies hurled down at me. On those occasions I went on singing my song, just a bit louder, that's all. Sometimes I would pull the audience round with a joke, sometimes with a gesture, sometimes I answered back. In this way I found out that an apt rejoinder would silence them or turn boos to applause in a moment.

It is true that Music Halls accepted me after Colchester and my first London appearance at the Victoria Palace; but I had to fight for months before I really felt at home. Perhaps I tried too hard. The reputation I had earned in my father's musicals did not impress them. There was Marie Lloyd, George Formby, Harry Tate, Wilkie Bard, Nellie Wallace, Nora Delaney (now Mrs. Prince Littler), Florrie Ford, Charles Austin, George Lashwood, Little Tich, Vesta Tilley, G. H. Elliot, Fred Kitchen,

Fred Barnes, Talbot O'Farrell, and George Robey, to mention only a few of them. Most of those I have mentioned are no longer in the land of the living, but in 1917 they were the great stars of the Music Hall with tremendous personal followings. They commanded big salaries even compared with present-day standards. But they were, most of them, so open-hearted and generous that they gave away most of what they earned.

An exception to this was George Lashwood. When he died in 1944 he left, for a music-hall artiste, the astonishing sum of £131,000. When I think of it this is astonishing for anyone.

A more typical example of the times was a friend of ours, Fred Karno, whose road show, *The Mumming Birds*, employed no less an artiste than Charles Chaplin. Fred Karno was a rich man in 1914, rich enough to spend £70,000 on Tagg's Island, which lies in the Thames at Hampton. Here he built a kind of casino to attract wealthy week-enders in search of good dancing and dinners. He hoped to run it for a couple of seasons and then sell out at a good profit. The war came and 'Karsino', as he called his venture, proved a flop. In 1918 he told me about another brilliant idea which had seized him, a spectacular revue at the big London Opera House, starring Charlie Chaplin. The revue was to be written by no less a person than Horatio Bottomley. He offered Charlie £1,000 a week to come over, but Fred told me that Charlie replied: "Yes, £1,000 a week is a lot of money and I should like to see the old town again. But over here I am making £10,000 a week and they won't let me go." Poor Fred Karno. He died a few years later leaving only £42.

Up to the time I went on the Halls I had always worked for my father and, whatever I may have earned on paper, I was never allowed to handle more than £2 or £3 a week. At the time I resented this, but at least it trained me to be careful without being mean. I was glad of this training when I began to earn big money on the Halls. Within a few months I was getting £75 a week, and before I returned to a West End theatre I was earning even more.

Just as I was establishing myself in Music Hall my voice went back on me. There were no microphones in those days and although my voice had proved strong enough for Musical Comedy I was never sure I had enough volume to take the impatient music-hall audience by the ears. And as I believed that was the only way to take them I sang at the top of my voice, particularly in the vast auditoriums like Bristol Hippodrome, Glasgow Empire, and the London Palladium. I believe I sang so loudly that when I was playing at one of these Halls I could be heard at the other two. The result was that people heard me but within three months my voice had gone.

It happened when I was playing on a Bill with the late Wilkie Bard, who specialized in character impressions. That week he was doing his studies of the patronizing Peeress, the bathing-machine attendant, and the office cleaner. He came into my dressing-room after the last performance on the Saturday night and said, "Young lady, you've been taking me too seriously."

"What do you mean?" I asked him in a whisper.

"This," he said, and began to sing in his curiously jerky voice the song by which he is still remembered. It was very apt.

> "I want to sing in opera, I've got that kind of voice.
> I want to sing in opera, if I could have my choice,
> Signor Caruso told me I ought to do so,
> So that's why I want to sing in opera,
> Sing in op-op-opera-a-a."

I thought he was making fun of me and I said, angrily, "Mr. Bard, I have never imagined myself an opera singer."

He smiled. "I should be more tactful, Miss Courtneidge. But you are losing your voice, now aren't you?"

I nodded, and he continued: "If I were you I would go to see a doctor before it goes altogether. I am sure you need to rest. And if you don't mind taking some advice from an 'old pro', don't try so hard. I've watched you, and believe me, you get over as soon as they see you."

"Thank you, Mr. Bard," I whispered, "but I want to be sure that everyone in the House hears me."

He smiled, and patted me gently on the cheek. "They'll listen to a pin drop if they like you," he said.

I caught the night train to London and the next morning went to see a throat specialist. His verdict sounded alarming. I had nodules on my larynx and the only cure was complete rest. I had to postpone all my dates. I rented a four-roomed cottage, for fifteen shillings a week, at Radlett, which was near where Jack was stationed. I was forbidden to talk at all, and for the only time in our married life Jack was able to have the first and last words in all our discussions.

It was months before my voice was strong enough for me to work again, and I used this time to go and see the two artistes I most admired, Vesta Tilley and Gertie Millar. I had always admired Gertie Millar. So had everyone since they first saw her at the Gaiety in *The Toreador*. The Gaiety was famous for the beautiful girls it produced, but Gertie Millar was the star of them all. In *The Toreador* she captured London from the moment they set eyes upon her in a bridesmaid's gown and a large hat. Those who saw her said that it seemed as if a swan was floating on a lake as she swam down-stage. It is difficult to pinpoint her appeal; there was something about her which at once arrested the attention. There was a brightness, a freshness, and a charm, which crossed the footlights at once. I think that Mr. Macqueen Pope, the Theatrical historian, has captured in words, as well as anyone could, the magic of her personality when he says:

"Here was someone with a piquant face, a slim, graceful figure, who, despite the ease and grace of movement, made everyone feel the life and the vivacity she radiated. It is not possible to convey the extraordinary appeal of Gertie Millar. The Gaiety-goers met it that night in June for the first time, and all of them, men and women alike, surrendered at once. This new girl, unknown to all of them hitherto, just stole the show and captured all hearts. It was not only looks and indefinable charm, for hers was not beauty of classical lines, or baby chocolate-box prettiness. It was something better. It was pure fascination which this girl possessed, and that much misused word, Glamour. She had it in full. You could not resist it, yet she exerted no force to make it reach you. It was there, like an invisible net which enwrapped the entire house, from gallery to the boxes."

Gertie Millar was approaching the end of her theatrical career when my lost voice gave me the chance to see her in *Airs and Graces* at the Palace Theatre. She was then nearly forty, but her beauty and personality were as vivid as ever. I think, over and above everything else, she had style, and that is what drew me to

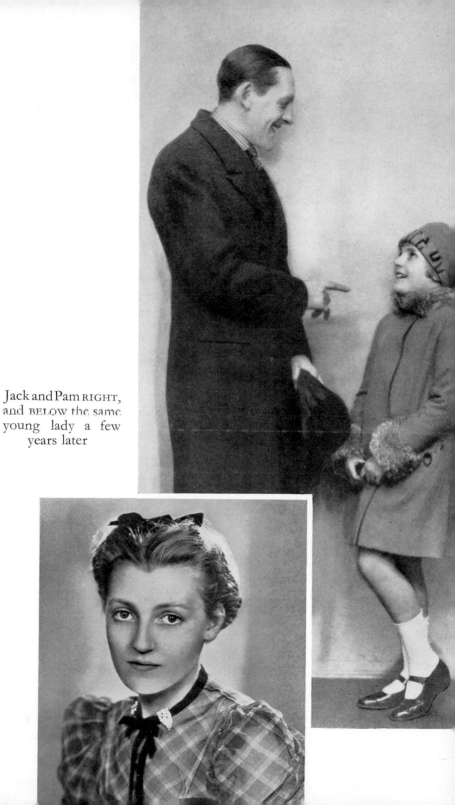

Jack and Pam RIGHT,
and BELOW the same
young lady a few
years later

Who's baby are you? As if you didn't know!

her most of all. Her great successes were, of course, associated with one theatre, the Gaiety. And although she had successes at other theatres, the Gaiety was her Palace. Crowds stood every night, to give little gasps of admiration and applause, as she went from the stage-door to her carriage or car. And as she came through the stage-door the crowd fell apart, leaving a gangway for her to pass down, and stood adoring her, and treating her like royalty. She would trip to her waiting vehicle, with a bright smile for all, a wave of the hand, and drive away, treated like the Queen she was.

Curiously enough, although the two women I most admired, Gertie Millar and Vesta Tilley, were utterly different personalities —one was the Glamour Queen of all time and the other a great comedienne—they had one theatrical achievement in common, both reached almost regal status in the Theatre.

I think Vesta Tilley enjoyed the most successful career of any woman who trod the music-hall stage. At the age of five she piped out a little ditty, a habit she maintained for another sixty years. She was the creator of the male impersonator and I followed in her footsteps. Her long continued run as 'Top of the Bill' was due to the fact that she mastered the technique of the Music Halls more thoroughly than any woman had ever done before. She had attack, warmth, and vitality, and an instantaneous, almost radar-like, feel for the mood of an audience. Whatever song she sang, she made, by some strange alchemy, her very own, whether it was 'Jolly good luck to the girl who loves a sailor' or 'Piccadilly Johnnie with the little glass eye'. She certainly made her mark on the Metropolis, where she was known as 'London's idol', and on Music Hall, where she topped Bills for thirty years. She made her mark on me too. I went night after night to see her; youth has ambitions as high as Mount Everest. Mine were, I wanted to be as amusing as Vesta Tilley, and as glamorous as Gertie Millar.

My enforced rest, waiting for the nodules to disappear from my larynx, did me a great deal of good. When I returned to work I found the time I had spent studying Music Hall as one of the audience had not been wasted. My confidence grew, and when it was suggested to me that I should do a pantomime with Harry Relph, who was known as Little Tich, I was brash enough to say, "That depends on the pantomime."

Little Tich was to all intents and purposes a freak of nature, being a bare four feet in height with a perfectly normal body, but dwarfishly short legs. To complete the misfortune, he came into the world with five fingers and a thumb on each of his hands, plus six toes on both feet. Nevertheless, as so frequently happens in such instances, he was gifted with an abnormally keen brain and a determination to overcome these disabilities. Life always had its humorous side for him. He went on the Halls and as time went on his reputation grew; there was something appealingly attractive in this comical little creature who came bounding on the stage to roll out a song with such energy. In burlesque evening dress, about ten sizes too big for him, top-hat, and a huge cigar, he brought a completely novel humour to audiences tired of comic songs and sketches.

When I was invited to play with him he was earning as much as £300 a week, but despite his importance as a star I was still bold enough to say, "I would love to play in pantomime with Mr. Relph if it is the right one."

I knew the management wanted me to play *Cinderella*. I wanted to play *Aladdin*. After all, I was specializing in male impersonation. I made it quite clear that nothing anyone could say, including Little Tich, would shift me from my determination to play *Aladdin*. I opened in *Cinderella* at the Theatre Royal, Manchester. The management thought they had won until they saw my interpretation of *Cinderella*. There never was, and probably never will be, such a forward, boyish, strutting performance of *Cinderella* in the history of the Theatre. There never was a *Cinderella* so unafraid of the ugly sisters. I think I convinced my Prince Charming, and the audience, that he stood more in need of my help than I of his. I not only got away with playing *Cinderella* as *Aladdin*, but I still remained friends with Little Tich.

We liked each other from the start and despite his reputation for being a difficult person to work with he encouraged me to get all the laughs I could. Harry Relph—I am going to call him that because he never liked being called Little Tich outside the Theatre—was always very much on his dignity and quick to resent the slightest reference to his disabilities. Anyone calling him Little Tich got no answer. If he had not been so small I am sure he would have wanted to have been a serious musician.

Sometimes, in between shows, he used to play the violin to me. I did not feel any pity for him. My eyes were not attracted by the curiosity of his six fingers. I admired him for the great artiste he was. To me he was a big man. He felt this, and that is why I think we were such good friends. During the pantomime Harry was in love with a famous and beautiful star of the theatre. One of the beautiful things about her was that she saw beyond his stunted figure, into his heart, and returned his love. He was never very happy but he was with her.

Harry Tate was one of the greatest music-hall stars I have ever known. His motor-car act is still a legend. All that happened was that everything went wrong with the car; like all good ideas it was basically simple. A door would fall off, the steering-wheel came away, the seats collapsed, and the radiator spurted water. Harry's act used to keep me in fits of laughter from the wings each night. So too did Harry Tate's method of entry. He loved 'a-little-of-what-he-fancied' to the extent of staying in the pub across the road until two minutes before his act. When his call came, Harry would empty his glass, walk across the road to the stage-door, up the steps, and on to the stage. As he approached the wings, his dresser had his white motoring coat ready to slip on, a motoring cap would be crammed down on his head, and without stopping in his stride Harry would put on his moustache and walk on stage, straight into his act.

He was always an immediate success. I watched every show of his. His timing was out of this world.

One of the main differences between Music Hall and the Theatre is that in the first you are on your own. Not only, as I have already said, when the moment of truth arrives between yourself and the audience, but after the show is over. It is a lonely life, forever on the move, and this loneliness got on my nerves, so I decided to put it right. I engaged assistants to help me in my act and later on I became even more ambitious and took out a complete company of my own.

One of the first people to tour with me was my brother-in-law, Claude Hulbert. He was the second undergraduate in my theatrical life and used to tour with me during his school holidays from Cambridge.

NOTE FROM JACK HULBERT
I have told my wife repeatedly that Cambridge is a University and not a school, and that they do not have holidays but vacations.

As I was saying, Claude toured with me during his school holidays. He was wonderful company and I was sorry when he had to go back. Fortunately he sent me one of his school friends in his place. He was the third undergraduate in my life. His name was, and still is, Peter Haddon, and he subsequently became my brother-in-law. He took over Claude's job of stage manager and played a small part in a sketch which I introduced into one of my cameos.

Claude had one or two handicaps. At the beginning they were obstacles to success; today he has turned them into advantages. The first was his complete inability to close his mouth. As a result he just could not throw his voice at all.

I would go to him and say, "Claude, throw your voice forward, close your teeth and mouth like this for heaven's sake!"

"But I can't close it, Cis, it won't go."

"Rubbish," I would yell, "of course you can! Everyone can close their teeth if they try." And I would actually put my hands on his head and on his chin to try to force his teeth together. But it was useless, Claude's mouth remained open. I would drill him, working out lines he could speak clearly and words that he could articulate clearly.

His second difficulty was his hearing. Claude was inclined to be deaf, and this made him speak so quietly. So quietly he could not be heard at all. True, he was my stoodge, but what use a stoodge who could not be heard? Poor Claude, how he dreaded the Halls! He was often depressed and convinced he had no future. There were times when I felt like agreeing with him. And yet if we could only have seen ahead for a few years we would have known that his crazy voice and queer articulation would be the very things that would eventually win him success.

Peter Haddon was quite different. You could hear everything he said, or should I say drawled, even when he spoke in a whisper. He had an easy manner on the stage, too easy at times, because he was so slow at first there were occasions when the Second House had started before he had finished saying his lines in the First. He took criticism, though he tried to answer back, but I was too quick for him.

The only word he got in edgeways was "Er."

I used to call him the 'Duke of Er'. Peter is another example who has turned an apparent disadvantage to advantage, and did

A scene from the film I made in Hollywood

Holiday snaps in England and Switzerland

so well he cornered a market for himself playing Dukes, Earls, Peers, Baronets, and Knights. If you look him up in the stage *Who's Who* you can easily imagine, when you read a list of the parts he has played, that you have strayed into *Debrett*.

There is a point I would like to make here. During the years I was touring the Halls I was always introducing new material. This was regarded as quite unusual. In those days when artistes of known repute found a good number or a good sketch, they would go on singing or playing it year in year out, until they faded away. This policy was eventually to hasten the decline of the Music Hall, as not only the artistes faded away but so did the audiences.

Putting in new material did not always have a happy ending. Once it resulted in me walking off the stage. And then it was nothing to do with a tough audience. It was to do with a tough Watch Committee. Ivor Novello, in collaboration with Jack, had written me a song. Now there was a rule in all contracts on the Halls that if the management objected to an act, or part of it, they had to notify you immediately after the First House or not later than the Second House. This gave you time to change your act and rehearse another one.

I was playing Birmingham when I put in my new number. It went down well, so I kept it in for the Second House; again it went well. Then suddenly, on the second day, just as I was about to go on the stage, the management told me the Watch Committee objected to the song and it had to come out. I was astounded that a Watch Committee could take objection to a song written by Ivor Novello and Jack. I must have been pretty innocent because the lyric did not seem suggestive to me. On reflection, I realize that the lyric could be judged suggestive. But I really did not think so at the time. It was called 'The little dog's tail went up', and it told the story of a man meeting a girl and, 'The little dog's tail went up'. They went for a walk in the park and home to tea and, 'The little dog's tail went up'. Next day they went to the races, to the theatre, out to supper, and eventually they kissed, and 'The little dog's tail went up'. Subsequently they married, and, 'The little dog's tail went up'. But when a family arrived and the wife produced twins, 'The little dog's tail went up twice'. And as for the Watch Committee, their eyebrows went up a dozen times.

F

There is nothing so infuriating, to my mind, as being accused of bad taste, or anything else for that matter, when you honestly believe you are innocent.

I pointed out to the manager that they had not given me time to get another song ready, and anyway they should have warned me the day before or in the morning. I had no one to advise me. Jack was in the Army, way down South. I looked at the manager and tried to sum him up. Then I decided to make a stand. "It is too late for me to change now," I argued. "I can only go on with the act I have rehearsed, and that includes the song."

"You must cut the song, by order of the Watch Committee," insisted the manager.

"I have nothing to put in its place," I protested.

"That is not my worry," he replied.

"Oh yes it is," I said, "because I can't go on without the little dog's tail. I am billed to appear in three cameos, I am not going on just to do two."

"If you don't go on," he said angrily, "the management will sue you for breaking your contract."

I showed him I could be just as obstinate as he was being. "I will sue the management," I declared, "for breaking their contract by not giving me sufficient warning." I realized it was useless to argue any further with him, and as my song had been cut I would not go on.

I packed, walked out of the theatre, and caught the next train to London. Afterwards I had the consolation of being told by my agent that I was in the right. But I did not feel triumphant, because, whoever was proved right or wrong, the audience who had paid to see me were the losers.

One day in 1921, when I was playing at the Liverpool Empire, my agent, Hartley Milburn, came to see me with a suggestion that I at first refused to countenance.

He said, without batting an eyelid, "Cicely, why don't you get a small company together, take over the Bill, and play some of the fit-ups?"

I replied: "It has taken me three years to build up a first-class reputation on the Music Halls and here are you suggesting I should go on some one-night stands. You must be out of your mind."

Hartley Milburn shook his head sadly, lit a cigarette, and said,

"Oh well, I suppose I shouldn't have mentioned it, but I did think you would like to make some extra money."

There was nothing I liked better and Hartley Milburn knew I had swallowed his bait, and pretended to leave. "Come off it," I said. "Let me see what you have in mind. If the figures are good then perhaps it may be worth the effort."

He showed me the estimated box-office receipts of some of the smaller towns like Ripon, Newark, Filey, Skipton, Thirsk, Northallerton, and Withernsea. His figures proved to me that if I alternated the bigger dates with weeks of one-night stands I stood a fair chance of nearly doubling my income. I was thrilled.

I got a company together and became one of the last people in Music Hall to play the fit-ups. It was not long before I was to be glad of the Northern Scots blood in my veins. It was not long before I was to be proud of any blood in my veins. There is nothing in my experience in the Theatre which takes it out of you so much as fit-ups. Before I go into detail about fit-ups let me tell you a theatrical lie: I adored one-night stands, I loved the out-of-the-way towns, and any success I may have made is entirely due to this experience. Now for the truth: I would exchange any one-night stand for a long run in a West End theatre. I know this is hard to believe in view of the testimony of so many theatrical autobiographies, but I beg to differ.

I suppose I must have played over a hundred one-night stands. In the main they were remunerative, but when I think back I remember a jigsaw of incidents when things went wrong. It is true that people, usually, are apt to remember only the good things, but in this case it is the bad that come flooding back to me and I think it is because in retrospect they are amusing. In particular I remember a day on one of my first fit-up tours when nothing went right.

I was up at 5 a.m., had a quick cup of tea, and then made a quick dash to the station to catch a 5.45 a.m. Emett special. I arrived at the town where I was billed to appear at 8.30 a.m. I left the staff to unload and get the luggage and scenery into the hall in which I was playing by 10 a.m. I soon discovered that no arrangements had been made for my visit as no one was expecting me, although I could see bills up all over the town announcing my arrival. There was no piano in the hall, and no battens, or tumblers, or anything on which to arrange our lighting, hang the curtains, drapes, and fly our scenery. From 10 a.m. to 1 p.m. I tried to organize a piano, a piano-tuner, a pianist, and some wood to improvise our stage requirements.

During a lull, when I was sipping a cup of tea, a young man arrived who said he was a pianist. While I was trying to investigate his claim another man appeared who said he had worked at the hall and knew someone who knew someone who might be able to find me some wood. While I was investigating his claim my staff were improvising the scenery. Meanwhile, I had accepted the pianist at face value and asked him to go through the music for the whole Company. This was not as easy as it sounds (not that he sounded very good), as he played by ear. He was also hard of hearing.

For the next two hours I tried to teach him the piano while the cast were ironing and pressing their clothes and trying to squeeze themselves, eleven people, into two small dressing-rooms in which there were no wash-basins, no mirrors, no cupboards, no chairs, no shelves, no windows, but still they were labelled 'Dressing Rooms'.

Around five o'clock in the afternoon I took a look at the box-office sheet to see the plan and discovered that Hartley Milburn was quite wrong in his estimate and that if I was lucky I'd play to £7 10*s*. on the two houses and not £80 as he had forecast. I wondered if I had come to the wrong town. I checked and found the name of the town was the name of the place I was in. There was no way out. The show had to go on because I was in need of the money to pay the fares to the next town.

A few people arrived in the hall and began an animated conversation about local matters which made me once again take seconds. Then I realized they were supposed to be the staff of the local hall. My clue was their complete lack of interest. There was only one way to attract their attention and that was to join in their conversation, a political one. I did this when there was a suitable opening between Lloyd George and Campbell-Bannerman and after about half an hour I was able to slip in a sly reference to the job on hand—i.e. the show that evening. They went right on talking, but this time about local affairs, so I went right on talking about the show. I was fairly confident that if they gave up talking before I did I would win the day. It was as easy as that. Once I had converted them to the idea of doing their job they would be second to everyone. In fact it would have been far better for my peace of mind to have paid them to go away, but I was stubborn enough to believe that the programme girl should sell programmes, the box-office girl should sell tickets, that one of them should work the curtains, another the switchboard, and, of course, the ushers should ush. I tried to get rid of the pianist but he refused to go.

Once I had everyone organized and an apathetic audience was filing into the hall for the First House I remembered I had nowhere to sleep that night, but I decided to postpone that problem until between the shows, when I found that the only difficulty about obtaining a bed for the night was that no one was particularly keen to take me in. If I had let them know earlier it would have been all right, they told me, but they were full right up. So I had better ask Mrs. Jones, who had a vacancy but could not possibly call me at five o'clock in the morning. She directed me to another landlady who would call me at five o'clock in the morning but was full up, so I had to settle for Mrs. Jones who wouldn't call me at five o'clock. This meant that I spent a sleepless night worrying in case I overslept, until at half-past four I fell exhausted to sleep. Thirty minutes later Mrs. Jones, who had taken pity on me, woke me up with a five o'clock call.

I hope I am making one-night stands sound like hell because they were. So was the show. Judge for yourself: First of all, a gentleman I used to call Mr. Jam-Jars came on and played previously popular songs on jam-jars. Meanwhile the pianist composed some music. The audience regarded this strange combination as rather wonderful because Mr. Jam-Jars always retired to a couple of healthy tabs. He was followed by a lady who played violin solos. Meanwhile the pianist composed some music. So far so bad, but there was worse to come: a sister act which sang and danced. They were a sturdy couple who took no more notice of the pianist composer than he did of them. We also had a vocalist who sang 'Drake is going West', and, usually, an uninvited encore, 'On the Road to Mandalay', with one hand in his pocket. But this time the pianist had both hands in his pockets, and he only started playing again when a cross-talk act came on who fought each other for the attention of the audience.

I was the last turn and I went on determined to do or die.

I died. It is very difficult to sing a song when a pianist is composing music.

Getting into the town had its problems but so did getting out. There was the settling up to do with the local management, packing, loading the trucks, taking the scenery down to the station, off-loading them at the siding ready for the morning, then back into the town for a late supper and so to bed, round about 2 a.m., and, as I have told you, about half an hour's shut-eye. So far as the routine of fit-ups is concerned, what I have told you is typical of any of them when you combine the roles of artiste and management.

In the early days of touring my own Company I was not helped by my manager, a charming man who could not manage himself. He used to disappear for days on end and I used to search for him. When I found him he always promised to reform, and really meant it at the time, and I believed him until one day I decided he had gone too far. I think we were playing Ripon, an important date, as we were there for two nights. When we arrived he was already missing and he had made no preparations for my arrival, so I put on the show as best I could in the time and afterwards went in search of him. It was Friday night, Mr. Missing Manager had the money, and everyone had to be paid.

I finally tracked him down in the only Temperance Hotel in the town. He was lying fully dressed on the bed in a small attic at the top of the hotel, and when he had handed over what money was left he said, "I suppose this is the end."

I felt sorry for him, he looked so ill, but I could not help but agree. "Yes," I said, "I am going to get myself a new manager. You must return to London."

I gave him his fare, and then, thinking of his wife and family at home, I asked if there was anything I could do.

He thought for a moment and then he said, "Yes, I wonder if you would mind getting me some fruit salts?"

I said, "Is there really nothing else?"

He thought again and shook his head. "No. Just the fruit salts." And with that parting gift we parted company.

Despite the trials of one-night stands, I was quite happy on the Halls and always enjoyed my weeks in the big towns. But after five years of touring, although I was established as a comedienne, I was anxious to return to the West End of London in a musical comedy. Apart from any other consideration I wanted some home life, to be near Jack, who was at the Lyric Theatre playing in *A Little Dutch Girl*. My opportunity came in 1921 when I was offered a part in a new revue which was being presented by Tod Waller, the son of Lewis Waller, at the Royalty Theatre. My acceptance of the part meant that I had to cancel some very lucrative music-hall contracts, but I thought it was worth the risk, particularly when Jack was also engaged to appear with me. We had a cast which included Eric Blore, Phyllis Dare, Marie Blanche, and Ivy St. Helier.

The revue was called *Ring Up* and after the critics had finished with it the only thing left for us to do was to ring down. This we did, but we were not beaten. The show was re-written and re-produced by Jack and transferred to the Vaudeville Theatre, where we had slightly better luck, under a new management, and ran for three months. This was by no means the triumphant return to London for which I had hoped, but at least it was a return.

When the run of *Ring Up* ended I went back to the Music Halls, where I had to pay the penalty for cancelling my contracts by accepting less money. This did not upset me as much as it might have done, as I still remembered what it was like to be out of work.

IX

At Home

THERE are very many rewards for a theatrical life. For one thing there is plenty of variety even if you are doing the same show night after night. No two audiences are alike, their mood is affected by the weather, good news and bad news, and a number of other conditioning factors such as what they have eaten for dinner. So every time the curtain goes up the audience represents a challenge, and when you have won them over you have a feeling of triumph which never palls. The social side of the Theatre is another attraction. You meet a lot of interesting people, not only in your own profession, but from all walks of life.

But I suppose that most people would say that the biggest reward that the Theatre has to offer is in the form of money. There is no doubt that if you have what the public wants you can earn a lot of money, and you do so while you are still young. Against this you have to debit high expenses, running two homes, especially when you are on tour, and of course you can never be sure how long the public are going to go on wanting you. Insecurity is the never changing backcloth to theatrical life and ninety per cent of the people in the Theatre are lucky if they make a bare living. Why, you may ask, do they go on? I know why I did: the whip was earning my daily bread and the carrot was fame.

But however successful we are, and however sweet the carrot, I sometimes wonder if it is worth the sacrifice nearly every artiste has to make, the sacrifice of home life. Of course we have homes, but we are never sure how long we are going to be in them. I know there is an answer to this: give up the profession, get an ordinary job, and stay at home. Oh no! We couldn't do that. You have only to go into our history to find the reason why. First of all we were rogues and vagabonds, then we became strolling players, and now we are called ladies and gentlemen. But between you and me we remain a mixture of all three. That doesn't prevent us, however, from having a tremendous nostalgia for home life. I know that two years after the First World War I was becoming very dissatisfied with only seeing my husband when I was playing near enough to London to go home on a Sunday. Of course Jack sometimes used to come up to see me, but still only for a day, as always he had to return to London for his show on the Monday. We both longed for an opportunity to enjoy some home life in our flat in Great Portland Street.

When my opportunity came it was not entirely unexpected. The doctor said, "You are going to have a baby."

I said, "I know I am."

He said, "You must cancel your tour."

And forthwith I did so and caught the train to London, where I started work on my son's trousseau. I made it of pure white *crêpe de Chine*, very extravagant no doubt, but after all it was my first baby. I used to do miles and miles of tucks all kept to their size with a tiny white piece of cardboard. Then I would whip on miles and miles of real lace, and finally thread through whole rolls of baby ribbon. I naturally chose blue for a boy because I was certain I would have a son.

When I had finished making the trousseau I looked round for another anodyne to keep me occupied and found one in dusting. Most people dislike this form of housework. I love it. I like to do it completely though. That means pinning up curtains, pulling out books, moving furniture, and going behind everything. And I also like polishing. So I spent every moment dusting and polishing until even the furniture must have wanted a rest.

I probably drove Jack mad during this period. He used to come flying home from the theatre, shoot up in the lift, and bounce in through the door, shouting, "How's the boy behaving himself?"

"He's behaving very nicely," I would say proudly.

We used to discuss our son's future. How we used to plan, Jack and I! I would never tire of talking about him, but Jack inevitably turned every conversation back to the Theatre. The Theatre was everything to Jack and still is. I doubt if it is ever out of his mind. When he is eating, drinking, driving a car, or shaving; particularly when he is shaving. The concentration of all his waking thoughts on the Theatre is the reason why he has no sense of time. I am sure, when he goes to sleep, he dreams about the Theatre, although he denies this. And if he ever makes any appointments in his dreams I believe he must be as late for them as he is in real life. Even in the early days of our married life, when it was easy to forgive, he used to drive me frantic with his last minute scrambles. He still does.

I am quite different. I like to plan. I planned to have a son. I planned the exact moment when he was going to arrive, but he took after Jack and kept me waiting three weeks. Jack was wonderful during those weeks. He kept me laughing and took me out on nightly promenades and even encouraged me to tap dance and jump to try and hurry the baby along.

He would come rushing in from the theatre and call out, "Am I in time?" when he knew quite well nothing had happened. A nurse was with me by now and so was my mother's sister, Edith, and the family kept calling and ringing up for news of the baby.

And then at last, early one morning, I felt certain my son had decided to arrive. The doctor agreed on twilight sleep and I was given a mask to put over my face. I remember pushing the mask as hard as I could, but no sleep came. Indeed, I was conscious all the time.

My aunt kept saying, "Not long now, darling, you're being so brave."

I wasn't, but it was beyond me to be silent. My father came round and he and Jack waited together until it was over and the child was born. I heard whispering in a corner of the room, and then some slapping noises. Are they clapping their hands? I wondered. Funny moment to applaud. Then I heard a sound which was a mixture of a grunt, hiccup, and squeal. My baby had taken its first breath of air.

They handed the little bundle to me and Jack said, "It's a girl, darling," and kissed me gently. "She's a lovely baby, weighs over eight pounds," said my aunt.

I had to take her word for it. For the bundle in my arms had a bright red face, all puckered up, and tightly closed eyes, and a mop of shaggy dark hair. I had to smile. Pamela Rosemary was the funniest little object I had ever seen.

I recovered well after the birth but my daughter did not make good progress. She had to be artificially fed and we just couldn't find a food to suit her. We tried dozens but she still lost weight. At last we went to a specialist.

"She's all right," he assured me, "nothing organically wrong at all. It's just a matter of finding the right food to suit her."

It was all very well for him to talk, but by the time we had found the right food I was scared there would be no Pamela Rosemary to eat it.

It was dear old Nannie Kennedy who came to the rescue. The doctor had recommended her to me.

"She is a widow," he said, "and she lost her husband in the war and adores children; always wanted a big family herself. She's got a slight limp—had some shrapnel in her foot—but you won't mind that, will you?"

How could I? For Nannie Kennedy was a mother of a woman and when I met her she went straight to my heart. She had a way of talking about babies that was like the light of the sun. And so the moment Pamela Rosemary was born Nannie came to live with us. And I never cease to thank heaven for her sweetness and patience, but above all for the love she has given the whole family. She is still with us.

When I look back on my life so little of it has been spent at any one time at home that I am grateful for the memories I have of my life at Portland Court in the early part of the 1920s. Sunday was the great day of the week, particularly in the summer, when it was picnic day. We would pack a hamper with a basket of extras for Pam, a blanket in case it got cold, a sun-bonnet in case it got hot, sterilized milk in the thermos flask, strained prune pulp, orange juice, boiled water, a silver spoon and a dribbling bib. When the hamper, basket, Pam and I were in the car we would sit while Jack rushed from pillar to post organizing his last minute scramble.

At last we would be off to the country. We had our favourite spots which Jack would look out beforehand on the map. But the idea each Sunday, of course, was to find somewhere new. We would speed along the lanes with me holding a shawl over Pam's head to protect her from the wind.

Jack would say, "We'll stop round the next bend, I think,"

and I would shout, "Look, just there . . . no, we've passed it now, never mind."

Claude was often with us and my sister Rosaline too. We would all try to get Jack to stop at the spot we liked best, but he drove so fast we had usually passed them before we could point them out to him.

We were a very happy family. Jack was forging ahead in the West End of London. Claude was still at Cambridge and had made up his mind that he was going to follow in his brother's footsteps. My sister Rosaline had left school and gone straight on to the stage, where she was quickly building a reputation for herself as a Shakesperean actress.

My brother Charles was a regular visitor. He had got through the war but not without being twice wounded. He had joined up as a private and come out as an officer. He had come back to the Theatre but had not succeeded. Charles was one of the most sensitive and shy people I have ever known. It is possible for people with these characteristics to be successful in the Theatre but it is very rare, they need a great deal of encouragement to give them confidence. Father did not understand this and was often impatient with Charles; the result was that Charles stood on his head to try to please Father. If he had stood up to him he might have received the encouragement he needed. As it was, Father insisted on telling Charles what he should do, and when Charles tried to do as he was told he was never right, so far as Father was concerned. It was not surprising, therefore, under these circumstances, that Charles was not a success in the Theatre. Eventually he went to America, where he played in one or two shows. He stayed over there for two years and married Cecile Dixon, who was George Arliss's leading lady, and brought her back to England, where he established himself in book publishing.

I do not think the world ever looked so bright to the Court-neidge family as it did in the 1920s. Father was making a wonderful financial recovery and he had paid off most of the £20,000 he owed to his creditors. He had also written and produced three revues, with unqualified success, on the Music Halls, until finally *The Man from Toronto* and then *Paddy the Next Best Thing* restored him to financial health. When he married again, two years after Mother's death, Jack and I found Rosaline a small flat near us in Portland Court.

I loved having Rosaline near to me, particularly after Pam was born, and anyway since my mother's death I felt that I had taken her place, so far as I was able, with my younger brother and sister. Rosaline had all her meals with us and I was even responsible, though I did not know it at the time, for introducing her to her future husband, Peter Haddon. He was an elegant, good-looking young man who, after touring with me on the Music Halls, did not find it difficult to make his way in London. He went to the Winter Garden, where for three years he understudied George Grossmith. He also found plenty of time to make sheep's eyes at my sister. She must have liked sheep's eyes because they announced their engagement a few months after they first met, on Rosaline's nineteenth birthday.

Pam's arrival made me very reluctant to go back to the Provinces on the Music Halls, and when eventually I did so I could not settle down. A few months after my return Jack came to see me in Aberdeen with some wonderful news; Edward Laurillard was putting on a revue at the Little Theatre and it was a revue with a new idea. It was to start at nine o'clock. There had been a great outcry in the Press at the time about late-comers to the theatre. The curtain used to go up in those days at 8.15 or 8.30, never later, but still people arrived late even for the shows which started at 8.30.

Laurillard hit on the idea of catering especially for them, and his idea attracted a lot of interest. I was interested whatever time the curtain went up so long as I could return to London, be with Jack and Pam, and my sister Rosaline.

The Little Revues were an important milestone in my life. They marked the beginning of eighteen years' uninterrupted success for myself and Jack. They introduced a young man to the West End for the first time who was to have a brilliant career. His name was Bobby Howes. Our juvenile, Harold French, has had an equally successful career in films, and one of the sketches I originated, 'Laughing Gas', has sold three million records, and is still selling. The Little Revues were a success although people still arrived late for them. This did not worry me. I was far too happy at home in the day, at the theatre with Jack at night, and back home again after the show.

X

Rosaline

I HOPE there is truth in the pagan statement that those whom the gods love die young. Certainly there was everything to love in my sister Rosaline. She was blessed with natural talent, intelligence, and beauty. By the time she was twenty-one she was already a leading lady in the West End of London, and a year later she had accomplished her greatest ambition and she was leading lady at Stratford-on-Avon, and her Juliet was applauded by the critics. Like Juliet, she was in love. Like Juliet she was destined to die young. But in 1924 when I attended her wedding to Peter Haddon only life seemed near and death an unthinkable intruder.

I remember at her wedding reception pushing past Ian Hay and Leslie Henson and exclaiming: "Oh! Rosaline, you look so very lovely."

She laughed. "That's what happiness does for you," she said, and added: "I feel it is almost too good to last."

Not long afterwards I went to America with Jack in a revue called *By the Way*. It had been a great success at the Apollo Theatre. I was to return a year later to find Rosaline and her husband living in a house in Hampstead. The first time I walked up the drive of that house I had a strange apprehensive feeling which I cannot explain. I felt something tragic was going to happen.

Before Jack and I left for America we gave a little party in our flat in Portland Court. Our dearest friends were there to wish us well in the path of Columbus; there was Shaun Glenville, and his wife Dorothy Ward, who looked nearly as young then as she does today; there was Fay Compton, who in those days used to have great crushes on new flames. I remember I kept talking about the trip to America and Fay kept talking about her latest flame. I don't remember who was the flame and I am certain that Fay doesn't remember I was going to America. But as we did not allow what each other was saying to interrupt our flow of words we were both quite happy. Rosaline and Peter were there, and so was Harold French, who was coming with us to New York. Harold had been an usher at their wedding, and had endeared himself to us all because on that solemn occasion he had unwittingly given us the biggest laugh of the day.

Before the ceremony he rang up Jack and said: "I say, old man, I haven't got any morning clothes for the wedding. Can you possibly lend me some of yours?"

Now, Jack was always well supplied with morning clothes and dress suits for his stage shows. At that moment he was playing an idiotic sketch in which he was the perfect civil servant with walrus moustache, rolled umbrella, exaggerated striped trousers, and a tight-fitting, comically cut, black jacket. In addition he had in his wardrobe several other dark suits of elegance and dignity. The civil servant suit was a tailor's joke. "Of course you can borrow anything you like," said Jack, generously. "Just pop along to the theatre and help yourself, by all means."

The service at All Souls, Langham Place, went off according to plan and then we all drove to the Savoy Hotel for the reception. We were all too busy and bride-conscious at the church to take in much, but at the reception we had time to look round.

"Oh, my lord," said Jack, suddenly, "do look at Harold!"

I looked. There stood Harold, sandwich in hand, face flushed with social services and eyes a trifle glazed. He was dressed in Jack's comedy clothes, the exaggerated striped trousers which concertina'd down his legs, and the comically cut jacket. I began to laugh, and so did Jack, and when we had explained to Harold that he had picked out the wrong suit, he said, solemnly, "But I thought it was a better fit than the others."

We led him to a mirror, he took one look at himself and tried to make a run for it. Jack held on to him while I went and got him another drink. He needed something to deaden the shock.

Paul Murray, who was Jack's partner, also went with us to America. He was an Irishman with all the charm of his race, a lovely sense of humour, and what was more important an excellent knowledge of the Theatre. He had very good ideas, was a hard worker, and today would certainly be one of the great men of the Theatre, instead of one of its tragedies, if he had not had a weakness in his character which was not apparent to us at that time.

By the Way was backed by William Gaunt, one of the greatest little men I have ever met. He had started life in the cotton mills at Bradford and had gone on to make his fortune in the still expanding days of the 1920s. He spoke with a broad Yorkshire accent that took some time to get used to. But his heart was an open book. He loved the Theatre and its glamour, in which I believe he found compensation for the dull hardness of his early life. He trusted Jack at once. He liked me and believed in me. He was rough, ready, and generous to a fault, and he became a friend to both of us.

I believe that very few people know that William Gaunt was also the backer of Jimmy White, the financier who became a great figure in London Theatrical Management. People who did not know that Gaunt was in the background regarded Jimmy White as the Golden Boy of Theatrical finance. When things eventually went wrong with Jimmy White he turned to Gaunt for help, as he had done so often before, but this time 'The Little Man from Bradford' refused to be Jimmy White's financial prop, and it was not long afterwards that we were all shocked by the news that 'The Theatre's Golden Boy of the '20s' had made as dramatic an exit from the Theatre as he had an entrance. He committed suicide. I remember Gaunt saying to me in an astounded voice, when he heard the news, "Jimmy never told me things were as bad as that."

We took the entire London cast of *By the Way* to America, including my brother Charles. We opened in Brooklyn to the toughest audience of my life. Thank God they took to me. They liked me as a 'boy', they adored my fooling as a woman. The more I hurled myself about and unglamorized my sex, the more they howled with delight. But Jack they just didn't understand.

So he re-wrote and cut and rehearsed himself off his feet and then altered and slashed and rebuilt his part before we opened in New York, where *By the Way*, after a quiet opening, grew into a big success until the heat wave of an American Summer caught up with us and the season closed down.

With Mr. Frank Morgan

With Mr. Jack Hulbert

All the King's Horses

In *Full Swing* at the Palace Theatre with Nora Swinburne and Jack

It was in New York that I was caught out in an American habit of which I knew nothing at the time. It was a wet and dreary afternoon and I had gone off to a matinée and was sitting quietly and rather uncomfortably in the audience. I looked quite frightful. An old mac, an old umbrella, and splashed stockings. I am afraid I'm one of the women who kick their heels up so much at the back that they cover their stockings with mud from ankle to knee. Some of us do and some don't. I had rammed a small hat on my head, 'that didn't matter if it did get wet'. Suddenly Al Jolson, the star of the show, came down to the front of the stage.

"And now, friends," he said, "now I want to introduce you to someone new. Someone you're going to fall for in a big way. A little lady from over the sea. Miss Cicely Courtneidge, from London, England. Stand up, little lady, and take a bow. Come on, boys—give her a big hand."

The first part of the build-up had interested me. The second part had got me wondering who on earth was in the audience. But when I heard, "Miss Cicely Courtneidge," I nearly fell through the floor.

But Al Jolson was insistent and the audience were applauding so I had to get up and go on to the stage. They gave me a big hand but I could have died from embarrassment. Twisted muddy stockings, wet hat, bedraggled hair, crumpled dress, and clutching my umbrella. What a picture!

"Say a word to the folks," said Al, as they put me on the spot.

"Good-bye, folks," I said.

They thought this was funny, and laughed and applauded.

"Say a few more words," said Al Jolson. "They like to hear your English accent."

"Good-bye again, folks," I said, and suiting the action to the words made my exit.

It taught me a lesson. From that day forward I have never gone out in public without being properly groomed and polished. There is no such thing as being off-stage if you want to be a star, except in the seclusion of your own home. In my opinion it is not fair to the public, who are, after all, your employers. In the Theatre we create an illusion and to break that down outside is not only unfair to yourself but to them. I suggest that the young women who think it proper to wear slacks, an old jumper, and

G

windswept hair off-stage, or off the film set, should take note of what Aunt Cicely has to say: don't let your public down or you will soon wind up with an audience of one, and a non-paying audience at that.

My ill-dressed public appearance is not my only remembrance of 'Life' during my first visit to America. Jack and I drove out one Sunday to see life in an Indian reservation and part of the schedule was to nurse the children and meet the big chief and his squaw. The chief's baby son was the prettiest little child I have ever seen; a little red-black angel with button black eyes and long tangled hair. I picked him up and sat on a stuffed crocodile for an official picture. 'Miss Cicely Courtneidge and Chief's son in the Indian reservation'. It went along nicely until I looked down at the child's head. I was really seeing life. It was literally crawling with inhabitants. At that moment Jack turned and saw my horror. He says my face portrayed the most frightful terror he had ever seen. And even today the thought of it makes me scratch. So if you are laughing at me I hope this story will make you want to scratch too.

One night in a night club in New York we met Irving Berlin, who took us back to George Gershwin's flat, hours after New York should have been in bed. In fact they never go to bed and I don't know how their population increases at the rate it does. Gershwin played for us his 'Rhapsody in Blue'. Its effect on me was to make me feel blue. I did not think it would have much of a future and here I must admit frankly that my judgment was not quite right! Another night when we went out we met a young footballer who had just come down from College. He was trying to be a comedian, just like Jack. His effect on me was to make me feel blue. I did not think he would have much of a future and here again I must admit quite frankly that my judgment was not quite right. His name was Bob Hope!

Another character I met in America, who had a great future, was Fred MacMurray. He took Jack and me on a sight-seeing trip and ran over a skunk. We had to get out of the car and walk because Fred's car smelt so badly, and so after trying to clean it did Fred.

The '20s were also the days of Prohibition. One night Jack and I went to a very hot night club where we were introduced by a Damon Runyan character who I will call Letmesee.

"Oh, Al," he said, when they let us in to the speakeasy, "letmesee if you know these two actors who are well known in a place called England."

The man called Al, who was florid, and Italian looking, looked at us from beneath his heavily lidded eyes and said, "Letmesee if you can tell me."

"They are famous British stars," said our guide. "Don't you know them, Al?"

"No," said Al, "I don't know them. Why should I?"

"Let me see if they can drink," said our guide.

"Okay," said Al, who did not seem to share our guide's enthusiasm.

We were ushered into a smoke-filled room where some coloured musicians were playing as though they had to catch a train, and people were drinking as though they were really thirsty. I caught the atmosphere and so did Jack. I pretended to look hard and knowingly around me, and Jack walked slowly, with purpose, like the villain in a Western. As we were in the Middle West this seemed fairly reasonable characterization.

Everyone around us looked like gangsters and their molls. I thought they were then, but I realize now that many of them were probably respectable American politicians on a night out from Congress.

Jack and I ordered a drink and they brought us two cups of dark fluid.

Suddenly Jack said to me, "Don't drink that, Cis."

I slammed down the cup, which broke on impact. A very nice Sicilian-looking gentleman strolled over, hand on hip, and said to Jack, who was not related to him in any way, "Brother, why shouldn't the dame drink the coffee?"

"I didn't know it was coffee," I said quickly, "and now I do I'll drink it."

"Sure you will," said our guide, Letmesee. So he ordered another and I drank it at one gulp.

"You are a good baby," said the Sicilian.

"Please," said Jack.

"Let me see you do that again," said the guide.

"Sure I will," I said. "This may be strong coffee but we English can take it."

Land of Hope and Glory, I represented you.

It was strong coffee, but I drank it. Jack objected, the Sicilian approved, and our guide, Letmesee, kept on saying, "More."

Finally the guy called Al came over. "You're a good dame," he said.

"Don't you dame me," I said.

"Don't you like the coffee?" said Al.

"It's weak," I said.

"Say that again," said Al. So I said it again.

"No one accuses me of serving weak coffee," said Al.

"I do," I said, despite Jack kicking me, Letmesee nudging me, and the Sicilian eyeing me.

"In England," I said, boldly, and quite untruthfully, "the milk is stronger."

"If you want to make trouble," said Al, menacingly. . . .

"This guy here will settle it," I said, indicating Jack, who was speechless.

For some reason or other these words of mine, which were spoken in an ordinary conversational tone, brought silence to the speakeasy.

"So you're a guy who wants trouble?" said Al to Jack.

"I am a guy who wants to leave," said Jack with conviction.

We left at once, but outside I stopped to ask the doorman a question.

"Who is that man who spoke to us so rudely?" I asked him.

"Which one?" said the doorman.

"The one they call Al," I said.

"Oh," he said, "you mean Mister Capone."

I never met Al Capone again because the American Government eventually gave him a long holiday. But I can testify here and now Al Capone made the strongest coffee in the world.

After a year in America we returned to London back to Pam and Nannie Kennedy. We had given up Portland Court on leaving for America, so now we had no home, but Rosaline and Peter came to the rescue and invited us to stay with them. Rosaline could see I was rather surprised when she said, airily, "I want you to stay with us in our new house."

I said, "You two must have made a lot of money if you've been able to buy a house during the year we've been away?"

Rosaline laughed. "It's not our house, really. It's been lent

to us by Edgar Wallace. He says we can have it rent free for as
long as we like, two years if need be."

"Why two years?"

"Because he's taken it furnished for that time," explained
Rosaline.

In the ordinary way I would have been surprised to have been
told that someone had given anyone a furnished house rent free
for two years. But with Edgar Wallace it was different. He was
the soul of generosity, especially to his friends.

On the way to the house Peter told me how Edgar had come
to make them the offer. "I was telling him that Rosaline was
expecting a baby," said Peter, "and that we would have to move
from our flat in Marylebone Lane."

"Then I've got the very place for you," Edgar said, impul-
sively. "It's an old house on the Hill with a large overgrown
garden."

"How much rent?" said Peter.

"Nothing," said Edgar, "but that may be too much."

"You're joking," said Peter.

"I'm not joking," replied Edgar, "but I don't think you had
better have it after all. You can stay in one of my other places."

Peter insisted on seeing the House on the Hill. "It looks
perfect for us when the baby arrives. But why aren't you using
it?" he asked Edgar.

"I can't explain," Edgar replied. "I should think it is because
I just don't get on with the house."

Peter said, laughingly: "What do you mean by that? Anyone
would think that houses are people?"

Edgar replied: "Perhaps they are. Anyway, if you like the
look of it perhaps that means it likes the look of you."

Although Edgar had not admitted it to Rosaline and Peter
he could not work in the house. It unsettled him. It is not easy
for a grown man to admit to things of this sort, any more than
I found it easy to mention my nervousness when I walked up the
drive of the House on the Hill for the first time.

The house itself was rather shapeless, a mixture of archi-
tectural styles, showing that different owners had added to the
building over a period of 200 years. It was bounded by a wall,
webbed with creepers; the wall high enough to prevent the
outside world from looking in and ourselves from looking out.

I say this because its immediate effect on me was to make me feel shut in.

To me, the house was even more unsettling than its exterior. It is very difficult for me to explain why. Except to say that as I walked along the corridors, or up and down the creaking staircases, I felt as though I had no business to be there. At first I told myself these were foolish thoughts. How could I possibly feel that bricks, mortar, woodwork, and furniture were against me? I only know I did feel this and I wanted to leave at once. I have since reproached myself for not expressing my feelings to Rosaline, for I believe, though without any real justification, that had I done so Rosaline would not have been affected. At the time, of course, I did not wish to disturb her, as I would have done if I had left at once.

As soon as I had the chance to have a good look at her I could see that she did not look nearly so well and blooming as she should. I pretended however that she was on top of the world. But all the time I was in that house I neither felt happy nor did I sleep well. In fact that is a gross understatement. I not only slept fitfully, I had nightmare after nightmare. Nightmares that had woken me up at all hours, so terrible that I had felt paralysed and I could not even stir to waken Jack. I would wake up, stiff, and sweating with terror, and for the life of me not know what it was all about.

Then one day my maid came to me. I can remember her so well; a placid, common-sense sort of woman, whose lack of imagination was reflected in her cooking.

"Madame," she said, "I must talk to you."

It appeared that she and Hilda (Rosaline's maid) and her friend Mrs. Williams had the same foreboding as I had and she urged me to tell Rosaline to leave the house before her baby arrived.

"I dread to think what will happen," she said.

I sat forward on my chair. I am not easily frightened, nor am I easily bluffed. But I most emphatically have a feeling about things supernatural.

I sent for Hilda and I talked to Mrs. Williams. Each confirmed what my maid had told me.

I did not know what to do. I felt the same way as they did. I loathed my nightmares. But Rosaline was happy there, or so she told me, and the last thing I wanted to do at that moment was to upset her.

Then I thought of other disturbing incidents. We had a lovely Alsatian dog, called Bayard, which Philip Astley had given Rosaline, and to which we were all devoted. Soon after the dog had been brought to the house he used to howl and growl at something invisible to us. Sometimes his hair would stand up on end with anger and fright. This went on for weeks and weeks until the dog died. The vet could not tell us the cause.

Finally, I made up my mind to speak to Rosaline. "Darling," I said. "I think you ought to go away to the seaside. Just for a time until the baby arrives. I don't think this place suits you. It doesn't suit me. I'm not sleeping at all well here, and we have had a lot of nasty luck, haven't we?"

"What are you trying to tell me, darling?" said Rosaline. "That I will come to harm here in this house?"

"If you put it that way—yes," I replied.

"But I love the house and I am sure nothing will harm me here," Rosaline answered.

Then I told her about my nightmares and about Hilda, and Mrs. Williams. But Rosaline laughed and said I was too superstitious. I argued and pleaded with her, saying in the end: "Look, just come away for a time with Jack and me. We'll take rooms in a hotel and be together."

Rosaline knew I was serious by this time, but would not agree. "I'm going to stay here just as long as Edgar will let us have it," she said, and then went on: "Honestly, darling, I don't feel anything wrong here at all. But if I ever do, I promise you, I'll let you know at once."

There was nothing more I could do, and as Jack and I were rehearsing for *Lido Lady* we could neither of us afford sleepless nights. So we left Hampstead and took rooms in a hotel in the Strand.

Soon after I left London and went on tour with our new show I received bad news. Rosaline had had a very difficult time, and after prolonged labour a Caesarian had been performed and she had given birth to a daughter. I visited her at the week-end and rushed back to my show. Two weeks passed and Rosaline was still in the nursing home. The baby was fine. But Rosaline was not. Sir Arbuthnot Lane, the most distinguished surgeon of the day, was called in and ordered an immediate operation. Shortly afterwards, when she was terribly ill, she suddenly became frantic with anxiety about Peter, and she sent for me.

"Darling," she said, "please get Peter away from that house. Get him away at once. I understand it all now. Please promise me you will not let him sleep there tonight."

I promised, and I kept my promise, and Peter never went to live in that house again.

Four weeks to the day after the baby's birth my sister Rosaline was dead.

Theatreland, which is easily moved, was genuinely moved by Rosaline's death. On the following day *The Times* said:

> "All Theatrical London at yesterday's matinées and evening performances was talking of Rosaline Courtneidge. So much touching and genuine sympathy has not been aroused since the equally sudden and premature death of Meggie Albanesi."

But as I look through the yellowing clips of newsprint which reported her death I do not think I can do better than quote my father. He said:

> "She had the acute sensibility, the vivid imagination, and the physical qualifications that seemed to assure her of a foremost place in her profession. In private life she was so bright and merry that few suspected the solid foundation of her character, and even I, who viewed her so critically, never gauged, until all was over, how great was her courage. She left the memory of a sweet girl suffering patiently and without complaint, who, knowing the end was near, faced the unknown with perfect calm, her only concern being that others should not grieve. In this serene and gentle mood, she said good-bye to all she loved, steadfast in her faith that we should meet again."

XI

Our Partnership

★

SOMETIMES I feel that as an actress I have let my public down in my private life as I have only been married once and I am still happily married. I realize that this must seem incongruous to the entertainment world, and to the public, who are used to stage and film stars becoming restive if their marriages last more than a couple of years, or even a couple of months.

Jack and I have been married since 1916, and although we are aware that by present-day standards this is a drab and un-glamorous arrangement, it has not proved so to us. Not that it has always been easy. Now that I look back I think that the difficult days of our marriage were the early days, particularly when I was touring on the Music Halls, Jack was playing in London, and we had long periods of separation. I think that enforced separation causes the breakdown of more theatrical marriages than any other factor.

When you come to think of it I suppose this applies to all marriages. Don't start telling me that absence makes the heart grow fonder. No matter what the poets may say, hearts have very poor memories. Ask your own heart and you will agree with me. Absence invariably makes the heart grow fonder of someone else.

Long separation can also play funny tricks on our memory. I know a number of women in my profession (doesn't that sound awful?) whose husbands went away to war, and I also knew their husbands. At least, I thought I did until their wives began to talk about them after about a year of absence, by which time the far-away hubbies all became handsome, generous, kind, thoughtful, and also great lovers. This was quite apart from winning the war on their own.

105

The wives were often surprised when their husbands returned home from the wars to find that some of them were ugly, bald, tubby, mean, thoughtless, and sometimes not even great lovers. How, they wondered, had he changed? The answer was of course that he had not. He was just the same old *him*. This sort of thing can put a marriage on the rocks quicker than almost anything, including cold tea in the morning.

Husbands are just as bad. I remember, during the war, how soldiers would produce a photograph of the little woman out of their A.B.64s. Usually the little woman looked a homely body whose quality was that she was homely. That is a very good thing to be. But that was not how the husband remembered her.

"Isn't she beautiful?" he would say, his eyes lighting as though he was holding a picture of Ava Gardner.

I discovered two ways of playing this: you could either go off at a tangent and say, "What colour is her hair?", and whatever colour he said, say "Ah! I thought so," very knowingly. Or you could just agree with him. Either way you knew he was building himself up for a let-down when he got home, and there was nothing you could do about it.

Well, just as most people are separated during a war, theatrical husbands and wives are separated for long periods during peace-time. I know I used to guard against the pitfalls of separation in the early days of my marriage to Jack by taking a quick look at him, even if only for a couple of hours on a Sunday, to keep him in perspective. Whenever I started to think of him as being tall, dark, and handsome, a quick check would prove that although he was tall, he was neither dark nor handsome. He was attractive and proud of it, but that's not being handsome. And while we are on the subject of looks I think that Ronald Colman, with his regular features and startling blue eyes, is handsome, and so is Gregory Peck, whose bone structure is in the classical mould, like that of Gary Cooper and Michael Wilding. Jack is in a different class like Danny Kaye, Jack Benny, Jimmy Durante, or any other comedian. They do not have to rely on their looks, which you may say is just as well. But they do rely on their personality, and that is something which does not fade like looks.

Anyway the first thing you have to guard against in a theatrical marriage is losing your sense of proportion about the other person, during separation. And, let us be frank, you also have to guard against your heart growing fonder of someone else. This is a very real problem. The Theatre is full of people who are physically attractive, more so than in everyday life. Personally, I always try to remember that people in the Theatre are naturally prone to exaggerate and dramatize their feelings. And it is also the home of scandal, where even a long handshake may be interpreted as a violent affair, and how they gossip????

I try never to listen to gossipers. I just wait for them to finish what they have to say and then I tell them what I have to say. Seriously, I can gossip with the worst of women, but I honestly try to keep to the facts although I know this limits the field of conversation. I do this because I have so often been the victim of gossip and I know how harmful it can be. Time and again, though not so often now as before the war, Jack and I have had to deny rumours that all was not well with our marriage. I have rarely been able to trace the origin of these rumours. So I put them down to the desire so many people have to talk scandal about people in the public eye.

As I have said, the theatrical profession is one of the worst offenders in this respect. But my journalist friends tell me that this is because I don't know Fleet Street. My political friends tell me it is because I don't know Westminster, and to cap it all, my medical friends (who really should know better) tell me it is because I don't know Harley Street. So it is a bad show all round.

But how, oh! how does gossip start?

I mean in the first place. I have sometimes wondered whether there is a Gossipers' Association which meets at regular intervals and decides upon subjects for scandal. The sort of thing I have in mind is as follows:

Scene: The lobby of a smart restaurant.
Time: The present.
The two characters could be played by any member of the Gossipers' Association with two or more years' service. They are both smartly dressed and speak in what I call a Peter Haddon whisper. By that I mean their voices can be heard in the furthest recesses of the restaurant, and even in the street outside, above the roar of London traffic.

1ST GOSSIP: Darling, I hear Jack and Ciss are breaking up.
2ND GOSSIP: No!!

1ST GOSSIP: But, my dear, yes. Do you mean to say you don't know? It's all over Town.

2ND GOSSIP: But it can't be true. Tell me more.

1ST GOSSIP: Well, you know that pretty Mrs. What's-her-name . . .

2ND GOSSIP: You mean that short, dumpy little woman you were just talking to?

1ST GOSSIP: Yes. Well, she told me that someone told her . . . mind you, this is in the strictest confidence.

2ND GOSSIP: Cross my heart.

1ST GOSSIP: That Jack and Cis have had the most terrible row . . . and it really is the end.

2ND GOSSIP: You don't mean it?

1ST GOSSIP: But, darling, I do. And what's more they're living in different hotels.

2ND GOSSIP: Fancy! You can never tell. Even the best of marriages. Well, good-bye, darling. See you soon.

The 1st Gossip exits. Enter 3rd Gossip, who is a carbon copy of the one who has just left.

2ND GOSSIP: Darling, have you heard the latest?

3RD GOSSIP: You mean about Jack and Cis breaking up?

2ND GOSSIP (very disappointed): You mean to say you know . . .

3RD GOSSIP (happily): My dear, it's all over Town. You'll have to pull your nylons up, old girl, or you'll be dismissed the Association.

CURTAIN

That little scene, in my opinion, Ladies and Gentlemen, shows you in dramatized form how gossip starts. You don't need any facts, just a lively imagination, and of course someone prepared to listen. It is easy to get them to repeat your scandal so long as you remember to make them promise not to tell a living soul. Although I am treating this lightly, it is only out of consideration for you who have paid so much for this book and must be feeling depressed already. For those of you who have borrowed the book from a friend, or a library, here is what I really think about gossips. I hate them!

They have caused Jack and me a lot of annoyance. They seem to find something irritating in our marriage because it has endured for so long. They might as well know, here and now, Jack and I intend to irritate them even more. Not that Jack is an easy person to live with. A creative person never is. Some women might feel that he is too preoccupied with his work to make an ideal husband. He is not an ideal husband. But he is the one I want and the one I am going to keep. If you have only met Jack as a member of the audience then you may be saying to yourself: "I don't blame her. It must be wonderful to have someone at home so gay and ready for a laugh. Why! he must be the life and soul of the party."

Take parties, for instance. Except for rare occasions, the noisier the party gets the quieter Jack becomes. He goes into a corner and stays there on the outside looking in. It took me years to realize this was not his lack of interest in the party but sheer shyness. So long as the party was going well he preferred not to call attention to himself.

When we are alone he can be entirely different and very amusing. One of the things I like about him most, apart from his sense of fun, is his love of surprise. I remember one very sweet example of this. It was over my wedding ring in 1931. My first wedding ring had been a plain gold one and, in the fashion of the time, rather wide. I had always refused to take it off, it was just another of my superstitions or sentimentalities, if you like. But you cannot have an actress who is playing the part of a single woman wearing a whacking great wedding ring on the stage, so every night before I went on I used to disguise it by sewing over some white material. For years Jack had watched this ritual.

And then, one day, Jack said: "Cis, I've bought you a beautiful new platinum wedding ring. We've got half an hour to spare. Let's go to Bond Street and try it on."

He rushed me into a taxi and, full of protests about bad luck, not wanting a change, and refusing to take off my old one, we arrived at the jewellers, and there I was shown a lovely new platinum wedding ring with an inscription inside in his handwriting.

He slipped the new one on and then in front of a rather dazed audience of shop assistants I had the old one filed off. So I was never without a wedding ring on my finger. And what was the inscription on the new one after fifteen years of married life? The same as it was on the old one. And what was that? The same as it was on the new one.

I am sure you won't mind my sharing this, as I always have, only with Jack.

XII

Jack and I

THE first person to cast Jack and me together was my father, but afterwards we cast ourselves together. Jack always had a high opinion of my work. He believed in me when I was still playing romantic parts. He believed in me when no one else did, including myself. His faith in my ability kept me going when I was out of work for two years. He believed I could switch from romantic parts to the hurly-burly of the Music Halls. This is not to say he was uncritical. But Jack has the sort of critical faculty which leaves a sweet taste in the mouth. For example, when I did something wrong Jack used to tell me I was doing it well but he was certain I could do far better, and he would show me how. It is because he understands me so well that I have always produced my best work for him.

There is another important factor which has always entered into our professional relationship. I was brought up by my father to believe that minute attention to detail coupled with self-discipline was the only way to achieve success in the Theatre. By success I mean not only having one's name in lights and earning high rewards, but the ultimate aim of all artistes to give the best possible performance of which they are capable. My father believed that on no occasion should an artiste attempt less than this and on no occasion did an audience deserve less. Jack was also a perfectionist. I realized this from the first time we worked together. Later on, as Jack found his feet in the Theatre and added writing and production to his acting, I became aware that here was someone with a similar purpose to my father whose methods were different but, in fairness to my father, he was a product of his generation and Jack of his.

The only real school that Robert Courtneidge attended was the Robert Courtneidge school. So perhaps it is not surprising that their methods differed so widely. Where Father would pour out his wrath at an artiste who was late for rehearsal, Jack would arrive later than the artiste, but in the time at his disposal, with charm and good humour, produce the same result as Father. If an artiste failed to respond to Father's direction he would show him the stage-door, whereas Jack would suggest that the fault was his own because he was not explaining himself properly.

I think I can sum up the difference between the methods of the two men by saying that although both wanted their horse to drink from the same pool, Father drove but Jack led. I know he led me. That is why I always enjoyed working with Jack. If the decision had rested with Jack and me we would always have worked together, but this was by no means easy. Today, for example, we have an almost unparalleled record in the theatre for a husband and wife partnership on the stage, but we are not working together, much as we would like, simply because we cannot find suitable material. Therefore you can imagine how much harder it was to get our stage partnership under way, in the first place, before we were properly established.

One success does not do the trick. We had to make several attempts before we could say truthfully in 1929 that the Managements and the public accepted us without question as a husband and wife team. By this time we had four major successes to our credit in the space of six years, beginning with *By the Way*, at the Apollo Theatre, *Lido Lady*, at the Gaiety Theatre, *Clowns in Clover*, at the Adelphi Theatre, and *The House that Jack Built*, also at the Adelphi. We had an uninterrupted run in these shows, and Jack's contribution to them was—the lot. He wrote, organized and produced them all. They not only made us a lot of money and consolidated our position for all time in the West End but gave us the chance to be together, on the stage, and at home. *Clowns in Clover*, with June, afterwards Lady Inverclyde, was without doubt our greatest success. It ran for two years to capacity business. It has always been one of my happiest thoughts that the show which followed, *The House that Jack Built*, should have received such an appropriate title: believe me, Jack built a very good house.

This run of success would have made us very rich if Jack had not had to concentrate so much on the creative side of our partnership. But we could not have it both ways. If he had not concentrated on the creative side we would not have been the success we were, but it meant that he had to leave the administrative and financial side entirely in the hands of someone else; this was Paul Murray.

Jack trusted Paul implicitly and signed the cheques as they came along. Paul rarely told us the full details of our transactions; he would, for instance, announce that he had 'fixed' a deal, such as taking over the Adelphi Theatre. He took it over first and told us afterwards. After *Clowns in Clover* we knew he had taken a further lease of the Adelphi, but we did not know at the time that this transaction was the beginning of trouble until one fine morning, while Jack was abroad, my theatre cheque was returned by the bank.

"What on earth is this?" I asked Paul, innocently. "Haven't I signed it right? What do they mean?"

He took the cheque and stared at it as though he was surprised. He said: "What's this? Not honoured? There's some mistake here, Cis. Just leave it to me. I'll see that it's put right. They've muddled the accounts. I'll make out a new cheque and see you have the money over the week-end."

I was quite satisfied with this explanation, and I did as he suggested, but the cheque came back again, and again and again. By this time even I was beginning to believe Paul's repeated explanation that there must be some mistake. I was also beginning to suspect that it was not the bank who was making the mistake, but someone else. That left Paul and me. It wasn't me. That left Paul.

Then rumours began to reach me, so I tackled Paul, who I now addressed somewhat coldly as Mr. Murray. He certainly kept to his story and would not come out into the open; he was a very proud man and would never admit defeat. Finally I lost my temper. "But it cannot be the bank," I said, furiously.

"It must be," he insisted.

"Jack and I should have several thousand pounds to our credit," I said. "Are you suggesting the bank has mislaid all this money?"

"No," he said, "I'm not suggesting anything of the sort. I'm saying they've made a mistake somewhere."

Just a spot of war work

Jack's the boy!

Arriving at Gibraltar with Vic Marlowe,
Maggie McGrath and Thorley Walters

"Then it's one of the biggest mistakes in the history of banking," I said, "because I've had a word with them and according to their figures we are in the red, and I can't believe that any bank can be as careless as that. If you do, then I suggest you had better come along with me and tell the bank manager to put things right, otherwise I'll have to take action against them."

Paul Murray knew that I meant what I said.

Slowly, but painfully, he told me what had happened. In good faith, and I am sure it was in good faith, Paul had engaged us, as he was empowered so to do, in a series of theatrical commitments beyond our resources. He had gambled and lost. He had tried to hide the losses from us for as long as possible, hoping that a miracle would come to the rescue.

I went to meet Jack on his return home and told him what had happened. Jack tried to pull the chestnuts out of the fire but they were burnt to a cinder. We had lost all the money we had earned over the years and we were thousands of pounds in debt. So after the horse was out of the stable we locked the door by dissolving the partnership. It seemed incredible at the time that Paul, after working so closely with us and knowing how we trusted him, had waited for us to find out what he had done instead of telling us in time to help him or ourselves.

Jack and I had grown very fond of Paul and we also admired his ability in the Theatre, and aside from the financial blow we lost a friend. Paul's weakness was that he allowed his ideas, some of them basically sound, to get out of hand, and when they did he would not face up to reality. Eventually, his refusal to face life led to his death. Two years ago he gambled and lost. He took out a show into the Provinces, and he did not have the money behind him to pay the salaries at the end of the week, unless the Monday Night audience proclaimed the show a success. That Monday Night audience, which Paul hoped would influence business for the rest of the week, unwittingly pronounced his death sentence. They did not like the show and consequently Paul knew that he would be unable to pay the salaries at the end of the week. So he returned to London and was found next day, dead in a gas-filled room. What a tragedy!

Our financial crisis would have ruined us professionally if we had not been so well established. From the moment it broke we could not afford to be together, in view of our debts, as we could earn more money apart. Jack went to the Winter Garden Theatre in *Follow a Star* with Sophie Tucker and I went to the Piccadilly Theatre in *Folly to be Wise* with Nelson Keys.

Nelson Keys, or rather, Bunch as we all called him, was an old friend of my early Shaftesbury Theatre days. Like many small people he was highly strung, moody, and quick on the uptake. He was a brilliant mimic and he did not mind whom he upset with his mimicry. These were the days when Jack and I were living in Curzon Street and trying to conform with its dignity. Bunch rather upset our pose as a quiet young couple as he decided that Curzon Street needed cheering up. He would come along and start a most frightful Cockney act on the front-door step. Sitting in our drawing-room, we would be shot out of our seats by a shrill yell of "Foine juicy oranges, all foine and sound, lidy, four a penny; 'ave a juicy orange, lidy, they'll do somethink to yer—as if you didn't need it." This racket would go on plus a nice back answer from Bunch for any unfortunate inhabitant of Curzon Street who opened a window, or stepped outside, until Jack hauled him in. Sometimes the act was oranges. Sometimes a banjo. But whatever it was, once Bunch decided that Curzon Street needed brightening up there was no escape. And here was the crowning humiliation. Whatever the act, Bunch would always go through, complete with filthy cap to collect the pennies. Nothing put him off, even an advancing policeman, because he knew he could slip into our home the moment he felt he had given us the full value of his friendship.

I think it is fair to say that Jack and I would still be paying back our creditors today if we had not had the good fortune to run into the biggest boom the British Picture Industry has ever known. If you say, "it is the only boom", then you are forgetting Mr. Rank and American frozen assets, in that order. The first film boom started with the coming of the talkies, and Al Jolson saying, "You ain't heard nothing yet!" And going on to prove it with a song which caused more tears than Johnny (Cry) Ray will ever know. I am referring, of course, to 'Sonny Boy'. The effect of the American Talking Picture boom was felt over here several years later when our people suddenly realized that *we* originated the English which was being spoken on the talkies, and that *we* possessed artistes who could speak and sing their native tongue passably well. The Film Boys told the City Boys, who simply poured money into the industry. I think Alexander Korda was more responsible for the enthusiasm of the financial backers than anyone else. He had made a picture, *The Private Life of Henry VIII*, in which Charles Laughton showed that our great Tudor King not only liked his wives in quantity, but also his food, which he ate like a dog, a well-trained dog, mind you, but nevertheless a dog.

This film, which was made on a shoe-string, turned over a great deal of money, and encouraged other people to join the Gold Rush. I believe I am right in saying that during this boom period the sum of £8,000,000 was invested in the British Film Industry by the City. This represented quite a lot of money in those days as Gabriel Pascal had not yet arrived.

A large proportion of that £8,000,000 found its way into the pockets of the actors and actresses. This may have been due to an oversight on the part of the producers and directors, but it really did happen. It was a golden time for everyone in our profession, including Jack and myself. We had no intention of leaving the Theatre for any length of time. We thought we could make one or two films just as people think they can eat one or two salted almonds. But once we were in the film business we were there to stay for longer than we imagined.

I shall always be grateful for the help and encouragement which we received from Sir Michael Balcon, but it was Herman Fellner to whom we were originally indebted for our entry into films. He arrived early one morning out of the blue when things were really looking black. At a time when I hated to answer the telephone or go to the front door lest a summons had been pushed through the letter-box or a gentleman had arrived with a bowler hat in one hand and a writ in the other. And then suddenly in the midst of all this chaos I found Herman standing in the hall. How he got there I was never able to discover. He was a big man, with a tiny head and enormous feet, and when he smiled his face wrinkled like a crumpled piece of paper. He spoke in a high-pitched voice like Lee Ephraim, although, unlike Lee, he had a strong guttural accent. You always wanted to laugh *with* Herman, but never *at* him. He possessed a heart of gold and had that happy knack of averting his attention from surrounding distractions so that he could concentrate his full energies on you. He suggested that Jack should go into films, and to my utter amazement he also suggested that I should go too. And that was the beginning of an association which was only broken by his untimely and tragic death. Dear Herman. You are not forgotten.

In the beginning we had a strong motive for accepting every film offer that came along: the money seemed ridiculously large for the amount of work done. Mind you, I am not trying to decry film acting, goodness knows I've done enough, but I must confess it really is far easier on the artiste than almost any other form of entertaining. In films you are not required to make a sustained effort for more than a minute or two, and it is the sustained effort that takes it out of you in the Theatre. I know that some people think that the Theatre is pretty easy going once you have settled down to a long run. These people imagine that you only have to go on and do the same thing night after night and it becomes progressively less exacting. I can assure them this is not so.

A very distinguished doctor once told me that I burn up more nervous energy in one performance in the theatre than an office worker does in eight weeks. I am not a doctor, but I would say that there is not much difference between the emotional strain of office and film work. I don't want my friends in Hollywood to get angry with me over this. I know that you have to get up very early in the morning to make films, but so you do to go to an office. I know that conditions in some film studios are trying, but no more trying than in many offices. The biggest strain of film work is in the first few days, when you are settling down, getting to know your director, fellow artistes, and the tea boy. And if I am going to continue the parallel, which I am because this is my book, the most difficult time in an office is when you are settling down, getting to know the boss, your fellow workers, and the tea boy.

Now I suppose I have set you wondering why people work at all in out-of-the-way places like Hollywood when they could easily have a nice steady job in an office. The answer to this question is money. Just think of it. In offices they put your pay in one thin envelope, but in film-land they often have to use a cabin trunk. That, children, is the great attraction the films have for film people. It is time someone blew the gaff.

I swear to you that when Jack and I received our first pay packet for our first film we both thought they had made a mistake and added too many noughts. But we needed the money so badly we decided to keep quiet in case no one found out. When they went on paying us these astronomical sums we soon adjusted ourselves to the situation and it was not long before we had a credit balance at the bank and we were telling each other the moment had come to return to the stage. But we kept on putting off the day of return, arguing that one more film would not make all that difference. Oh, my sainted salted almonds! Films were very tempting and we were tempted.

There was no financial risk for us to underwrite in films, and one picture, which took, say, eight weeks to make, earned us more money than a year's run in the theatre. Sometimes we felt we were renegades, but we consoled ourselves with the thought that we could play to an audience of a million in one night in the cinema as against one thousand in the theatre.

The first film that Jack and I made together was *The Ghost Train* and it was a very big success: so I went off happily to make another, this time on my own. At first I felt absolutely fearful. Imagine what it was like to prance on, lines ready—funny lines, do all the gestures and all the inflections to get a really good laugh, and hear nothing but cameras turning.

As far as I was concerned everything in film-making depended on my director. Perhaps to film people who have never been on the stage the director does not have so great an effect. But to me, who had been trained to make an audience laugh and react, only the director could spur me on. If he encouraged me and laughed at what I was doing all was well. But if he merely shouted instructions, "Cut", "Shoot", "That's awful", and so on, I felt worse than being out alone on a music-hall stage up against a tough Saturday Night audience.

Albert de Courville was one of the craziest film directors with whom I have ever worked. He directed me in a circus film. Now I can ride a pony, but naturally I have not attempted Handstands in Hyde Park on my morning canters. For some days I rehearsed around the ring with the usual tent wires fixed to me. Then de Courville wanted something sensational tried, so he brought on the circus 'Queen' to show me what to do. The girl was nervous. Several times she complained that something was not quite right with the ponies or the trappings. "Rubbish!" shouted de Courville, "get on with it. Everything's fine." She did, and was carried off on a stretcher. And I carried myself home with a very clear idea of one 'Sensational Act' I was not going to do for Mister de Courville.

I was one of the first English actresses to go to Hollywood and I arrived at the M.G.M. Studios in great excitement and anticipation of success. The film was called *The Improper Gentleman*. It was a bad film and the part was quite wrong for me. We made the opening shots and they were shockingly unfunny. So we remade them again and again. I was trying as hard as I could but the producer was unsympathetic. Then, one day, he sent for me.

"Now, Miss Courtneidge," he began in a hacksaw voice, "tell me, what do you do in England? What kind of parts do you play?"

I was stupefied. I had been sent for as a British star and here was the boss without the faintest idea of my work! I politely gave him a résumé of my career and in due course he sent for some of my earlier films. He must have been impressed because he immediately gave orders to rewrite the entire film and make my part three times as strong. The whole story, which had been written round Frank Morgan, who was playing the male lead, was now centred on me. I did not think the result very good. I will go further, I thought it was rubbish. We remade the rubbish, twice with different directors. Finally Jack tried to advise them, but it was just patching up a bad film. And so from the original contract, five weeks' shooting time, I was in Hollywood for over three months. But apart from Hollywood I did make some good films and so did Jack.

The most amusing one we made together was *Jack's the Boy*. In this we had a sequence in Madame Tussaud's, ending in the Chamber of Horrors, which is still talked about today. This was an occasion when I did not miss the stimulation of an audience. I found it quite easy to register horror surrounded by the 'Brides in the Bath' being done in, Dr. Crippen, Major Armstrong, and Mr. Seddon doling out arsenic, and all the other murderers at work. Come to think of it they were not actually at work, but my imagination soon supplied them with poisoned phials, guns, daggers, baths, in fact anything they required to get on with the job. The sequence ended when I turned to Jack and said, "You've arrested Charlie Peace."

The most successful film I made on my own was *Soldiers of the King*. I played a grandmother who sat in a box listening to her daughter sing 'There's something about a soldier that is fine, fine, fine'. I also played the daughter, proving that one of the advantages when making a film is that you can be in two places at once. Through a mixture of Jack's direction with Maurice Elvey, and a script which gave me the opportunity to give of my best, the result was a film which people saw more than once; in fact it was usually not so much a question of "Have you seen *Soldiers of the King*"? but how many times?

Jack had a similar success in *Sunshine Susie* with Renate Muller. This was a light, gay-hearted musical-comedy film, made at Shepherd's Bush and directed by Victor Saville. The budget was modest even for those days and I think it was the very simplicity and the complete lack of pretentiousness which made *Sunshine Susie* into such a box-office success.

Jack's the Boy, Soldiers of the King, and *Sunshine Susie* were our outstanding successes. I also made *Me and Marlborough, Falling for You, Everybody Dance, Happy Ever After, Please Teacher, Take my Tip,* and *Aunt Sally*; whilst *The Camels are Coming, Bull Dog Jack, Jack of All Trades, Jack Ahoy* will always be happily associated with Jack.

The longer I worked in films the more nostalgic I became for a stage-door, my name on the bills outside, 'Overture and beginners, Miss Courtneidge, please', and real people in front when the curtain went up. Naturally, I wanted to make my return to the stage with Jack, but he was still working in the film studios when Lee Ephraim came to me and said, in his high-pitched pleading voice:

"Cis, I've got the very show for you called *Hide and Seek*. Now that's a good title, don't you think so?" And before I could answer he went on: "There, I knew you would agree. And as for the numbers, Vivian Ellis has never written better. He's written Bobbie Howes the best number in the show."

This last piece of information was by way of a brick being dropped heavily on my toes, but when my friends drop bricks I pretend not to notice. Lee's enthusiasm persuaded me to read the script and I was won over. In case Lee congratulates himself too much on his salesmanship here I ought to add that he was on a seller's market.

Lee was quite right when he said Vivian Ellis had written some wonderful music, and I shall never forget Bobbie singing 'She's my Lovely'. Bobbie Howes is, in my opinion, one of our great artistes. He has the quality which we in the profession describe as 'Heart'. It is not easy to define exactly what this is, you can only say that you recognize it at once. Chaplin has it, so has . . . well, not many people; but Bobbie has.

Hide and Seek was a delightful show with all the charm of the true English musical comedy which has now been replaced by importations from the U.S.A. or something very like them. The first night at the London Hippodrome was like coming home, and I don't know anything better than that.

XIII

Peace and War

I LOVE family life and I think it is sad when families separate, either through circumstances over which they have no control or of their own choosing. The point of departure in my family life was not so much my mother's death, but when my father married again. During the later part of my life on the Music Halls, and then during my early shows with Jack and the years when I was filming, my father and I saw progressively less of each other. The reason for this must remain locked in my heart. Sufficient to say that a gap opened between us. I thought at first I could bridge it, but as the years passed the gap widened until we saw very little of each other. I was always hoping that there was something I could say or do that I had not thought of before, which would bring us together again. This was particularly in my mind early in 1938 when my father and I had not seen each other for several months. It may not be unusual in some families for father and daughter not to see each other for long periods, but to me it seemed that all communication between us was cut. Did I say all? Well, not all. Of course my daughter Pam used to go and see her grandfather frequently. I would always say, "Give Grandpa my love, darling," and he would always send his love back to me. But we did not meet. Pam was in her early teens, and had grown from a flaxen-haired, pink-cheeked, blue-eyed baby into a solid little girl, happy at day school and adoring her outings at the theatre. I allowed her a great deal more freedom than I had had and always made a point of seeing she had plenty of pocket money. This is not to say I spoiled her. When I said 'No', she knew that I would not change my mind unless she waited for at least an hour. I had to make a show of discipline to offset Nannie Kennedy, who always spoilt Pam.

Despite the nature of our work Jack and I did our best to see that Pam was separated from us as little as possible. Sometimes during the holidays Pam and Nannie came with us on tour. If I was playing in Town when Pam was at school then I would go back from the matinées to have tea with her.

Jack was a loving father but did not really understand how to communicate with children. Their world of make-belief had him baffled. I remember an example of this when Pam was about seven years of age, and she spoke to him on the subject of my birthday.

"Can I have some money for Mummy's birthday next week?" she said.

"Of course, darling," Jack replied. "How much do you want?"

"You say, Daddy."

"Go on, you say," said Jack, as though he was dealing with a member of the cast asking for a rise.

"Oh, fifty," said Pam, looking very wise.

"Fifty!" exclaimed Jack, incredulously. "Fifty what?"

"Just fifty," repeated Pam, who knew she was on to something.

"But it must be fifty something, darling," Jack insisted. "Pounds, shillings, or pence?"

"No. Just fifty, please, Daddy."

Jack settled for a fiver, and with that Pam withdrew.

But if Pam was an enigma to Jack, as all children are, she was completely understood by Nannie Kennedy, who anticipated her every wish and always thought of her as a baby in arms. Nannie was so kind and loyal and generous that I was glad of her influence on Pam, excepting one thing, and that was her gift for using the wrong word in the right place and the right word in the wrong place. (She's got me at it now.) To Nannie a 'running commentary' was a 'running coventry', and a Protestant, believe it or not, was innocently termed a Prostitute in the Kennedy vocabulary.

The curious thing about Nannie's mischoice of words was that they did not run true to any pattern. A startling example of this was the time when she returned with Pam from a visit to my father in Brighton while I was still in *Hide and Seek*. I was waiting to hear news of Father as Pam and Nannie came into the drawing-room.

Nannie put down her usual collection of parcels, umbrella,

and sunshade, flicked the dust of travel from her peacock-blue
art silk dress, and said breathlessly:

"I've got a message from Mr. Courtneidge for you and
Mister Hulbert."

"What is it?" I said.

Nannie paused to get her breath and collect her words. "He
says that you and Mr. Hulbert ought to hang together."

"Hang?" I exclaimed.

This was indeed surprising news from Brighton.

"Are you sure you have the message right?"

"Certainly, Madame," said Nannie Kennedy, who, like the
Bank of England, did not like to be queried.

"Grampie asked us to tell you," said Pam, "that he thought it
was about time you and Daddy were on the stage together again."

For a moment I pondered as to how Nannie could possibly
translate a message that Jack and I should be together again on
the stage into hanging us there, until I saw there was a relationship between being together and, as Nannie put it, 'hanging
together'. I was tempted to discuss this with Nannie, but I wanted
to hear the rest of the news as quickly as possible as I had an
appointment with Lee Ephraim.

Lee has played such an important part in my life that I would
like to introduce him to you as fully as possible, so, Ladies and
Gentlemen, come and meet a great impresario. The best place
to meet him is at his office, which is in a little street just off
Shaftesbury Avenue, a street you can easily miss called Denman
Street, a narrow, undistinguished street which probably started
off in life a century or so ago as one of the lanes in London. It
houses a few garish restaurants, a garage, the stage-door of the
Piccadilly Theatre, a small coffee shop and Magnet House. If you
walk up Denman Street to the end you get into Soho proper, but
if you stop at Magnet House you arrive at Lee's office.

Its entrance is as unpretentious as the street, and you may be
rather surprised, as I was, to find that, small as it is, there is a lift
to take you up the three floors to the place where Lee works.
When you arrive on the third floor there are no signed photographs of stars to tell you the sort of office you are in. But if you
look past the girl at the switchboard into the waiting-room you
will see your first sign of the Theatre; young men and women
waiting with the patience of 'pros' to see the great impresario.

His office is the first on the left. Next door, his right hand, Betty Farmer, works. She has been with Lee thirty years and is assisted by a Pekinese called Winky. I have never found out exactly what Winky was supposed to do but I suspect he is an assistant casting director because of the disdainful way he eyes visitors.

Lee's office has two doors. One opens out on to the corridor, and the other opens into Betty's office. On her desk are two volumes of Lee's bible, thick black books which represent fifty years of work in the Theatre. They contain programmes of shows he has seen, been interested in, or put on. They are not just souvenirs; besides the name of each member of the cast are Lee's comments, and underneath the title his judgment on the show. He never forgets a show or an individual performance, and if he needs to refresh his memory he has only to refer to the bound volumes of his programmes.

Lee says he was born in Kentucky in 1877. I am sure he was born two or three hundred years before that. No one can become as wise as he in one lifetime. When my business association with Lee began in 1937 with *Hide and Seek* he had already presented between forty and fifty shows in the West End of London. It was Lee who gave us such musicals as *Rose Marie, The Desert Song, Lilac Time, Rio Rita, Gay Divorce, On Your Toes,* and *Sunny*. And artistes like Fred Astaire, Sir Godfrey Tearle, Leslie Faber, Jack Buchanan, George Grossmith, Rex Harrison, Gladys Cooper, Violet Vanbrugh, Isobel Jeans, Lady Forbes Robertson, and Ellis Jeffreys have all appeared under his banner.

When I first met Lee he was, according to his reckoning, only sixty; according to mine he had just passed his two hundred mark. Today he is a little bird of a man, quick of movement, full of energy and hoods for eyelids which shut out the world for a few minutes' sleep whenever he is bored or tired. This does not happen very often. That is how he looks today. Fifteen years ago he looked exactly the same.

In his office he plans shows, reads shows, discusses shows, casts shows. The only reason he doesn't put them on there is because there is not enough room. He usually dresses in a neat dark suit and wears an Anthony Eden. For the life of me I don't know why it is not called a Lee Ephraim. He usually thinks about four things at once, which has given him the reputation for being absent-minded. A typical example of this is the way he sometimes greets an artiste by complimenting them on a performance of theirs he has recently seen, discussing the show in detail and then, just as they are beginning to think they have made a tremendous personal impression, he says, "By the way ... what is your name?"

You have probably guessed by now that I am very fond of Lee. I always have been, but never so much as one day towards the end of the run of *Hide and Seek*, shortly after Pam and Nannie Kennedy had come back from seeing my father. Lee was at home ill in bed when I went to visit him. And after I had enquired about his health (he really looked a sick man), I said: "I've brought someone else to see you. Do you feel well enough?"

He looked at me from under his eyes, smiled weakly and nodded.

I raised my voice and said, "He'll see you."

This was Jack's cue for his entrance and he tiptoed into the room to the weary-looking patient.

"Lee," I said, "Jack and I have a great idea."

A lot of people have said that to Lee in his time and he did not react visibly.

"This news will either kill or cure you," I said. "All the plans are changed. We want to act together again. What do you think of that?"

In a moment Lee was out of the bed, calling for his clothes, shouting into the telephone, ordering a car, telling his office to expect him, and before we knew what was happening the three of us, Jack, Lee, and myself, were on the way there. Lee did not speak a word until we were upstairs in his office. Several times Jack and I tried to draw him, but he hushed us with a gesture. Once in his office he sat behind his desk, carefully took off his hat and put it on the hat-stand, folded his arms and said:

"Now, Cis—Jack—I've got a great idea. You two ought to work together."

He kept a straight face for a moment and then burst out laughing and so did we, and without more ado he set to work to plan the new show. What a man!

At this time Lee had been negotiating for me to do a new show by Archie Menzies to follow the run of *Hide and Seek*. Now our plans were changed it was decided to call in Archie

Menzies with Arthur Macrae to work together on the book for Jack and myself. It took about three months, from the day we decided to go ahead for the delivery of the script of a new musical comedy called *Under Your Hat*. During this three months there were daily conferences with Lee taking the chair. At these conferences Jack represented three people, himself as an artiste, himself as part author, himself as our producer. There were times when his three selves quarrelled with each other, but fortunately not often. Arthur Macrae and Archie Menzies represented the rest of the authorship and Vivian Ellis all the music and most of the lyrics. I say 'most of the lyrics' because Claude contributed some, including the title song of the show, 'Keep it under your Hat'. I was also at these conferences representing myself. They took up hours of our time, sometimes, believe it or not, twenty hours out of twenty-four. If you had sat in on one of them—so at variance with each other did we sound—you might reasonably have imagined that far from being a group of people working together for a common objective, we were delegates to a peace conference.

Even three months of hard work on the script, lyrics, and the score did not mean we had the finished article. Musical comedies are not created as easily as that. What we did have was material in which we had enough confidence with which to start rehearsals. Most of our rehearsals were at the Lyceum Theatre, which as far back as 1938 had been condemned in the interests of a road-widening scheme of which Waterloo Bridge was a part. I must say I felt a little sad rehearsing in a theatre which had such a great past and was under sentence of death. Today the Lyceum is still there, enjoying, at least in my opinion, a fate worse than death, as a dance hall.

I think I am right in saying that the entire cast of *Under Your Hat* found it more difficult to concentrate on the work in hand than they have ever done before or since. The reason for this was that we were rehearsing our play, which we hoped would bring laughter and happiness to people, whilst on the stage of the world the political players were working out a grim drama at Munich. We all knew that our lives depended on the outcome of that drama. Every half-hour or so rehearsals would be interrupted to read the latest edition of the newspapers which were pounding off the presses like the beating of an anxious heart.

This tension, which we felt like everyone else, was only relieved when Mr. Neville Chamberlain came home from Germany to tell the country that he had secured peace with honour. It was fortunate for our peace of mind that we did not know enough then to translate 'peace with honour' as a year's grace.

The show was due to open at the Court Theatre, Liverpool, which had been rebuilt after a fire. Did I say 'had been'? They were still at it when we arrived. There were no proper passages down from the dressing-rooms to the stage, men were nailing down carpets, and windows were being fitted. Jack was determined to get on with the job whatever the conditions. He called the Company together and spoke as follows:

"They may not finish building this place by the time we open but that is not going to affect us. Just ignore everything that is going on and concentrate on the show and your part and you'll have nothing to worry about."

My! How that man can kid himself.

This meant that in addition to our own musical score we had to rehearse against what I call 'The Builder's Song', which, as you know, consists mainly of hammering, sawing, shouting, and an infinite variety of bangs. In the midst of all this I was sitting in the stalls with the late Frank Cellier and Leonora Corbett when I was overcome with a fit of the giggles. I am like that when I am worked up at rehearsals and the trouble is that my giggles are catching. On this occasion I infected the entire Company and it was some time before Jack managed to quieten us all down and we could go on with rehearsals.

Jack shouted his instructions over the building noises. The lights were the worst trouble. They were operated by remote control instead of direct from the stage. But there was no remote control. He could not telephone his instructions to the electrician in his box up in the gallery, so he had to come forward and shout, for example: "Take out your Pink. Come up with your Blue." The poor dears who could hear, up in their box in the gallery, as little as us, would promptly take out the Blue and come up with the Pink.

And this was not all. The actors could not hear each other and so could not take up their cues. This went on without a break from Saturday midday, when we arrived in the theatre, until Sunday morning at 9.30 a.m., when Jack gave us three hours off, to get our breakfast and a night's sleep. We returned at one o'clock and went on working throughout the afternoon and evening, well into the night and through until Monday morning. Jack had maintained some sort of outward calm all through this, rather in the tradition of a captain in a doomed ship, until at last he could stand no more. Suddenly he rushed towards the front of the stage and shouted, without response, for lights. He sounded at breaking point.

"Can anyone tell me how to get the lights working?" he yelled.

"Why not try a carrier pigeon?" Arthur Macrae suggested quietly, and the tension was relieved with laughter.

You know what they say about it 'being all right on the night'? Well, it was. We were all so tired, almost to the point of desperation, that we only had enough left in ourselves to give a good show.

After twelve weeks in the Provinces polishing and re-polishing the show, rehearsing every day and rewriting every night, we came to the Palace Theatre, London. Here I want to say something to theatre-goers in the Provinces, as I think it is possible that they may take exception to what I have said about polishing and re-polishing the show, rehearsing and rewriting, on tour. It may sound to them as though Jack and I think of the Provinces as trying it out 'on the dog'. That really is not so. The truth is that we, like everyone else in show business, would like to present a show that was perfect on the first night. Indeed, that is always our aim, but our business is one of trial and error, particularly when we are presenting as complex a piece of entertainment as a musical comedy. We cannot tell for sure whether a scene will go. The audience can. We cannot tell for sure whether a number is right. The audience can. We cannot tell for sure if a line is funny. The audience can. They tell us where the dead wood is and where the live wood is, too.

In a very real sense our provincial audience helps in the creation of the finished product which London sees. Sometimes the London verdict does not tally with the Provinces. But for my money the latter is the one I accept. So does Jack. You may say, "Why not have your try-out in London?" We would like to do that very much, but the economics of the theatre are against us. Musical comedies have always cost tens of thousands

"Posted" in Italy

Sergeant Ronald Shiner
watches me make a
clean sweep in
Something in the Air

My brother Charles and
my sister Rosaline

Colonel and
Mrs. Sheepshanks in
Under Your Hat

of pounds to put on. We could not afford to gamble our capital
and our livelihoods on the one throw of the dice in the West End.
They don't give you second chances there. The Provinces do.

In November 1938 *Under Your Hat* opened at the Palace
Theatre, London. Our reception echoed our success in the
Provinces, and after eight years of professional separation on
the stage Jack and I were together again. Sir Charles Cochran
wrote to Jack and me and said, "Thank you for saving the
Palace and putting it back on the map again." I would remember
Under Your Hat, which ran for nearly two years, as the happiest
show of my life if it had not been marked by a deep personal
sadness.

During the run of the show, early in 1939, my father, who
was then within a few months of his eightieth birthday, became
seriously ill. One night, just before I was due to go on the stage,
my brother-in-law, Peter Haddon, paid his customary visit to
my dressing-room. While we were talking he was called away to
the telephone. I don't know why I felt there was some special
significance in him being called away to the telephone that night,
it had happened before, but I know I did. I did not see Peter
again until he came on to the stage to play a scene with me. He
seemed his usual nonchalant self, but indefinably different. I
tried to catch his glance. His eyes avoided mine and we went on
playing our scene. Then suddenly I looked him straight in
the eyes, during one of those pauses which we actors can take,
during a big laugh. I knew then why I had felt some special
significance in the telephone call. I knew then why I had felt
there was something indefinably different in Peter's manner
on his entrance. My father was dead. My eyes told Peter that I
knew and, without a word, he nodded gravely.

The opening bars of my next number almost caught me
unawares, but I pulled myself together and sang:

> "Keep it under your hat.
> We must agree to do that.
> Everything I say to you
> Is absolutely *entre nous*.
> And it's more than that,
> It's between us two, so,
> Keep it under your hat."

I

XIV

War and Peace

IF I were going to give a name to the last war I could call the last war the Flying War because it was a war dominated by the aeroplanes. I remember, not long before it began, going with Jack one afternoon to see the film of H. G. Wells' *The Shape of Things to Come*, in which practically all the civilized world was shown laid waste by the aeroplanes. I said to Jack as we came out of the cinema, "Do you think it could really ever come to that?"

Jack shook his head. "No, the prospect of what might happen will put them off," he said, and as time went on Jack became more and more convinced that no politician would be foolish enough to risk the destruction of modern war. In this view he was in good company. I recall that Lord Beaverbrook was even more emphatic and right up to the outbreak of war told us through the *Daily Express* that there would be no war that year.

Under Your Hat had been running in London for nearly a year when the war eventually came, for me at least unexpectedly only in the manner of its coming; not with the roar of bombers overhead or the sound of guns, but with the announcement by a tired and patently disappointed man over the radio. When I heard the news I was with my family and close friends down at our farm in Essendon, near Hatfield. The farm had for many years been Jack's main interest outside the Theatre. I suppose it was his only outside interest. All his life he had longed to be a farmer, and for months, even years, he had spent every available week-end touring the countryside in search of an ideal place to live. West End Farm was that place, and it became the centre of our private lives. Here we found peace from the Theatre. Here we hoped, when the time arrived for us to retire, we would also find peace for the rest of our lives.

On that Sunday morning, like the rest of England, we turned on the radio to listen to Neville Chamberlain's announcement, and like the rest of England we heard the air-raid sirens blaring out over London and the Home Counties. I did not speak for a moment. I was thinking of my brother Charles, who had died not long ago, how he had gone off to fight in a war that was to end all wars. Charles was always an idealist and I was glad, in a way, he had not lived to see the peace he had fought for, and many others died for, broken after so short a time. I thought of my mother, my sister Rosaline, and my father. Suddenly I felt lonely. I turned to Pam and made one of those mundane remarks that so often come to mind in moments of great stress. "Well, darling, your first holiday abroad will have to be postponed," I said.

She turned to me and tried to speak, but the words were lost in the emotional impact of the news we had just heard. There were tears in her eyes, which brought the whole thing straight home to me.

My first thought was to comfort Pam, and my next, that's the end of *Under Your Hat*. Suddenly we all began talking at once, as though to find comfort in the sound of our voices.

"What can each of us do?" was the predominant thought.

"Well, I for one shall join the Police Force," announced Jack, and we all turned and stared at him. "I mean it," he insisted, and the stern set of his eyes stopped any bright gags that any of us had on our lips.

We wandered round the farm looking for spots for a shelter, and made long lists of seeds and vegetables to plant against the food shortage. We also planned an increase of chickens and pigs, and perhaps several cows. I had entered so much into the situation that when one of our guests suggested we should kill a chicken for dinner, I said, with a reprimand in my voice: "Chicken for dinner—in wartime? Of course not, I've never heard of such a thing."

All theatres shut down at once and the rest of the week we spent moving everything we wanted from our house in Curzon Street to the farm and the rest of our belongings we stored.

We also reorganized the farm to sleep eighteen people instead of six as we wanted to give shelter to as many of our friends as we could. There were beds everywhere, upstairs, downstairs, under the cupboards and in the cupboards. Feeding and sleeping eighteen people is no small matter, particularly if you only have, as we had, one domestic help. There were potatoes to peel, food to be cooked, smalls to be washed out, and all the outside work of shelter digging, sand-bag filling, and farm work. We worked to a plan, each man and woman was given a job to do, and in a surprisingly short time wartime life at the farm was running smoothly.

Once life at the farm began to settle down I began to get restive. Surely, I thought, there is more for me to do with my country at war than vegetate on a farm? And as though in answer to my question the Government decided that, bombs or no bombs, in the interest of maintaining public morale the theatres were to be reopened. So Jack and I went back to work in *Under Your Hat*. We had quite good audiences, though they were inclined to be restive and the black-out naturally worried them, and us. But everyone soon accustomed themselves to that.

Jack joined the Police Force and was on duty daily. He loved the work and had to pass examinations like a schoolboy for a scholarship. The great difficulty of that time to me was the fact that London, my London, seemed to have disappeared. I would dial a familiar telephone number—the line had gone dead. I would walk round to a friend's house, to find it closed down and no one knew the new address. I could walk within a mile radius of my old house in Curzon Street and not meet anyone I knew. It made me feel as though I was lost.

In 1940, after the run of *Under Your Hat*, Jack and I decided to put on a show called *Hulbert Follies*. It was largely a family concern. Jack, Claude, and I, with Dorothy Hyson, Pam, and the best chorus we could find. We didn't expect to make a great financial success, we just hoped to make a living and give people something to brighten up their evenings. On nights when we ran into raids we took only a few shillings. At other times on 'quiet nights' we did well. We packed our props and clothes into lorries and travelled either by train or by car all over the country. When the raids became worse we used to rush, immediately after the show, to charabancs parked outside the theatre and try to beat the bombers overhead. This way we never slept with our wardrobes or props in any of the big cities, but always outside.

Often we used to rehearse in a quiet spot on the way to the theatre and drive up at the last moment. If we were organizing as we went along, so too were some of the Theatre Managers, who had great difficulty in keeping their staffs together. They did a great job and got very little thanks. Here, better late than never, I give them mine.

I admit that working during the raids was hard on the nerves and on the voice. Don't expect any stiff upper lip stuff from me. I have stood on the stage trying to get my lines across when all of Goering's Air Force seemed to be overhead. I doubt if I got one word across to the Field Marshal's twenty. But when I did, the laughter that came back made my effort worth while. People laughed easily in those early wartime shows. They laughed at the black-out, the bombs, the Germans, the Italians, gas-masks, air-raid wardens, and all the problems of wartime living. Like everyone else we had some near escapes, but one of the worst moments was when we arrived in Liverpool to find the whole town on fire, including the theatre. It was one of the most terrible sights I have ever seen. I really believed, at that moment, that H. G. Wells' *The Shape of Things to Come* had arrived and we were seeing the beginning of the end of our civilization. The sight of a great city in flames can easily make you feel like that.

In 1942 we came back to the Palace Theatre, London, in *Full Swing*, which was followed a year later by *Something in the Air*. By this time the war had changed the habits of theatre-goers. Going to the theatre was no longer the social occasion which began with dressing up, a few drinks, dinner, followed by the theatre at 8.30 p.m. and then home at leisure. People were either home on leave from the Services or taking time off from the factory or some other war work. For all of them, the Theatre was, more than ever before, an escape from the world outside. But however much they laughed at that world, in the comfort of theatre seats they still had to reckon with it, which meant getting home as early as possible before the bombing began. This meant, for a start, the curtain rising for an evening performance just after tea-time instead of dinner. Jack and I used to get out of London the moment the show ended.

A big raid the night before, or a full moon, had a bad effect on our houses, otherwise business was good. Our greatest difficulty was rehearsals. Most of the cast slept in the suburbs or the Home Counties, and many of them did war work as well, so that after a night of 'incidents' we never knew who would turn up the next day. People were bombed out, transport was cancelled, and it took all Jack's inventiveness to pull us through. Quite early in the war I began to give Sunday concerts for the troops. My great standby in this was Bob Probst, my pianist and conductor. He had tremendous enthusiasm and never said 'No' to any request I made on his time for a concert. He became one of my Services entertainment unit, which consisted of Jean Gillie, Mary Martlew, Thorley Walters, Ronald Shiner, and six to eight lovelies in the chorus. Each week I used to invite a guest to the Unit, usually a well-known star such as Arthur Askey and Richard Murdoch, and then we would drive out to the camp, or barracks, and give a three-hour show. I did my cameos, the lovelies did their dances and songs, and Bob Probst supplied the music. These concerts developed from once a week to full-time shows.

I was playing at Nottingham when Jevan Brandon Thomas, whose father wrote that all-time perennial *Charley's Aunt*, came to see me. "Cis," he said, "do you know what the Ack-ack men are going through? They literally have no comforts at all, no recreations, no books, nothing. Do you think you could give them a hand?"

Many of them were stationed in out-of-the-way places and were on duty day and night.

I told Jevan, "Of course I'll do something." I soon collected for them records, books, a piano, games, cricket bats, footballs, mufflers, blankets, and gloves. After every performance at the Palace Theatre, and twice on Wednesdays and Saturdays after the matinées, I would go to the front of the house and collect the comforts, after appealing to my audience from the stage. And what comforts they gave! For many months the comforts poured in, the public giving with both hands. They could not give with one. I wouldn't let them. Then I decided on another idea, to ask for money to buy the comforts my Ack-ack men needed.

Although I say so myself, I was a good beggar. No one had a chance to escape. As soon as the curtain rang down I would lift up my petticoats and run to the front of the house and there hold out a big hat and beg the departing audience to fill it. I did not mind what they gave, so long as they gave something, preferably notes and cheques. I did this for over two years and in all collected over £10,000. This was in addition to gifts in kind. Sometimes, in the early days, I used to hire lorries to take the gifts to the boys, but eventually, when funds allowed, I bought two vans. Sometimes I had to hire a room to store the stuff while it was being allocated. When it came to the cash collections, I don't recall one single member of my audiences trying to pass me by.

The third phase of my Ack-ack Comforts Fund was perhaps the most exciting. First I had collected the comforts, then the money to buy them. Finally, because the shelves in the shops were empty, I hit on the idea of buying miniature cinemas to send round the sites.

Right through the war my audiences went on laughing, through all the bombings, black-out, and bad news, whether in the theatre or in the N.A.A.F.I. huts; until the fly-bombs came. I don't know what it was, perhaps the fact that there was no one up there controlling them, but I do know that the moment the fly-bombs began we found that audiences gave us only one ear at the time, the other ear was cocked to listen for the cut-out of the fly-bombs. And we couldn't joke about them. We could get laughs out of Hitler, Haw-Haw, torpedoes, the Blitz, and anything else that happened, but we couldn't get a laugh out of fly-bombs. For the very simple reason there was nothing funny about them. They were far too impersonal, and in my view they were better than Goebbels claimed. We, in the Theatre, are barometers of public morale, and as far as this barometer is concerned fly-bombs had the British Public more worried than any other weapon used during the war. They also had this barometer worried.

I shall never forget the cartoon of the little man listening for the fly-bombs with one ear overgrown to the size of a great cabbage. Our audiences were all like that. And the queerest thing of all was the fact that I might be singing, going all out in the middle of a number, the orchestra playing full blast, and *still* I heard the fly-bomb cut-out and swoop earthwards. And, brother, we were on earth.

In 1945 E.N.S.A. wanted me to go abroad with a small company. Our first call was Gibraltar and I had to go by air. It was my first flight of any kind. Years ago I had turned down flying as a means of transport and that had been in the good old days of peace. Now, in the midst of war, I had to fly for my maiden trip. I was so frightened I had to hold my chin to stop my teeth biting my tongue in half.

The Governor of Gibraltar, Sir Ralph Eastwood, and his wife, Lady Eastwood, were wonderfully kind to us.

Lady Eastwood said: "You can't rehearse in comfort in the tiny little theatre. Would you like to come up to Government House and rehearse?"

Very nervously I said, "Yes, we would."

In the most perfect surroundings of Government House I tried to keep my Company up to scratch. But you know how difficult it is with a lot of young people. I would find them smoking and be terrified of cigarette burns. "Look here, you are not in the theatre now, you know." I would read the Riot Act to them. "This is a private home, full of beautiful things, you mustn't smoke here."

All went fairly well, though I was on tenterhooks the whole time, for Government House was beautifully furnished and Lady Eastwood didn't seem to mind where we went. Then one day one of the Company nearly gave me a fit. We were having tea in the drawing-room out of beautiful porcelain cups, when one of the cast merrily stepped back, bang on a cup of tea, and sent it all over the carpet. Lady Eastwood brushed my apologies aside in the most charming way, though what I said afterwards to the culprit is unprintable.

From the Rock we went to Malta, North Africa, and Italy, and there mislaid an army. We chased around to locate the regiments we were booked to visit, and only with difficulty and delay found them.

Hartley Power was one of our Company and one night in Rome I had a great deal of fun at his expense. Now we all have our fancies and our foibles and Hartley has an aversion to buying a round of drinks. He and Jack Benny ought to go out together one evening. They would die of thirst. I know that during my Italian tour Hartley would stand on his head to be absent when his turn came to buy the drinks. We would be having a gossip, and a drink, the glasses would get empty, and it would be Hartley's turn. And as sure as night follows day he would say: "Well, that's been fine . . . let's call it a day . . . I've had enough . . . let me buy you all one tomorrow." And it was always tomorrow. This had been going on for some time and then I thought of a lovely plan. Naomi Jacob, the novelist, who was a Welfare Officer for E.N.S.A., was with us and we all congregated early and I ordered a bottle of champagne to each table. We sat down and began to drink and then Hartley arrived with a big thirst. There were quite thirty of us by now, all with our bottles of bubbly. The moment I spied Hartley I stood up.

"Come on," I called out. "Come and have a drink . . . a bottle for Mr. Power, please." It was quickly delivered by the waiter. "And now raise your glasses," I said happily, and the entire Company stood. "It's been so difficult to get hold of you, Hartley, so I'm afraid we've already begun, but here's to you . . . our host, Mr. Hartley Power. Your very good health."

Hartley stood there, glass in hand. I must say he took it quietly on the chin. There was no other way he could take it, really. "Well, Cis," he said, "that's fine." He looked round at the thirty-odd glasses raised in his name. "That's fine, I'm sure." Then, lowering his voice a little to me, he added, "Um—er—er—I'll sign the bill tomorrow."

"Oh no," I said. "You'll pay the bill tonight. Here it is." I wonder how his champagne tasted. Mine tasted fine.

One day on a trip from Naples to Rome by road we got lost near the war-shattered monastery of Cassino, now rebuilt, which I was anxious to see. We drove up mountainous roads, until jets of steam began pouring out of the radiator and I wondered whether the car was going to explode. By this time the sun was setting and the driver got out and decided he could go no farther. We were on the outskirts of a small village which looked as though it was deserted.

"We must find some food," I announced, majestically, "and somewhere to stay the night."

None of us spoke Italian, and my smattering of French was useless as the Italians who eventually appeared all spoke Italian. Perhaps if we had spoken their language we might have fared better, but as it was none of us could find anywhere to sleep, except one room, in one house, containing one bed.

The room was large and clean, the owner quite cheerful and hospitable. The bed was a large double one, which in the Italian tradition took up most of the room. We were all tired and far from home. So the four of us got into the bed, and, tired with our journey, we were soon asleep.

I was dozing in the early morning, about 4 a.m., when there was a loud knock on the bedroom door and a sergeant in the Highland Division after knocking came right in. I take off my hat to that sergeant. He never batted an eyelid.

He merely saluted smartly, and said: "Miss Cicely Courtneidge, ma'am. There's another car waiting to take you to Rome."

I put my head out of the covers, the other three did the same, and I said weakly, "Thank you very much."

The sergeant saluted again and without a smile on his face turned and walked smartly out of the room, leaving the four of us, two men and two women, wondering what he thought of four in a bed.

I was in the San Carlos Theatre in Naples in June of that year singing, 'Home is the place where your heart is', when the news of the Cease Fire came through. A British soldier got hold of a huge Union Jack from somewhere and rushed up over the orchestra and on to the stage and hung it round me. I went on singing and soon it seemed the whole of Naples was singing that song with tears streaming down many a cheek, including mine.

We did not return to England at once but went on to Florence and Rome and round the hospitals giving our shows. Finally, we went back to Gibraltar, and it was at the end of the tour that I had the most wonderful holiday of my life. Wonderful because it was my first holiday of the war. The Governor of Gibraltar told me of a tiny seaside town near Malaga and provided me with transport. There I lay and soaked in six years of longed-for sunshine and warm salt water. I shall never forget that little seaside town in Spain and the peace and warmth of it all. One day I shall go back for another look.

During the war I did many broadcasts for the B.B.C., and this brought me the widest audience of my life. But my favourite broadcast of all time was when the B.B.C. asked me to join the Victory Variety Programme in 1946 and I was given the most wonderful chance to reach millions of listeners and tell them what

I thought of them. It isn't a chance that comes to all of us. Jack and I talked the project over with Harold Purcell, who had already written material for some of my shows. Harold Purcell wrote some inspiring words for me for the Victory Variety Programme. I said them over the air and I said them again at the Albert Hall. And as a tribute to the people they are about I reproduce some of them here. They represent a salute to the people who did not march in the Victory Parade.

They were never in the headlines—did their jobs without a fuss,
Such as Ada Smith 'the daily'—who came to do for us.
Seventy, and every evening down the tube with counterpane,
Seventy, and every morning up the stairs to work again.
When they dug her from our kitchen in the May of '41,
I still hear her from her stretcher, "Mind the steps, they've just been
    done."
Then I see a heap of rubble and I hear the postman say,
"Lady, where'd you like your income tax?—the letter-box is blown
    away."

THEY ARE UNIMPORTANT PEOPLE AND THEY ARE NOT
    IN THE PARADE,
AND THEY DIDN'T WEAR THE BADGES AND THEY DIDN'T
    HAVE THE BRAID.

The war is done—the fighting's over—the N.F.S. and all the larks,
There is trouble and frustration and remarks,
What have we got out of winning? Has no one told you? Then I will.
We've got England, shabby, hungry—but England with a future still.
As it is we're still together—we can vote and have our say,
We can dig our bits of garden—and bring the kids up our own way.
We can grouse and we can grumble—we can throw our weight about,
We can criticize the Government—we can even chuck them out.

And those splendid unseen armies of the Fallen lead the way
Down the years from 1940 to the Triumph of today.
And with all our hearts we thank them for the job they had to do,
But we must still remember all those other people too,
All those unimportant people who are *not* in the Parade,
From the never-heard-of places where our Empire has been made,
For these people are the Empire—and the whole world understands,
We are not frightened for its future, while we leave it in their hands.

XV

"Under the Counter"

★

I CAME back to a London, in the late summer of 1945, with the lights shining through the windows again; not a gay London but quiet and relieved. Things would be better now, I told myself, and at any rate there would be no more bombing at night. Like most people, I also imagined that all the wartime shortages would soon be replaced by plenty.

My first objective was to find a London home. The farm had sheltered us but it was not our home. We did not want to go back to our old house in Curzon Street, which was far too large. I wanted a smaller house to suit my post-war needs and it had to be in the centre of Theatreland.

Wanting was one thing—getting another. I don't know how many streets I tramped, how many blasted walls I gazed at, or premiums I blanched at, but I do know that the total amount of 'key' money I refused to pay would have bought me the American Embassy in Grosvenor Square. When I felt like giving up the search I was spurred on by the thought that I *had* to get a home. Jack had been living in hotels and flats while I was away and he, too, felt the need of a home of our own. At last I found it. Not the home of my dreams, for it had had a lot of rough treatment during the war and was really too big, but it was in South Audley Street, had lovely white oak-panelled walls, and what might easily be turned into a tiny roof garden at the back. The house was also in the heart of Mayfair and within walking distance of most London theatres.

Some women find their life transformed by a new hat. But to me, making a home is the most exciting feeling I know. Standing inside that rather battered first-floor drawing-room

in South Audley Street I purred with content. My eyes half
closed, I imagined a Regency chair there, my crimson and stone
curtains at the windows, my crimson carpet on the floor, my
piano under the far window, my desk—now where would my
desk go? By the inside wall or near the fireplace?

"I'll take it," I told the agent. "When can I move in?"

"But the War Damage," he stammered.

"Do that after I'm in," I informed him.

I had a glorious time moving in and I felt about seventeen
as I dashed from room to room placing my furniture as it arrived.
Jack is not a domestic animal when it comes to moving. He
will open a crate and heave a wardrobe with the best, but as
for colour schemes and arranging rooms he could not care
less.

"Now leave me my bookshelves in my study and the two
easy chairs, and that'll be fine," said Jack.

"I think you need new curtains for this room. What about
that striped green brocade I showed you?"

"Striped green brocade? What on earth is wrong with the
blue I had before?"

"Quite a lot," I told him. But Jack had not noticed a crack
in every seam. Given his books, his desk, his chairs, and some
fresh flowers from the farm, he plunged back into his world of
writing, production, and the Theatre. Come to think of it, he
never really came out of it. I didn't mind his lack of interest. It
left me all the more free to enjoy myself.

I remember one afternoon when I was standing in the middle
of the dining-room, trying to direct furniture, electricians, and
war damage repair men all at once. I had on an old navy suit,
a white apron, and my hair tied up with a flowered scarf. "Over
there with the sideboard," I yelled above the hammering. "Along
here with the bureau . . . chairs—put them against the wall for
the moment . . . no, not that side with the wall light . . . it must
shine on the bureau . . . will you be able to lime that patch over
the window? I don't want the wood to go yellow where you
have repaired it." To add to the hustle there were two cats and
my gay young puppy investigating chair-legs and crates. I was
dirty, tired, but in full swing, when the door opened and Jack
put his head round the corner.

"Hello, darling, busy?"

"Oh no," I replied, "just moving in, darling, nothing to do really."

"Well, I'll be dashing along now," said Jack hastily. "Don't rebuild the whole house while I'm gone."

And perhaps there was a hint of serious warning in that last remark. For there have been many times when my joy of rearranging homes has proved Jack's downfall. I have a habit, like most home-lovers, of suddenly seeing a complete change of furniture that would be a great improvement. Usually these inspirations come when I am sitting alone after lunch. No sooner the thought than the deed with any true housewife, so I get up and make the changes. Chairs go there, tables somewhere else, even carpets are moved to other rooms. And I am not in the least intimidated by the thought of moving a piano if the mood takes me. Unfortunately, on one or two occasions I have made drastic changes and not told Jack. And Jack has come creeping in, so as not to disturb me, without turning on the lights, and gone full length over a table or chair that stood in a new place. He has not been at all amused, judging by his language.

I am still having quite a lot of fun in South Audley Street planning my roof garden. Jack is having fun too, for Jack is a keen gardener. So while I plan tables and chairs and a corner for the sun-bathing mattress, Jack is building a small wall, into which he shoves bags of earth, ready for his flower border next Spring. The fact that we have to reach our roof garden by climbing up some steps, through the pantry window, and down steps on the other side, does not dismay me. One day we will probably knock the wall down. *Ah! that's an idea! I must ring up the builders.*

Perhaps it was all the moving, plus the war years and over-work at this moment, that suddenly affected my health. I had always been so full of vitality that I took my good health for granted. I had never pampered myself, but relied on sun, fresh air, and plenty of hard exercises in my shows to keep me fit. And then one day, without warning, I seemed all aches and pains and weariness. I looked wretched and I felt worse, and like all healthy people I was very cross about it, though it did not occur to me to find out what was wrong. Jack, however, insisted upon doctors and escorted me from one to another. Eventually, one of them diagnosed the popular complaint of the season, 'fibrositis', and so it was treated. I would get up early in the morning and drive to a clinic for massage and radiant heat treatment. I felt a trifle better while I was at the clinic but as soon as I got outside again I felt worse than ever. However, I was very obedient and went on with the treatment so that I could continue with the rehearsals of our new show, *Under the Counter*, which had been written by Arthur Macrae. I love working with Arthur—but then I love Arthur! His keen power of observation combined with his ridiculous sense of fun make him in my opinion the foremost writer of broad comedy and sophisticated dialogue in the country today.

He carries himself at rehearsals with a quiet and unobtrusive charm that allays the fears of the most nervous member of the Company who—believe it or not—happens to be me. He is a masterpiece of studied reserve. Ask him to write a scene which you think has a particularly good idea and which *he* thinks is not amusing—go on, ask him. I bet you don't get it!

Arthur usually stands at rehearsals on the side of the stage looking very self-conscious and embarrassed like a nervous schoolboy who, having delivered his homework and seen the headmaster reach for the cane, does his best to show that he fully realizes he has brought this on himself. And when at the end of a morning or afternoon session you turn to him to refer some point under discussion you find he has disappeared. Maybe he's got something there! But it is only at rehearsals that he develops this tendency to shoot out of my presence as if released by a spring.

He has an infectious, though nervous, giggle which if it dies solemnly away is usually ominous because it is the forerunner of a regretful but impressive "No!" I have never known him lose his temper nor an opportunity for a ready laugh. His success in the Theatre is a case of patient climbing up the ladder so there is no strut or swagger in anything he does. One works with a man whose field of interest might well be—and could well be—a First Secretary at the Foreign Office. His talk is poised and arresting, and when we are together our topics of conversation usually embrace the housing problem; the staff problem; and the 'do you know a little man round the corner where I can get something done cheap?' problem. There is a boyish alertness—a restlessness in him—even in the way he moves. Oh yes, I love working with Arthur, but then, as I say, I love Arthur. By the way, there is one thing I have forgotten to tell you about him—he likes antiques. Maybe that is why he likes me?

Those early rehearsals of *Under the Counter* were frightful. I had to lie back on a chair and learn my lines while my understudy went through all the movements. This went on for quite a time until I felt almost suicidal with aches and pains, tiredness and frustration.

At the clinic they kept telling me: "You must be patient. These conditions take a long time to improve. Now—the radiant heat *does* relieve you—doesn't it?"

But I was not patient. And I defy anyone who has always been fit and active and hard-working ever to be patient of illness.

After a few weeks I told Jack: "I'm just the same really, you know. I'm not a fraction better."

And Jack was even more worried than I. Here he was producing me in my first big peace-time show, which was my first starring vehicle on my own, and it was therefore most important for me to make a big success and my health was so bad I was not even able to rehearse properly. I did not know then, but I do now, that very few of the Company expected me to be fit enough to open. Jack was anxious for me to have a second opinion and a friend of ours begged to be allowed to call in his doctor, so one day Jack said, "Darling, I have found someone else and if you like we'll go along and see him."

That 'someone else' diagnosed I had a tired heart and not fibrositis.

I trusted this 'someone else' the moment I met him, and he has proved the most wonderful friend. I can never be too grateful for his help. I think that some medical men, and Mac is one of them, are born with the gift of healing. You can usually tell if they have this gift by something in their eyes, in their voice, in their understanding of their fellow human beings. But above all, I believe it is a God-given gift. Doctors who have it are aware of this, although they will insist it all comes out of the text-book. Twaddle! Absolute twaddle!

I remember Mac saying: "Now listen carefully, Mrs. Hulbert. You have told me what work you have to do and I have told you what is wrong. If you will carry out all my instructions we will have you on the stage for the first night of your new play and you will not miss a performance; but you must do as you are told. You must go to bed for two hours in the afternoon, take the

Under Your Hat. ABOVE from the film. BELOW from the show

Gay's the word

medicine I am going to give you, and you must stop worrying. You understand? Stop worrying. You have strained your heart with overwork and it needs a lot of rest and no anxieties. But you will get well, I promise you."

I walked out of his consulting-room half cured, at least the mental half was cured. I kept to my strict regime of bed and rest and medicines, and I was on for the first night of *Under the Counter* as Mac had promised. It had its funny side—that first night. You see, I had not been allowed to walk about on the stage during rehearsals at all, my understudy had done that for me. So when the first night came I had little knowledge of my movements. All round the stage Jack posted prompters, and funnier still he had large black notices pinned up for me to read all over the set. Hidden behind a chair, for instance, I would see a notice, "When the telephone rings and Mrs. B. is speaking, that is your cue to sit down." From behind a curtain I would read a note, "Go down-stage to fireplace when the door opens." There were even speeches written out for me as reminders in odd corners of the stage. It was a brilliant bit of organizing on Jack's part, and only one person in the audience knew what was taking place, apart from Jack. Mac knew how I was getting through the show.

Under the Counter was an immediate success and ran for two years to packed houses. Our story made fun of the lengths to which people would go to overcome wartime shortages and regulations, and the audience rose to every wangle, joke, and situation. After all, most of them had done much the same themselves and to share a joke with others is always to double it. A success in the Theatre is a strange thing. The critics come and the audience accept you. You are a success. And the very next morning, before most people have seen a single criticism or studied the theatre news at all, there is a long queue at the box office and every seat is sold out. How do people learn of a success so quickly, I wonder? It must be by word of mouth, or instinct. Perhaps people going home tell their friends? They talk in the buses or tubes? Anyway, public reaction to a show they like is instantaneous.

During the run of *Under the Counter* there occurred one of the strangest incidents I have ever known in the Theatre. It happened one night just before we went to New York, a few minutes before the final curtain, when Wilfred Hyde White was playing the part

K

of the Cabinet Minister. Like most actors, Wilfred Hyde White is nervous and anxious on the stage and likes everything around him to run smoothly. I was playing the final scene with him when he picked up the telephone and talked into it. Suddenly, and quite calmly, a man passed me and crossed the stage. Just like that. He was dressed in dark clothes and was completely sure of himself. I had never seen him before. He walked into the centre of the stage, sat down on a chair, crossed his legs, took out a cigarette from his case which he lit, and then he inhaled deeply, and exhaled vigorously at the audience. For a moment I wondered, and so I am sure did everyone back-stage, whether the script had been changed overnight. Wilfred went on with his telephoning and there I stood stiff with horror at what might happen if we could not get the stranger off. Presently he got up, walked to the mantelpiece, knocked off his cigarette ash, listened to Wilfred Hyde White, and nodded agreement at every telephone remark he made. The audience did not sense that anything was wrong. Wilfred was in a state of collapse, but somehow managed to keep going.

In the meantime, back-stage, the police had been 'phoned, the curtain was poised to ring down and men were ready to rush on and grab the intruder should he decide to take a more active part in the play. Wilfred Hyde White finished his scene like a man in a dream until I gave the cue to bring down the final curtain. And whilst the audience applauded our performance the police ran on to the stage and made an arrest. Who was the intruder? What was his motive? We never knew. All the police told us next morning was that the stranger professed a complete loss of memory.

While *Under the Counter* was running, London was filling up again and people were becoming conscious that peace was not a holiday and that the country had to work very hard indeed in order to survive economically. Consequently controls and restrictions were mounting, but in my business, show business, people were still coming to the theatre much earlier in the day than they had done before the war, but they were still coming. We had had a wonderful run in London and the big problem to decide now was whether to take *Under the Counter* to New York and have a shot at earning some dollars. Would the Americans find *Under the Counter* funny or even probable?

I asked Mary Martin. She said, "Yes."

I asked Mary Pickford, who agreed with Mary Martin.

I asked Noel Coward, who agreed with Mary Pickford.

I asked Kathleen Cornell, who agreed with Noel.

And then Lee Schubert, the well-known American impresario, came forward and said: "Yes. Bring the show over to New York and you will earn all the dollars you want."

Fair enough. We went. Straight over to New York with most of the original cast and fourteen girls from the Company. The girls were thrilled. It was their first trip abroad and to go to a land of plenty, and see the sights and have freedom from home problems must have seemed wonderful.

There were others who sent us off in high spirits. A good friend, Mr. A. V. Alexander, who was then Minister of Defence in Mr. Attlee's Government, and is now Lord Alexander, came to a party the night before we set out. He is tremendously fond of the Theatre and had found *Under the Counter* amusing, despite our political jokes making fun of Cabinet Ministers.

"It's a marvellous show," he told me, "and you are going to be a good ambassador for us over in the U.S.A., but you know, Cicely, you'll have to be very careful in America or they won't understand it at all. Why don't you have a prologue explaining the 'under the counter' business of shortages, or perhaps something printed on the programmes?"

"I think it might bore them," I said, "and most people never bother to read programmes, anyway."

"Well then," A. V. went on, "explain the plot of the show in your advance publicity."

What a pity we did not take Lord Alexander's advice!

XVI

America

W HEN you take a show to America you do not, as a rule, go straight to New York. You go to Boston or Washington and try it out, and I was keen to do this. It was a very important and difficult thing to take a show abroad in 1947, or any other time for that matter; but especially so then as all the dollars for salaries and expenses had to be earned over there. If we did not succeed immediately it meant we had no reserves to fall back upon. This would have worried me if Lee Ephraim had not been so confident we would be a smash hit and that the Americans were ready to give us a big hand.

On our arrival in New York we had a series of previews. They were ghastly. To my horror, half the laughs missed altogether and quite obviously the selected audiences had not a clue to what the story was about. It reminded me of a film, which I made in Berlin, where the interpreter kept coming forward and asking me: "Why did you laugh there, please? Herr Director says it is not shown as a laugh in the script."

After the previews we had what one of my intimate friends calls 'A Hulbert'. We sat up and rewrote and rehearsed and reorganized the entire show. I was feeling a little despondent.

On the first night, every member of the cast was on their mettle. They were fine and to my joy and relief with that first-night audience *Under the Counter* was a stampeding, riotous success. They roared at our jokes, whether they understood them or not, and the curtain went up and down so many times at the end of the show that in my exuberance I promised to buy them a new one. I still did not know if it meant anything until Lee Ephraim said: "What did I tell you? You have a smash hit." And I felt he must know.

I went to bed that night after cables had been sent home to England describing our success. I believed I could afford to relax and that everything was all right. This, despite my previous forebodings and the previews. But try as I would, I did not get to sleep easily that night, for somewhere at the back of my mind I was still restless and unsure. "It's all the change and travel and excitement," I told myself as, at last, I slipped off into my dreams.

Came the dawn. And what an awakening! There were newspapers all over my bed. Success? Praise? Laughs? Not a bit of it. Utter and complete failure. Believe me, I have read bad Press notices in my time but nothing so sudden or so violent as the New York Press. They could not damn *Under the Counter* enough. The show was a flop. It had not a laugh. It was not even a show. And as for me? Well, here are some samples of what they said:

New York Journal:

"BRITISH SHOW SICKLY AFFAIR

Lend-Lease still works in favour of the British. It's show business I've got in mind. Didn't we Americans lend those Englanders our *Oklahoma*? And haven't those Englanders leased us their *Under the Counter*?

The *Under the Counter* those Englanders have leased us is 'a comedy with music' written around Cicely Courtneidge and a telephone. Both instruments are on stage throughout the evening; neither is silent from curtain rise to curtain fall. And when the two act up together, Britannia waives the rules of lend-lease and fair play.

Even with a line of 'Oh what a Beautiful Morning' thrown in, all of *Under the Counter*, including Cicely Courtneidge, isn't worth one scene of *Oklahoma* without a single star.

And Miss Courtneidge is, as the programmes say, 'the idolized darling' of English music halls and shows with songs and dances. A commoner's Beatrice Lillie, as it were. . . .

Well, there'll always be an England for her to go back to! ! ! !"

New York World Telegram:

"A BOMBSHELL AT THE SHUBERT

Under the Counter jigs around the stage of the Shubert like a relic of the '20s when dozens of small-scale musicals were cashing in on the boom.

Its loose-jointedness, its posing chorus, and its punchy enthusiasm, suggests that time stood still.

The show is tweaked now and then with some remarkably languid dance routines. Their salvation is they are trotted through by some very handsome gals.

Miss Courtneidge is undisputed titleholder: Miss Benzi-drene 1947!"

New York Herald Tribune:

By HOWARD BARNES

"For much of an act *Under the Counter*, at the Shubert Theatre, makes one beholden to our cousins across the sea. From that point on, it is only possible to wonder why the Arthur Macrae comedy with music ever lasted for a couple of seasons in London.

The trouble is that the latest musical offering to reach town has three acts and the last two are deplorable. All the laughter which is quietly conjured up for a brief interlude in what amounts to an over-blown Music Hall sketch is converted into yawns in the latter stanzas of the work. Miss Courtneidge tries valiantly to rescue a curious combination of didoes by interminable telephone conversations, pratt falls and supposedly comic costumes.

The supporting company does not even get in the few antic licks that the star contrives in the first act. Ballard Berkeley is distrait and dull as the actress's favourite. Thorley Walters, as a youngster precipitated into fast company, is more uncomfortable than comic, and Wilfred Hyde White as the Cabinet Minister goes through the motions.

Under the Counter might better have stayed in London."

New York Star:

"A VERY ENERGETIC LADY IN A QUITE ANAEMIC PLAY

From London, where it ran for two years, has come a very English play with music, starring a very English comedienne. The play is a sort of drawing room farce, a familiar British product that, whilst up-to-date enough in its allusions, seems well-nigh prehistoric in its general structure. It is agreeable for 15 or 20 minutes; agreeably silly for 15 or 20 minutes more; then uncomfortably silly, and at last, quite oppressively so. At last, moreover, means way past 11 o'clock.

Like many people who themselves seem inexhaustible, Miss Courtneidge can be very exhausting. But whether or not an evening with Miss Courtneidge is an event, it is definitely an experience."

New York Times:

By BROOKS ATKINSON

"With all proper respect to Miss Courtneidge as a person in the Theatre, this reviewer is not her audience."

New York Sun:

"UNDER THE COUNTER VERY FLIMSY

Good neighbour relationship between Broadway and London's West End won't be enhanced by *Under the Counter*."

New York Daily Mirror:

"UNDER THE COUNTER BELONGS THERE

Under the Counter is aptly named. That's where it belongs."

Now what had happened? I can think of only two reasons.
The first was that the idiom of the show was too English for
New York, and the second that we had arrived when the British
were most unpopular in America, or should I say New York?
It was in the middle of the Palestinian crisis with all kinds of
insults being hurled at the British. It was round about this time
that Ben Hecht was advertising, from the safety of his New York
penthouse, that there was a song in his heart every time a British
soldier was murdered in Palestine.

I did not let the cast know on the second night how serious
the situation was. Lee Shubert sent for Jack and me and Lee
Ephraim and told us he wanted to take the show off after the
evening performance. In the end we compromised and ran for
three weeks.

I felt responsible, as the star of the show, for our success
or failure, and this was an added strain. We held out with falling
audiences and continued disapproval from the Press. Then we
came off. But off to what? I wondered. Money was short. I had
moved to a cheap hotel and was living in the drug stores for my
food. We had no dollars. What should I do? The first thing was
to get the girls back to England.

My musical director, our ballet mistress, and one or two
other members of the Company were also wondering about the
future. They didn't want to go straight away home, any more
than I did. My argument to the management was something like
this:

"If we had a success I planned to stay over here a year.
And if we didn't, and we haven't, then I want to go on to Australia
or South Africa. We have two years' London success behind us,
and there is no earthly reason why we shouldn't be well received
in Cape Town or Melbourne."

I went out and discussed business with the Australian agents.
But you know what happens when the other man knows your
pocket is empty and you are desperate for the job he is offering. He doesn't suggest the most glowing terms, does he? So I
had to sign up for a year instead of the six months I hoped to
bargain for.

I asked a few members of the cast to come with me and that
really started something because, once it got around that I was
going, everybody wanted to come, including the chorus. But alas,

it could not be arranged owing to permits and pennies. The money was just not available to transport the entire company, so, in the end, only four of us went.

A few days after I signed my contract one of those really delightful things happened to me that sound so little and yet mean so much. A telephone call from Genevieve Tobin in Hollywood: Would I break my journey on the way to Australia and stay with her and her husband, Bill Keighley, for ten days? Would I? I would!

Genevieve and Bill will never know how much that invitation meant to me. When I arrived they gave me dollars and clothes, and they would not listen when I talked about a flop.

"Just bad timing, darling," Genevieve would say; "you couldn't have arrived at a worse moment." All this kindness coming on top of six weeks of living in drug stores in New York, in tiny hotels, and the bare clothes in which I stood up, pulled me on to my feet again. I did not feel very happy and I did not feel very confident, but I did feel ready to have another go at *Under the Counter*.

So I said good-bye to Jack, who returned to England, packed my trunks, my wardrobe, and my props on to a steamer and took off by air for Sydney, via Hollywood and Honolulu. It was mid-winter in America. We hoped to arrive in Sydney in blazing Summer weather just before Christmas. And we were happy to leave New York behind us.

I have been in the Theatre long enough to accept success and failure as and when they come. But for the rest of my life when I think of New York I will always be puzzled by that first-night reception, followed by those notices. It was such a paradox. When you have been on the stage for as long as I have you really get to know about audiences. You get to know how they feel almost as accurately as a doctor feeling a pulse. I know I had some friends in front that night; three of my oldest and dearest. Pat Stone, who was Bobby Howes's wife, Dorothy Ward, and Ivor MacLaren had crossed over to New York specially for my opening, and there were others; but not enough to sway an audience one way or the other. There were well over fifteen hundred people in the theatre that night and the laughs that came back to us on the stage were solid and spontaneous and from all parts of the house. The applause which thundered over the footlights at the end of the show was equally genuine. Now it is possible for an audience to differ from the critics, but not as much as they appeared to do on that night and the following morning. I don't say that *Under the Counter* was right up Broadway's street, but I do say it was not as bad as the Press made out.

I wonder if the death of a British show on Broadway that night was the cause of personal satisfaction to Ben Hecht? I wonder? . . .

XVII

Australia

From Honolulu the four of us flew straight to Sydney. It took three days and as we rose out of the Winter clouds we hoped to arrive in Australia into blazing Summer sunshine just before Christmas. But instead we arrived in pelting rain and we were told, of course, that it was most unusual and not at all typical.

The reception at the airport did not match the dismal weather. There were hundreds of people waiting to greet me—people who knew far more about my career and life than I had ever imagined possible outside England. There were flowers, handshakes, and introductions, and before I had time to put my hat to a more becoming angle a microphone was thrust in front of me and "would I please say a few words to the folks?" As it happened, this was my first mike interview. Fortunately, the compère kept up a flow of questions and I had little to do but answer them. Then we were taken off to our hotel to find more flowers, smiling service, and requests on every side for news of 'home'.

I had time for one or two brief glimpses of Sydney—I'll tell you more about that soon—and then got down to the difficult task of putting the show on by Christmas—that was in just over three weeks' time. It was difficult for quite a number of reasons, not the least of them being the fact that I did not know a single leading actor or actress in Australia. I would be introduced to one of their stars and would chatter away, but for the life of me I could not bring myself to ask "exactly what kind of part do you usually play?" So I had to feel my way as best I could until I heard some of them read the parts.

Once the Company was picked we went quickly ahead. The

chorus was splendid and some of the cast were excellent. But to my English eyes, used to high technical polish and efficiency in production, there was a great deal of grooming to do. I worked as hard as I have ever done in my life for those three weeks, rushing to the theatre to rehearse and sitting up late at night to work out the technical side of the production. But it was fun and for those weeks, at any rate, I had little time to feel lonely or homesick.

Then came a terrible snag. The four of us had only flown our personal baggage from New York. The trunks, with the wardrobes and props, had been put on board a ship. This meant that, during rehearsals, we had to work without the dresses which we were praying would arrive every moment. The show was due to open on Christmas Eve and there was not even standing room left in the theatre bookings. The weather had now turned hot and sunny and everything pointed to fair and favourable, when a dock strike occurred. What could we do? We kept going down to the docks to see if anything had or could be unloaded. We telephoned times without number, we begged and we pleaded. But it was of no avail. We had to cancel our first night. Notices in the newspapers, bills outside the theatre and returned bookings by the hundred. Christmas Eve came and it went, and *Under the Counter* did not open on time.

We dismissed the Company over Christmas and very sadly the four of us planned a quiet, no-party, no-presents, no-celebrations sort of Christmas. We all felt very lonely and horribly disappointed both for our Company and for the audiences who had hoped to get a Christmas laugh out of us. Christmas on the other side of the world in an hotel and without friends seemed a sad prospect.

It was Thorley Walters who broke the spell of dejection. Quite early on Christmas Eve morning he got up and went out to look at Sydney's shops. They looked so gay and so happy and he spied a whole lot of pretty decorations. In jubilation he bought an armful and came back to the hotel.

"Cis, look what I've found!" he called outside my room. "Shall I come in and show you?"

I was sitting up having my breakfast and looking at the notices in the paper about having to postpone the show, and the trouble it was causing.

"Oh, come in," I said, not too graciously. Then, seeing his arms full of Christmas, I dropped my papers.

I didn't drink any more coffee. I was out of bed, tying up a tinsel chain across the room, and when that lot was finished I shouted, "Give me two minutes and I'll be dressed and we'll go out and get some more . . ."

And we did. We went out and let ourselves go. We bought the lovely flowering branches that Australians call their Christmas tree, we bought yards of paper, tiny presents and bells and berries. And back we tore to the hotel and invited the waiters to come and help us make a Christmas story of our rooms upstairs. In an hour or two those hotel rooms looked as much like home as hard work and enthusiasm could make them. And when that was finished, to the complete astonishment of the hotel staff who were all brought up to see what we were doing, we shut ourselves into our separate apartments and began tying up our bundles of presents.

Like all Christmas stories in my life, excepting one when I was very young, that one ended as happily as it had begun sadly. The afternoon had hardly gone before some new Australian friends, Ben Arnott and his wonderful mother, rang up and said their home was open to all of us over Christmas and we were to come along just as though we had known them all our lives. We were greeted at the door with handshakes and affection, and taken into a huge drawing-room which had a Christmas tree up to the ceiling, and an army of relatives, from great-grandpa down to babes in arms. And to crown my pleasure and surprise, *I* was asked to act as Father Christmas and give away the presents.

From that kind first invitation, the Arnotts continued to shower us with love and friendship during our entire stay. Their home was always open to us, they rang up during our shows and they did everything humanly possible to make us feel happy in a strange land.

The Christmas night passed with traditional roast turkey, Christmas pudding, paper hats, silly games, and lots and lots of carols. In my bag I had the cables from Pam and Jack and my darlings at home and at the proper moment in time (remember it's night to our day over there) I telephoned Jack with my own greetings. By midnight on Christmas Eve I felt very, very different from when I awoke that morning.

Our clothes arrived at last and we had our first night early in the New Year. It was an instantaneous success. The Australians adored the show. They laughed their heads off and grasped at once what life was like in England. So different was their reaction from that of the Americans. We knew at once we were in for a big success.

But heavens, how hot it was in Sydney over the New Year! I had two electric fans working full time on the stage. I had a refrigerator in my dressing-room and I actually went on to play carrying two lumps of ice in my hands—and yet I felt so hot I could scarcely breathe.

At times the heat became quite unbearable. I found myself with a high temperature, fits of giddiness and a sore throat, and before I knew what had really happened doctors were called in and the show had to be closed down. There was no understudy for my part in Australia and I was now too ill to go on. It was a dreadful blow to all of us—most of all to me in the middle of a great success.

I called Mac, my doctor in England, and he advised the Australian doctors about treatment. The first thing advised was for me to move from Sydney to somewhere cooler. So I went up to the Blue Mountains. Their effect on me was to make me feel blue myself. They are bleak, desolate, and empty, though, in a detached way, beautiful. I sat with nothing to do but play draughts and card games and try to *think* myself into getting well again.

People were very kind to me. Flowers and fruit arrived daily, so did offers to nurse me free of charge, to read to me, to do my correspondence and to take me for drives.

While I was sitting in dismal isolation in the Blue Mountains some good friends had got together and found me a small house at Palm Beach—a lovely seaside town just outside the city. This was by way of being a miracle.

Why do I call it a miracle? Simply because next to dock strikes the housing problem in Australia is Public Enemy No. 3. Public Enemy No. 1 is drought. The housing problem is so serious that hotels are booked six months or a year in advance, flats are sought after and signed up before they are actually constructed, and all the time I was in the Blue Mountains, and indeed afterwards, when I was travelling, it was essential to keep up the booking of my hotel room to go back to.

But in spite of all this, my friends had managed to get me a house. And on leaving the mountains I went down to Palm Beach to continue my convalescence, and what a lot of curiosity I caused! The Press had been going full guns throughout my illness. One or two friends, members of my Company, had taken turns to stand guard outside my room to ward them off. In Sydney the public had their fun as well. We found that people in the houses opposite were actually focussing telescopes on my bedroom to try to see the invalid taking her nourishment! Some were even trying to photograph me.

I was ill for nearly six weeks, but by the time I arrived at Palm Beach I was more used to the heat and had had the rest I needed to make up for a very trying past year of anxieties and failure. The moment I felt fit again we continued with the run in Sydney and then set off across Australia just as her Autumn (our Spring) was beginning.

It seemed strange to me, as I looked around Sydney, to think that I had been born in this place. It has a most wonderful harbour—perhaps the most wonderful harbour in the world. The streets are narrow, crowded, and the shops crammed with goods—rather in the way we used to cram our best grocers' shops in Edwardian days. The buildings are very different to those in Europe. Some are beautiful and elegant. Others look as though they had been run up overnight. And the people? Well, I found the girls bigger and more buxom than our English lasses and the men much taller and gloriously suntanned. The men dress for open-air life always and their great passion seems to be the sea. I found that everyone, literally everyone, from home, shop, hotel, or office goes down to the sea in their leisure hours. Most of them sail, all of them swim and sunbathe, and the whole free time of Sydney seemed to be saltwater, sun, and exercise on the most glorious sands in the world. No wonder, I thought, Australians look such fine people.

The run finished in Sydney before it need have done as Hartley Power was due to open in the theatre, but my illness had held things up. Our next booking was in Melbourne and we were to fly there. One thing that never failed to astonish me in Australia was the huge distances. The towns are not a few miles apart—they are literally thousands of miles. You can go by train—but that means days or weeks of travel. Even flying may take a week of your time. This means that Australians are completely air-minded. They just think in terms of flying as we think in terms of Green Line coaches. It's as simple as that. If I had hated air-travel before, I told myself, I most certainly would have to get used to it now.

Melbourne was not such a lucky break as I had hoped. A very stupid piece of organization had taken place. Partly owing to the hold-up of the show in Sydney two English shows had been booked to run at the same time. The Oliviers in Shakespeare and our show *Under the Counter*. Now there is no reason on earth why in London a dozen shows should not run together and all be successful; there is every reason in Australia, however. The Oliviers had come with Government sponsorship and with tremendous advance publicity all over the country. They had official receptions, official pictures, and a 'grand tour' kind of propaganda all the way. And quite rightly too. We had to make our own publicity and we had also been given a huge theatre to fill—much too large for an intimate show like *Under the Counter*. With people coming long distances to Melbourne, most of them could only book for one English show—and that proved to be the Oliviers. Had we been there a few weeks earlier or a few weeks later, all would have been well. As it was, the two English companies were in direct rivalry. And sad to say, *Under the Counter* played to very small audiences.

It was mid-winter in Melbourne and I think it was the coldest city I have ever lived in. Icy winds howled round us, sweeping down the beautiful wide streets and on the stage of our theatre, which was as large as the Palladium. I felt more than once that what I needed really was a nice cosy box under the counter.

We finished our season in Melbourne and then flew off again. This time to Brisbane.

I think Brisbane is the most primitive place I have ever played in. It seems quite cut off from the modern world altogether. A sort of Mrs. Wiggs of the cabbage patch world in which hard work is only just catching up with good living. I was terribly afraid that *Under the Counter* would seem mere sophisticated nonsense in face of such down-to-earth living. But no, we went down well. Why? Because I found that in every Australian heart, be it in bush or city, there seems a fundamental love of 'home' and everything connected with 'home'.

After the investiture. Outside Buckingham Palace
with Jack and Pam

Inside the grounds of Buckingham Palace

Schnozzle Durante gags on my left at Ealing Studios

The Crazy Gang gag right, left and centre

Our next flight was to be to Perth—the most western tip of the Western Territories. To fly there meant to pass over vast stretches of arid desert. I did not know before, but I soon discovered that this flight was one of the worst in Australia. The air pockets over the desert were frequent and grim. The 'plane tossed, bumped, sagged, and seemed about to crash every few miles. Before we set out, the Company had been very excited as up till then only a few of us had flown and the rest had come by rail. For quite a number of the girls this was their first flight. I sat there, trying to pretend I was a seasoned flyer, while the rest gasped and moaned and went whiter and whiter. Presently, Thorley got up and asked the air-hostess if he might help in comforting the ladies. "Certainly, do what you can." And Thorley went around comforting them and suggesting brandy, books or air-sickness pills in what I thought was a most gallant way. His rounds almost over, Thorley came to me. "How are you, Cis? Managing all right? Can I get you anything?"

"No, thank you, nothing at all. I'm all right, really I am." I was feeling as sick as a dog, but I was not going to add to the distress of the trip if I could help it. I was too terrified to be ill. I thought my end was near and at any moment I would be shot out of the 'plane. "Are you sure you're all right?" pressed Thorley. "You look awful, I must say." I turned to answer and saw him suddenly turn green as he reached for his brown paper bag and practically brought up his boots. I have never seen anyone so suddenly and violently ill. If I had not felt so dreadful myself, or he had not looked so ghastly, it might have been funny. As it was, no one found it funny until we reached Perth. Then Thorley started to laugh . . . and went on laughing all the way to the hotel.

I found Perth a charming place and the people kind and hospitable beyond my dreams. They could not do enough to welcome us and each day we were besieged with folk bringing flowers and messages and asking questions about the way things were going 'back home'. As each city greeted me on that Australian tour I really began to feel very ashamed I had not known before how much they loved England. And how much they longed to keep in touch with her. Everywhere we were invited into private homes, given wonderful meals, and taken to see the famous spots. Everyone asked us for

L

news, photographs, and exactly how the old country was looking.

Our run finished at Perth, and we planned to go by train to Kalgoorlie and play one night to the gold-miners. I was very excited about it and all keyed up to go down a mine, meet the mayor, and have a gold nugget presented to me. Everything was laid on and a big reception arranged for me. Sad to say, it didn't happen. Another strike intervened. This time a rail strike. And we were held up in Perth and unable to get to Kalgoorlie in time for a show. Some days later we set off—the strike being settled—and steamed away across the bush and desert back to Adelaide. Passing through Kalgoorlie I was told I could have just an hour to have a look round. My name hung up over the queer shack-like theatre: 'Cicely Courtneidge in *Under the Counter*, to be presented . . .' The whole place looked so like a western film of the gold rush days that I was grinning with delight from the moment I walked down 'Main' street. There was plenty of husky help to show me around and I was even granted the privilege (?) of seeing a game of 'Two-up', where thousands of pounds are lost and won. To do this—a thing that no women are allowed even to watch—I was set behind some canvas barriers.

Drug stores, saloons, and houses all looked as though taken from a film studio. The voices of the men were rough, friendly, and coated with the thickest accent I have ever heard. The girls were feminine, pretty, and well aware of their minority value. I wish I could have gone down the mine, got the gold nugget, and played in the theatre. But I couldn't. We had now to go straight across to Adelaide or we should be late for our opening night.

What a journey that was across Western Australia! The news of my journey had reached every village or homestead within hundreds of miles and along they came to sit by the railroad track and shout and wave to me. Whenever we stopped there were people waiting to talk to me and give me small presents and ask for a handshake. I remember one night we halted for a moment by some small station. Some of the Company got out to breathe a bit of fresh air. Presently one of them tapped on my window: "Cis, put on a wrap and come out here . . . there's someone you must meet." Hastily I combed my hair, tied round me a long housecoat, and clambered out. There I found an old,

old man who had been waiting nearly all day to see me. Twenty years ago he had come from England and he would never go back, he said: "Ain't got the time nor the money." He loved the English comedy theatre, could remember every show he had seen when a young man—said he had never seen any like them since . . . could he shake hands with me? I felt my eyes begin to smart a little as I thrust out my hand. He seemed to be shaking hands with all the fun and laughter he had in his youth. I felt so proud and happy to see him grin like a boy. "The gentleman told me you'd come out the moment you heard . . ." he grunted happily. And then he went on to ask all the familiar questions. How was London looking? Had we enough to eat? Was it really true that St. Paul's and the Houses of Parliament were still intact and looking the same? What did the countryside look like? Green as emeralds still?

I'm glad we had that long train journey back—not so much as it avoided that nightmare air-trip, but because I saw a whole lot of Australia out of the windows which I should otherwise have missed. I saw mirages, for instance, in the desert—and they really were like the visions travellers tell you about. Whole cities suspended (usually upside-down) in the air, beautiful oasis pools and trees which may be somewhere, but certainly are not at the spot you see them in the mirage. I saw emus—though no kangaroos—and most distressing sight of my life, I saw aborigines.

The Australians are very ashamed about the way the aborigines live. What to do about them nobody knows. For they are far nearer to animals than men in mentality and they refuse to be helped in any way except by having food or clothes thrown to them. It is a quite shocking sight to see these men, more skeleton than anything else, come up to the passing trains. People throw old clothes to them out of the train windows, which they drape round their bodies. Sometimes they have carved rough boomerangs from the trees and these they offer to the passengers for sale. Among the better developed tribes it has been possible, of course, to send missionaries and build schools and hospitals, but among the worst and roughest in the bush help seems impossible.

I only missed one big thrill during my year in Australia, and that was a visit to the Great Barrier Reef. Like most schoolgirls, I had thought of the Reef as a stretch of coral out at sea to the north of Australia—and as nothing more. Over there, I was told that it was the most wonderful marine sight in the world. That from a 'plane you could watch sharks, porpoises, gigantic fish of all colours and shapes, and coral-strands of pink and red and every known shade of blue and green water—just beneath you.

There is much more colour in Australia than we have in England. The paroquets in the Blue Mountains were like jewelled flashes past my bedroom windows and the most astonishing colour scheme of my life was a trip by motor-boat to some tiny islands lying off Palm Beach.

We had set off on a small bathing trip and were looking for a nice secluded bay in which to harbour our boat. At last we found it: small, quiet, and with the most wonderful stretch of sands.

"Here," we all yelled, "look at that bay, let's go in there; not a soul about, what a spot for a swim. . . ."

We turned the nose of the boat straight on and bounced over the surf towards the bay. I was half standing up as we slid towards the shore, but as I looked I sat down with a bump. The whole stretch of sand rose up in a great smooth mound, and moved off! I screamed, the engines shut off, and we all stared over the bows. What had been a flat pink and blue surface of sands was now a moving mountain of tiny, tiny *crabs*! As the boat came in, so they got up and moved off to hide themselves. There must have been millions of them and none bigger than a five-shilling piece. By the time the boat grounded they had gone, leaving us a clear space of white sand. We had our bathe, for we were told they were quite harmless. But as we left the shore after our picnic we watched them coming back again—all pale pink and blue, covering the sands entirely as they came.

The little Koala bears were often to be seen near my house in Palm Beach. I spent my days searching for them, looking up in the trees. They are very hard to find and when you do invariably they are fast asleep. They are getting rather rare now, but are quite the most enchanting creatures I have ever seen. They look rather like a chubby poodle dog and they are extremely friendly. They have thickly fringed ears and pouches in their cheeks for storing the food you give them. And heavens, how they *snore* in the trees at night! I would like to have brought one back

At the
Phoenix Theatre
with my friend
Hartley Power

Down on the farm

Leading the chorus in *Full Swing*

Also from *Full Swing*

to partner Nanny at night, but no one is allowed to take them away as they are far too difficult to rear.

We finished our tour in Adelaide and we were getting more and more excited, counting the days of our return home, after eighteen months away from England. Adelaide was a lovely town full of hospitable people who kept sending us invitations to their homes. And how different home life is in Australia! In Australia there are no private servants. So everyone does their own cooking and cleaning. And the menfolk do quite half the jobs in the home. In many homes, indeed, it is the husband who cooks the evening meal and not the wife. And when it comes to the washing-up, host, hostess, and friends all leave the dinner-table, pop on overalls, and take a cloth to help.

What wonderful husbands they make, those Australians! I'll bet there isn't a job from polishing the brass to cooking an omelette and changing the baby that they can't tackle as well as a woman. So if any of you are thinking of marrying an Australian— don't hesitate.

I don't know how many homes I visited over there but it must have run into hundreds and in each one it would begin the same way, "Now tell us really, how are things back home?" They would drink in my 'accent' as they were pleased to call it and hang on to every word I said. And most lovely of all, they became real friends.

What a last night they gave us at Adelaide! They started throwing streamers, half-way through the show, and by the last act the Company had retaliated with their own streamers. The orchestra were covered so thickly that only Bob Probst's head could be seen above a thick skein of pink, blue, green, and red criss-crossed paper. He stood there with his head poking out, unable to see his musicians. The musicians, hidden beneath the streamers, could not raise their bows to their violins. But for Bob the situation was absurd. There he was, trying to wave his baton to an unseen orchestra, while down below strange noises were coming up at him.

After the Adelaide run we had ten days' holiday at Palm Beach before we set off on our return flight.

Wait a minute—here I am about to tell you of my return, but looking through my diary I find I have missed out New Zealand, where we went after our run in Brisbane. We played in Wellington, Auckland, Christchurch, Dunedin, and a few other towns. We flew everywhere—over torrents of water, rocks, forests, and mountains. We stood on the spot where Scott left for his Antarctic explorations.

One day I had a most exciting trip to see the penguins. I was lucky about this as at that time no one was allowed to come close to them. But by good fortune I met a professor who was in charge of the colony of penguins and he took me out to the rocks. I was photographed standing by a smart little penguin with his dress-shirt glistening and his tail-coat sleek and tailored. I saw lying on the rocks behind me a sea lion, the biggest I have ever seen, having a siesta. It was a thrill much more than any I had as a child in a zoological garden. The photo of me is not very good, but my friend the penguin is certainly looking his best.

We also managed to find time to get up to Rotorua—the hot springs district of North Island. Huge boiling geysers shot 100 feet into the sky, medicinal waters bubbled out of the rocks, and so hot do the geysers make the ground that you merely scrape a hole in the sand, fill your cooking-pot with water and food and plank it down in the open to simmer away for an hour. And then you can have either a nice sulphur bath (and what a smell it is!) and eat your casserole off a floating tray, or lean back on a deck-chair and read the newspapers while you sip your 'cure' in the mountain scenery.

In this part of New Zealand we met the Maoris and saw their dances. They were all ready at the time for the King and Queen's visit, which had to be postponed. Maoris are such beautiful and gentle people to look at and their natural skills and graces are superb. They gave me a lovely green brooch for luck, after an evening in which I sat entranced at a series of their dances done in the open air.

I cannot say the architecture of New Zealand is very inspiring. It seems to be all tiny log cabins, no brick or stone at all. But then I suppose there is the continual problem of earthquakes. Did I have one while I was there? Yes, apparently I did, but though the rest of the Company noticed it, I somehow missed it. The city of Christchurch is very lovely though—just like a miniature Cambridge without the height or spires. We made many friends there.

It was in Auckland, New Zealand, that I had the most un-dignified and disorganized interview of my life.

I was sitting in my room with friends when a message came that a reporter from the newspaper wished for a personal inter-view. "Just a moment," I said to a friend. "Hold him off for a moment. I must slip along next door first." I slipped out and into the little room 'next door'. But when I came to slip out again the door stuck. For fifteen minutes I shoved and banged and pushed and tried to get out of the little room next door. The household heard the noise I was making and came to my rescue, and so, too, did the reporter. Soon he was joined by a plumber and a car-penter. Still the door would not budge. So, with a background of saws, chisels, and hammers, I had to give my interview to the reporter through the lavatory door. Yes, I had a wonderful trip. Yes, I adored New Zealand. Yes, the audiences had been grand . . . Which town had I enjoyed most? Oh, the one I was in, naturally . . . Was I glad that I should soon be going home? . . . How was Jack? . . . How was England? . . . etc., etc. And the next morning, of course, my interview was recorded faithfully on the front page. No mention was made of the place of interview.

When the time came for my return home most of the Com-pany returned by sea but one or two of us flew via America.

We were so excited by the time we got to Honolulu that it took us an hour or so to realize that however hard we tried to organize we just could not be with friends in America for Christmas Day.

So we spent Christmas in Honolulu.

On Christmas Eve we went off to a midnight service in the English church there. It was very beautiful and so packed out that half the congregation were on the porch outside. We sang carols and we listened to the Bethlehem story that still sounds as young and sweet as the Spring . . . "And the angel said: 'Fear not, for behold I bring you tidings of great joy, which shall be to all people. For unto you is born this day in the city of David, a Saviour, which is Christ the Lord' . . . Glory to God in the highest and on earth peace, goodwill towards men. . . ." These familiar Christmas words did not seem strange to me despite the exotic setting. They took me back to memories of English churches as a child, as a girl and as wife. Christmas in Honolulu was not so lonely after all. Memories are good company.

After the service, which lasted, by the way, until nearly 2 a.m., we went back to the hotel where Christmas fun was well under way . . . even to a Father Christmas, a little the worse for good cheer, who greeted us with a stagger and yelled out with American flavour, "Say, folks, a real Happy Christmas to you." We drank Christmas Day in and decided on a few hours' sleep before further celebrations started, and I trust the local Father Christmas was able to do the same.

At 4.30 a.m. I woke up with a start—I had forgotten part of my decorations. I had no paper hat in which to give away my presents in the morning. That would never do. So I got out of bed, puffing with the heat, and carefully and artistically made myself a beautiful tinsel hat for Christmas morning. Then I took one look at the night—navy blue sky with white stars— and toppled back into bed and dreamland.

By 9.30 a.m. I was awake again, wearing my smartest wrap and with the paper hat on my head and a table covered with presents beside me on the balcony. Then I shouted for Thorley and breakfast. And in a few moments he came (and so did breakfast) with a huge and exquisite lei made of orchids which he proceeded to hang round my neck. And much more than orchids—for every inch or two round that garland he had hung a tiny message carefully copied from the cables from friends at home. There they hung, quite twenty-five of them, with a picture of Honolulu in bright colours above them. It must have taken him hours to have worked it all out.

The party that night was a typical Hawaiian one, quite unlike any other Christmas party I had ever seen. Dancing, music, flowers, singing—all of them soft and exotic and colourful.

And so it went on, Christmas Day, Boxing Day, and the next. Parties, drinks, music, and new friends. And Thorley and I could do nothing in return except to say 'thank you' and ask them to visit us when they came to England.

We arrived in Hollywood, at Bill and Genevieve's, just before New Year.

What a different pair we must have looked than on our outward journey a year ago! Then we had been despondent, tired, and anxious after the catastrophe in New York. Here we were back again both as fat as butter—at least Thorley was—and ready to go on to England.

After Hollywood we went on to New York and from thence to England. The big debate of that moment was—should we fly the Atlantic or not?

"I don't think I can," I told Thorley. "The idea of that awful water underneath . . . and the winds and fogs . . . oh dear . . . no."

"You managed the Pacific, didn't you?" he said.

"Yes, I know, but that was different."

"You had thousands of sharks underneath you then," he reminded me, "and don't forget the desert bumps in Australia."

"Don't *you* forget them either," I said.

"Look at the time we shall save, if we *do* fly," he persisted, and in the end persuaded me. I'm not sure that I want to do it again, but I wanted to get back to England and Jack and Pam. So we flew off through the clouds to home, and a new show—or so I hoped.

XVIII

"Tough at the Top"

★

SIR ALAN HERBERT wrote a show for Cochran called *Tough at the Top*, and he proved that he knew what he was talking about when he picked that title. I think an actor or actress who reaches the top of our profession is in a similar position to a champion boxer. With every new show, like every new fight, his title is at stake. On the way up people allow you a few failures, but once you have won championship status they expect you to deliver the goods every time. Keeping to the boxing simile, I, like many boxers, had to go to America to lose my crown. You may say that in common with some of them I, too, have blamed the referee. You may also say that one failure in America did not necessarily mean I had lost my crown and that anyway my British title was not at stake. Don't you believe it; failure anywhere, for *any* reason, resounds *everywhere* in the Theatre. People are very ready to applaud when you are at the top, but they are equally ready to join in the hue and cry if you stumble. I forget who said that phrase about 'there is something not displeasing in the misfortune of our friends', but I think it is more applicable to my profession than any other.

One of the outstanding figures in the contemporary Theatre, Dame Edith Evans, says about theatrical failure and success: "Don't go on the stage unless you want your heart broken. I went on the stage. My heart has been broken—shattered, bitterly and abysmally—several times. When this happens to us we just pick up the pieces and carry on. Stage people must be physically and emotionally strong. They work at a great emotional pitch for exhaustingly long hours in not very fresh air, with the threat of a failure and unemployment hanging over them every moment.

If they have an overflow of emotion that severs them from polite society in which the emotions are repressed they must also have a stoicism in the face of adversity possessed by few other people in the world." I reckon to have that stoicism in the face of adversity that Dame Edith talks about.

I knew I had a fight on my hands when I got back home. I knew I had to prove that I was still worthy of being at the top. I remember a notice in the prompt corner of a provincial music hall which said, 'Don't tell us what you can do—go on and do it.' The only way for me to do that on my return to London was to get a show together good enough for people to say, 'Whatever New York may think, Cicely Courtneidge is still the tops.' But good shows are not easy to find, and I am going to take this opportunity of giving the lie to people who say that it is no use writing a show unless you have a reputation or friends at Court. That simply is not true.

Everyone in the Theatre, at least everyone I know, and that is quite a lot of people, is always on the look-out for a new show, a new author, a new idea. We all read scripts or get someone to read them for us, and we don't care who has written them so long as they have merit. Mind you, and this applies to artistes, but not to managements, we naturally only read scripts which look as though they are suitable for us. Obviously, it would be a waste of my time and Jack's ploughing through the efforts of a potential Christopher Fry or Tennessee Williams. But show us a book or a story, with an idea for a musical, and we cannot afford *not* to read it.

During my absence in Australia I had hoped that Arthur Macrae would write a new show for me, but this did not materialize as he could not get the right idea that appealed to him. Jack read scores of scripts, by known and unknown authors, in the hope that he would find something suitable for me. Finally, as time was getting short, he called in Archie Menzies, who had what seemed a good basic idea, and he worked on this with Harold Purcell. But sometimes a good basic idea does not work out in practice and not long after I returned home I heard that the book was getting involved and tiresome and no one was satisfied with the result. The show was called *Her Excellency*, and we got through rehearsals and on to its first night, which went quite well. We had a good reception and we hoped for a run. But the

Press next morning was universally bad. There were one or two who praised me personally but that did not make it a good show. From a bad Press we opened in a heat wave, followed by two more. And each heat wave emptied the theatre as they always do unless you have heavy advance booking to carry you over. You see how I can use the excuses for failure I told you about earlier on. However, despite the notices and the heat waves, *Her Excellency* managed to run for seven months.

It was Winter when the show came off and I decided on a short holiday before we planned another first night. I had two weeks' Winter sports in Switzerland and came back refreshed and more determined than ever to find a show which would put me back at the top. During the run of *Her Excellency* Jack had had an idea for me. Briefly it was that I should play the part of an actress who becomes the owner of a Dramatic School. It was a good idea and one in which I saw possibilities for fun and burlesque.

"I think it's grand," I told Jack. "Ask Arthur Macrae to write it."

Jack replied, "I'll get on to him at once."

So before I left for my holiday, Arthur Macrae had promised to work on the new idea, which he liked at once.

The next problem was the music, and there a very strange thing happened. At least it seemed wonderfully strange at the time. When I was in Australia I had met an actress who had asked my advice about her chances of success if she came over to England, and when she arrived I was fortunately able to get her a small character part in *Her Excellency*. I could see, towards the end of the run, how worried she was getting. I knew she had sold up practically everything she possessed in Australia to come over here and had banked on succeeding in England. Then one night towards the end of the run, when our notice was up, she was waiting for me when I arrived at the theatre. "Miss Courtneidge," she said, "I'll have to go back to Australia if I don't get something soon."

And I knew very well she had next to nothing to go back to. I waited a few days and made one or two enquiries. I could not bear to face her anxious looks, so I telephoned Ivor Novello at the Palace Theatre, where he was playing in *King's Rhapsody*, and said: "May I come and see you after the show

Leonora Corbett and Jack resent my
intrusion in *Under Your Hat*

Ivor Novello

for ten minutes? There's something I'd like to talk over with you."

"Of course you can," said Ivor, "as soon as you like."

I went over to the Palace Theatre and found several of his friends in his dressing-room.

Ivor gave me a friendly wink and said, "Wait until they've gone and I'll have a word with you."

When, eventually, we had the room to ourselves, I said: "Ivor, would you do me a great favour?"

"Of course, if I can," he replied.

"Can you, or could you, find a small part for one of my cast in one of your shows? Or do you know anyone in London who would give her a chance?"

Ivor thought for a moment and then said, "I'll try to put her in one of my shows on tour if it can be fixed." He turned and filled up our glasses and then with rather a wry smile on his face he said, "You know, Cis, I'm very disappointed. I thought you had come to ask something quite different."

"Something different?" I was puzzled.

"Yes," he went on. "I thought you'd come to ask me to write the music for your new show—the one Arthur is doing."

"Write the music for my new show? You don't mean it?"

"Of course I do."

"But I didn't think you'd want to do my kind of music," I gasped.

"Why ever not? I'd adore to," said Ivor.

It sounded so simple and easy the way he said it, as though a famous and romantic composer was in the habit of writing the score for a comedy, and to cap his extreme modesty Ivor said, "Do you think Jack will agree?"

"Agree?" I repeated. "Why, he'll go mad with delight at the very idea."

"And Arthur? Would he like to work with me as well?"

I assured him that Arthur would be just as delighted as Jack and I.

How I got home to tell Jack I don't know. I sat on the edge of my taxi seat all the way home and chatted to myself in my excitement. "You can't get away from it—you're lucky. In trying to help someone else you've helped yourself. After three years, this is the turn of the tide, at least. Well, it's been worth waiting for. I can't go wrong with Ivor." I planned an immediate telephone call to Arthur Macrae to tell him my good news and I planned my opening explosion to Jack. "Ivor's going to write the music!" I yelled up the stairs as I burst in. "Did you ever hear of such luck? Isn't it wonderful? Where on earth are you?"

A long face came round the drawing-room door. "What's that you're saying? Ivor's going to write the music? When? Where? How did it happen?"

Then Jack and I got into an all-night session of plans and ideas. We were both completely enchanted that Ivor was so keen to write the score of a musical show for me. It seemed almost too good to be true.

"He always said he wanted to write music for you, didn't he?" Jack reminded me.

"Why, yes, so he did," I said, "but that was a long time ago."

So there we were. A new idea (Jack's), new music (Ivor's), and a new story (by Arthur Macrae), and the name of it was to be *Gay's the Word*.

All this happened at the end of the run of *Her Excellency*, and so I had plenty to dream about during my holiday in Switzerland. In fact I shouldn't have taken a holiday if there hadn't been something planned on the horizon. On my return from Zurich there was bad news. Jack broke it to me with a glum face.

"Cis, there's a snag about the new show."

"A snag," I said. "How can there be?"

"Arthur Macrae has suddenly had to fulfil another contract in a hurry—he just hasn't time to work on our show."

The question was, 'Could we wait for Arthur to be free?' Of course we couldn't. Jack and I both had commitments which had to be kept and Ivor could not put work on one side and start again.

I said: "We cannot lose Ivor. We must see him at once and ask him to work with someone else and find out whom he suggests."

So we decided there and then the best thing to do was to tell Ivor what had happened. I can see him so clearly in his room at the Aldwych that night when we went to see him. He looked handsome, elegant, and charming as always.

"Well, what's bothering you both?" said Ivor, as he moved

across to a small table. "Have a drink, and tell me what's the matter."

"It's Arthur," began Jack quietly. "He can't write the new show."

"He can't? Why ever not?" said Ivor.

And we both burst into explanations.

When the tale was over we began the real reason for our visit.

"We've come to ask if you can think of anyone else you would be willing to work with? Can you think of any other writer who would do?" And we mentioned names in the theatrical world that we thought might appeal to Ivor. He did not take up any of our suggestions, until at last I said, "Who would you be happy to work with?"

Ivor stood smiling at our worried faces, then he said quietly: "Happy to work with? Happy to work with? Well, I'd be happy to work with myself."

Neither Jack nor I grasped his meaning at first. We both thought he meant he would be quite happy to go on working at his music until a writer turned up to join him with the story.

He repeated the sentence: "I'd be happy to work with myself."

And then we tumbled.

"You don't mean . . . you can't mean . . . you do mean you'll do all the work?" said Jack, not daring to mention the word *write*.

"Just that," said Ivor, "if you want me."

"If we *want* you? I can't believe it!" I cried.

"If you want me," repeated Ivor, "I'll do it. I've always wanted to write a show for you."

We could hardly credit our good fortune and we sat silent while Ivor, in his modest way, continued: "Of course, say at once if you don't want me. And, of course, you are under no obligation if you don't like the stuff I write. Of course there'll be no hard feelings if you say it's not the kind of thing you want. And, of course, as it's Jack's idea I shall have to be in the closest touch with him all the time."

I think Ivor was the most modest and unspoiled man I have ever known. He never thought of his own importance, but always of the people he was working with. I doubt if he ever sat down and really thought about himself at all. I think he wrote and worked with his whole heart and all the time considered only the people who were going to play in his shows and sing his music. Before we left Ivor that night he had actually roughed out his entire plans.

"I dictate everything to a secretary," he told us. "I like working fast, it suits me. If I have the story roughed out in two to three weeks, how will that be?"

Nothing could be better, we told him.

"Don't worry if you don't hear from me except over the telephone. I shall be hard at it. I like to work on my own and then come up for air when I'm finished.

"One final thing before you go," he said. "I always work with Tom Arnold. May I bring him in?"

So Tom Arnold came into our new schemes that night as well, and we now felt we had the tops in all the necessary ingredients for a smash hit in the not too far distant future.

On my arrival home that night I wrote in my diary: February 28th, 1950. Ivor promised to write the new show.

XIX

Royalty

Down through the ages the great patrons of the Theatre have been the Kings and Queens of England. In fact the biggest slump the Theatre ever experienced was when we were without a king and that man Cromwell made himself Lord Protector, and for fourteen years it was Sunday every day of the week. Henry VIII was not only a good lyric writer, he composed the music as well. I am quite sure no one inspired Shakespeare so much as Elizabeth I, and without doubt the greatest stage-door Johnnie of all time was Charles II, although strictly speaking he never troubled with the stage-door but watched the show from the green itself.

Coming from the Stuarts to the House of Hanover it is true that William of Orange did not show a particular interest in the Theatre but that was only because he hardly understood a word of English. Queen Anne and her great friend Sarah, who was pleasured by her husband with his boots on, were great supporters of the Theatre. And the Prince Regent was not only a great lover of the Theatre but so adored dressing up that in my view he was a frustrated actor. This, by the way, was the only realm of activity in which he was frustrated. Nearer to our present times we have had Queen Victoria and the Prince Consort, who were both vitally interested in the Theatre, so much so that it was during Queen Victoria's reign that members of our profession were knighted for the first time. Queen Victoria was a great admirer of Sir Arthur Sullivan, who collaborated so successfully with Mr. Gilbert. Without wishing to appear disrespectful, I must register the opinion that Queen Victoria led Sir Arthur Sullivan astray, for it was at her suggestion that he turned from comic to grand opera. The result was a bore, which is the worst you can say of anyone.

But on the whole the effect of Royal patronage has been to raise the standard of the Theatre and the status of our players. During the last quarter of a century, when the Theatre has had to face the competitition of the cinema and radio sound and vision, Royal patronage has done more than anything else to keep the live Theatre alive. So long as Royal interest in the Theatre continues tens of thousands of people will follow their lead. And I think it is worthy of note that in America, where they have fine playwrights, producers, and artistes, but no Royal Family to lead the way, the Theatre is not as flourishing as it is here. As a matter of interest, the visit of the King and Queen to a theatre means almost certain success at the box office, and I speak from personal experience.

The first time I was at a performance attended by Royalty was at a Charity Matinée in March 1914 at the London Palladium when King George V and Queen Mary were present. It was only the third time that a British monarch had attended a music-hall performance, and the young beauties of the London stage acted as programme sellers; among them were Yvonne Arnaud, Gladys Cooper, Phyllis Monkman, and Cathleen Nesbitt. Somehow I was included, which in retrospect is hard to believe since I said 'Beauties'. However, it was in the newspapers so it must be true. The Bill consisted of Sir George Alexander in Max Beerbohm's sketch, *A Social Success*, Jackson's sixteen English dancers, Clarice Mayne with 'that fellow' J. W. Tate singing 'Nursie' and 'Faces', Sammy Shields giving a word picture of a Scotsman watching a football match, and George Robey singing 'The Pro's Landlady'.

A happy Royal occasion, but idiotically disappointing for me, was the wedding of Princess Mary, who is now the Princess Royal. I decided that to get anything like a proper view we must get up at dawn, before dawn in fact. Now, I simply cannot stand for any length of time. If I stand for more than two or three minutes I begin to wobble on my legs and I feel lightheaded. Maybe I had an ancestor in the Guards. So I armed myself with a canvas stool. I set off, well before daylight, and planted my stool in St. James's Street—not in the front row—oh dear me, no, there were already two rows waiting—but I had a good position.

At last the day dawned, the soldiers arrived, the sun shone, and the crowds moved in. The soldiers were horribly tall, and so too was the crowd in front of me, but I had my canvas stool to stand on. The crowd kept calling out, "Here they come!" and each time I clambered up on my canvas stool. If the call came once that morning, it came twenty times, and twenty times I stood on my wobbly stool. And then at last they came with one mighty shout, the clatter of horses' hooves, the cheers, and the swaying of the crowd against the soldiers. My big moment. I jumped up on my stool. Alas, I had clambered too often and not too well. For as I jumped for the last time the canvas gave way and I plunged through on to the ground, missing the Princess, the King, the Queen, and the whole procession.

During my career I have met most members of our Royal Family and the one to whom I was most devoted was Her Gracious Majesty Queen Mary. One of my most treasured possessions is a signed photograph which she sent me during the run of *Gay's the Word*. I think Queen Mary was a most marvellous person. Not only because of her dignity and presence, but because of her sense of duty and abiding interest in people. She loved the Theatre and had seen most of my shows. She had so many tragedies and sorrows in her private life, but never allowed them to interfere with her duty. She was out and about fulfilling her public engagements whatever sorrow she may have felt in her heart. To me she epitomized, more than anyone else, the continuity of the Crown and its devotion to service.

My first presentation to Queen Mary at a special matinée was a fiasco. We were all instructed, before it began, to line up in a corridor which was narrow and dark, and I was the last but one at the end of the line. I had practised my curtsey in my dressing-room and had tried out a number of bows in front of my mirror, and said, "Yes, your Majesty. No, your Majesty," in a variety of tones and expressions. I was confident I would pass muster. Her Majesty came down the long corridor, accompanied by her Equerry, and at last I heard someone saying, "Miss Cicely Courtneidge."

Now, I had been standing upright for some time, and to keep myself, or should I say to try and keep myself, from wobbling I had got very close to the wall. As my name was announced I bowed suddenly and, in doing so, caught my seat on the wall and shot forward. I tried to curtsey, but my head was almost between my knees and I all but fell into Her Majesty's lap. At last I managed to get up and grasp the Royal hand. Then came the final introduction and the Equerry should, I think, have moved straight on into the Royal Box. Instead, he seemed a trifle lost and stood there in the corridor. Suddenly, perhaps to fill the gap, the Queen turned to me and asked, "What is the name of the play I am to see?"

And here came the most awful moment of my life. I did not know what title they had given to the special matinée. I only knew what I was doing in the show and that it was in aid of King George V Pension Fund. I looked wildly at the woman standing next to me, hoping she would answer for me, but she was silent. I shifted from one foot to the other like a child who has not done her homework. I didn't blush, I went pale and could feel the blood draining from my head. And there stood Queen Mary and her most humble subject apparently refusing to answer her simple question. There was only one thing to do. In desperation I turned to Miss Unhelpful standing next to me and asked, "What is the name of the play Her Majesty is going to see?"

The reply was forthcoming and Queen Mary turned and walked into the box. And I turned and ran down the corridor telling myself I would never, never be presented to Royalty again. But I was. And so too were several members of my family, of whom perhaps Aunt Ada was the most memorable of all.

I was playing in *Folly to be Wise* at the Piccadilly Theatre and Princess Arthur of Connaught was in front. I was in my dressing-room with my Aunt Ada when a message came that Her Royal Highness was on her way round to visit me.

Aunt Ada was astounded at this news. "Oh, my good gracious!" she said. "Not in here—with me here—surely? I am far too nervous. I must go, Cis. I must go. I must. I must go at once."

I tried to reassure her. "Don't be silly," I said. "The Princess has been to see me before. She's absolutely charming. You must meet her. Sit down and keep calm and keep quiet." I tried to calm her, but Aunt Ada was so scared at the prospect of meeting Royalty she just fled. She could not fly into the outside passage because she heard the sound of footsteps, so she fled into my wardrobe and closed the door.

Princess Arthur came in and sat down and over a cup of tea we chatted and talked away merrily. All the time I was imagining my aunt either fainting, choking, or falling down flat among the clothes in the wardrobe, and as no sound came the thought crossed my mind that she was suffocating. When Her Royal Highness had gone I opened the wardrobe door and Aunt Ada emerged, a trifle bedraggled and even more agitated than before.

She kept saying, "Oh, my dear—what an experience—fancy me meeting a Princess!"

She sat down heavily on the couch, and I handed her a cup of tea, slightly stewed. Just to tease her, I said, "You are sitting on the very spot Princess Arthur sat on," and Aunt Ada squirmed with pride. Hardly, however, had the squirm subsided than there was a knock on the door and in came Her Royal Highness, saying: "I've left my hat behind. I had it in my hand."

I jumped up, but Aunt Ada was so transfixed with awe that she could not budge, not even when I presented her to the Princess. She was awed to the couch, no curtsey, no word, just open eyes and open mouth.

I skipped round the room looking for the missing hat. It was not on the chair, or on the floor, or on the table. Then I gently pushed Aunt Ada to one side as a dreadful thought occurred to me. There, under my aunt, who was a heavyweight, was the Royal hat, as flat as a plate, with creased bows and crushed roses. I picked it up, tried to push the crown back into shape, tried to prink up the ribbons, and twist the brim back to some semblance of its former line. But it was too far gone.

Princess Arthur took the hat and with a twinkle in her eye she said: "Please don't apologize. I hope we meet again soon."

At the beginning of the '30s, when Jack and I were at the Little Theatre, the Prince of Wales, the Duke of Gloucester, and the Duke of Kent came time after time to enjoy themselves at our Little Revues. The Duke of Gloucester, who had a high-pitched laugh you could not miss, found the show so funny he usually sat with a handkerchief crammed in front of his mouth to try to control his laughter, while the Duke of Kent enjoyed one of my sketches so much he could, and did, quote from it. It was a sketch about an undertaker and his wife playing whist with a publican and his wife. I played the pompous, bossy wife of the undertaker.

All the Royal Family have a wonderful sense of humour. They see us much as we see ourselves. Even my idiotic awkwardness at my first presentation to Queen Mary was passed off pleasantly by her. About a year later I met her at a Royal Garden Party and this time I made my curtsey, if not with extreme grace, at least without hitting myself on any shrub or wall. Her Majesty smiled at me and said, "Ah, Miss Courtneidge, did you make a lot of money at the Charity Matinée last year?" It seemed quite astonishing to me that a Queen should remember such a small thing in the midst of so many duties and so many worries.

I have had the honour of meeting her on many occasions, and at the opening of the Festival of Britain she called me aside and said: "You know my daughter-in-law, the Duchess of Kent, and her daughter, Princess Alexandra. I want you to meet the Duchess's sister, Countess Toerring. They have seen all your shows." Then she put out her hand and fingered my mink coat. "That's a very nice coat you have on." "It's a nice warm one, Your Majesty," I replied. Presently I said, "Won't you get tired walking all round the Exhibition?" "Look," she said, "I've got my little chair tucked away over there. I can go round in that later on."

When Queen Mary has attended my shows I have always had a few moments with her. I remember when she came to see *Her Excellency* at the Saville Theatre I was presented during an interval and I said I hoped she would enjoy the second half as much as the first. "I am quite sure I shall," she smiled. "But you talk a little fast in the play." "I'm very sorry, Your Majesty— do I?" "Oh well," she said, softly, "perhaps it isn't you, perhaps I'm getting a little old."

One of the happiest memories I have of the Royal Family happened on this occasion, and it illustrates a very human side to their nature. The manager of the theatre, Frank Sleap, was told during the performance that he was wanted on the telephone for an urgent call from Marlborough House, and with Queen Mary in the theatre attending a matinée he thought it must be very important for them to 'phone through, and indeed it was. Marlborough House wished him to convey an important message to the Queen's Equerry—the result of the 2.30, the 3 o'clock, and the 3.30 at Windsor races.

I remember a very moving conversation I had with the late

King George VI soon after he came to the throne. I went to a small reception at the Palace. There were not more than 200 guests in the drawing-rooms. Just before we arrived, Princess Margaret, then a small child, had fallen into the Palace pool. She had been pulled out and dried and changed, and was now back in the drawing-room, and, childlike, was hopping, first on one foot and then on the other, behind the King, and staring at us with childish curiosity. I was brought up to be presented to the King who, when we began to talk, noticed that my glance kept moving to the little Princess still hopping about behind him. Suddenly he asked, "Well, what do you think of her?" "I think she looks lovely," I said. "She looks healthy enough, doesn't she?" the King continued. "Why, yes, Your Majesty," I replied, "she looks fine." "Nothing wrong with her, is there?" he said. "No," I answered. His Majesty gave a wry smile and said, "Tell me, how do these rumours get about?" And I replied: "I wish I knew, Your Majesty. I only know they cause great unhappiness."

My last great Royal occasion was when I received the C.B.E. at His Majesty's hands early in 1951. I had imagined a Royal Investiture would be quite a small and intimate affair. I had forgotten that each person receiving an honour could bring two relatives or friends with them, and that to this there would also be present members of the Royal Family, the bulk of the Royal Household, and their entourage, with the result that about a thousand people were present in that great Reception Room.

The civilians were briefed in one room, those in the Services in another. I found that only three women were to be honoured, and I was to go first. The briefing was meticulous. So many steps in, so many steps out, so many steps right, so many steps left. Curtsey, three steps backwards after receiving the honour, and then out through the door. Then we were briefed about the pins. We were each given a pin rather like a double fish-hook. "Now if you lose your pin before you arrive at the dais, ask for another."

The long line at last began to move forward, everyone with their pins in place. We wound along the passages and then into the Reception Room. So many slow steps, with the band playing and the solemn audience looking on. Sharp turn right and along past a number of Court officials who were standing around His Majesty. One of them whispered, "Now, Miss Courtneidge, you're for it—it's your turn," and then a voice boomed out, "Miss Cicely Courtneidge—Commander of the British Empire." I stepped up, did my curtsey and looked up. The King was smiling. "I hear you are starting a new success," he said. "We've started, Your Majesty," I replied. "Well, congratulations and good luck to you," said the King, and pinned on the Order. Then he added, "And thank you for everything you have done."

Three steps back—golly! what long ones they seemed, but nothing, fortunately, to bump into, and then out into the corridor with a background of music where two charming gentlemen whipped off my medal, removed my fish-hook pin, and calmly put the medal into a case and handed it back to me. That wasn't quite the end of my greatest Royal occasion, however, because a few days later I was presented to His Majesty at a charity performance of *Gay's the Word*, and he asked me if I had been very nervous at the Investiture. "Terribly nervous," I told him. "I think you managed very well indeed," he assured me. Encouraged, I said, "But they took my Order away from me so quickly I could not wear it to show my family what you had given me." "I am sorry," said His Majesty, "but we wanted the pin back to use again," and he laughed happily at his joke.

A story was told afterwards of how as soon as I had received my C.B.E. from the King, I did an *entrechat* in the corridor. This is not true, although I was feeling happy enough to have done so. Happy and proud. I thought, as I trod the thick pile carpet in the Palace, of a young boy who had come from an Edinburgh cottage where there were no carpets but only an earthen floor. I thought of this boy who had had no formal education and had become a Shakespearean actor and an even greater producer of the Bard. I thought of his struggles until he became a proud West End manager. I thought of his family, of his wife who had died, of his son and daughter who had also died, and I thought of the one who was left, myself. I spoke to my father as I left the Palace, and I said: "All that training has worked out well in the end. You never thought that your Cicely would be a Commander of anything, let alone the British Empire." And then I thought to myself, Gosh! he would have been proud.

I am glad the Court officials did not notice my tears.

XX

"Gay's the Word"

★

THE most important first night of my career was that of *Gay's the Word*. Looking back over the three years which had preceded it, I had had a three weeks' run in New York, a year's tour in Australia, which although an experience did not advance me professionally, followed by *Her Excellency*, which had a comparatively short run and was not a financial success. I had then gone back to the Music Halls for a few months, but this was not a happy experience. I had been away from them for too long and I used material which had been proved in the musical-comedy theatre but was not broad enough for the halls. So I either had to make a success of *Gay's the Word* or retire to the straight theatre and challenge Vivien Leigh. I do not have to stretch my imagination very far to see myself as Cleopatra in Shaw or Shakespeare, and as for playing a cracked Southern Belle in *A Street Car Named Desire*, I think I could play it on my head—in fact, that is the way I think the part should be played. Next time I see Tennessee Williams I must discuss this with him. But I warn Dame Sybil, Dame Edith, Flora Robson, Diana Wynyard, Lynn Fontaine, and Vivien Leigh that the day I find the musical-comedy theatre is not a paying proposition they will have to reckon with me. And it is no good their taking this threat lightly on the grounds of my lack of experience in the straight theatre. I would remind them that I once played Peaseblossom in *A Midsummer Night's Dream*, and I spoke a line, and the dramatic critics said at the time that the line was spoken very well indeed and showed great promise. I knew the future of my career, built up over the years, depended on the success of *Gay's the Word*, otherwise I had to go back to Peaseblossom, that good old stand-by.

Ivor Novello was always a very busy man. In the February of 1950, for instance, he had two shows running on tour, he was appearing in his own *King's Rhapsody*, and was writing for me. He said he liked working at pressure but he was always driving himself too hard. Just before the rehearsals of *Gay's the Word* were due to begin Ivor collapsed and had to have a serious operation. Naturally we wanted to postpone until he was better, though he insisted Jack and I could manage without him. "I have absolute faith in you both to see the rehearsals through," he told me; so we carried on, keeping in touch with Ivor as much as we could.

We planned a four-months' tour of *Gay's the Word* in the Provinces before coming to London, and we opened on October 17th at the Palace Theatre, Manchester. Ivor had hoped to be present at the first night, but at last he had to say: "Look, Cis, I just can't make it. I have missed weeks of *King's Rhapsody* with my illness and the trip to Jamaica. I just can't let the public down any more. I'll come along the very first moment I dare." *Gay's the Word* was a success, and I was back on top; and you can imagine to whom I first telephoned when the curtain came down.

We finished our run in Manchester, where we broke more than one record at the box office, and went on to Coventry, and it was there that I had a message from the author that he would do his utmost to come and see the show. I told the Company at the very last minute, just before curtain up, as Ivor was not certain that he could manage to get away from *King's Rhapsody*. That night, just as the curtain rose, a tall, thin figure in dark sun-glasses slipped into the stalls. In the first interval he was recognized by members of the audience and one or two were brave enough to approach him for his autograph. "My autograph?" he said. "What for?" "You are Ivor Novello, aren't you?" said the member of the audience. "Good gracious, whatever makes you think that?" came the bland reply. "Surely Ivor Novello is in London playing in *King's Rhapsody*." Ivor was not being bashful. He loved the limelight and in the ordinary course of events went out of his way to satisfy his fans. The reason he denied his identity at Coventry was because he felt he had no right to be there, when his audience in London had paid to see him in *King's Rhapsody*.

Towards the end of the last interval, however, a girl appeared

who refused to take 'No' for an answer. She presented her
album. "Please may I have your autograph, Mr. Novello?"
Once again Ivor tried his excuse, "Surely Mr. Novello is playing
in London . . ." But this time it was not accepted. "Well, Mr.
Novello," she said, "as I am a member of the orchestra here, I'm
afraid I know you quite well. Please may I have your autograph?"
And she got it.

I took my call when the curtain came down on the final
scene and went forward for my speech. I began in the usual
way by thanking the audience for their enthusiastic reception.
Then I spoke at Ivor, sitting in the stalls, and said how wonderful
it must feel to be the author of such a success, to hear people
applaud the words you had written and the music you had
composed and to sit and watch your own creation come to life.
The applause grew to a crescendo, people began to shout:
"Author! Author!" and then I knew that it was common knowledge that Ivor was with us. So I went on with my speech.
"Somewhere," I said, pretending not to know where, "the author
is sitting in this theatre, and I hope we have not disappointed
him and he is as happy over *Gay's the Word* as we are on the
stage." At that Ivor got up and ran down the gangway and up
on to the stage and put his arm round me and kissed me. He
was beaming with delight just like a little boy who had won a
prize. Then he took off his own dark glasses and made his own
brief speech, in which of course, in his true tradition, he gave
all the praise to me and the Company and kept none for
himself.

After the show, when we had supper together, I said to Ivor,
"Were you furious with me for bringing you up on the
stage?"

He smiled happily, and said, "Darling, I should have been
furious with you if you hadn't."

Ivor only saw the show twice. He had meant to come to
every matinée, or so he had planned with Tom Arnold. I remember that subtle planning of his very well. It happened when we
were arranging our London theatre. "I've taken the Saville
Theatre," said Tom Arnold. "Matinées Wednesdays and Saturdays. Is that all right, Cis?"

"*Thursdays* and Saturdays," said Ivor, immediately.

"No. Wednesdays at the Saville," said Tom Arnold.

"Thursdays," said Ivor, firmly.

"Why Thursday?" said Tom Arnold.

"Because an author must be allowed to see his own show, and this author is working every night and Wednesday afternoon at the Palace Theatre, so that only leaves Thursday to go and see Cis."

"If that's the way you put it," said Tom Arnold, well and truly beaten, "all right then—Thursday it is."

Ivor was present at our first night when we opened in London at the Saville Theatre, and it was not only a great personal success for me but also for Ivor. His writing and music came into their full recognition at last. Beverley Baxter had this to say: "Once more Ivor Novello proves that he is immortal without being divine. No Cole Porter or Richard Rodgers or Irving Berlin can dethrone him. He has the gift of bringing happiness to the British breast through the British ear. It is time that some official recognition was shown of his achievement in keeping the British flag flying over Ruritania and giving so much pleasure to so many."

The next day we had long talks over the Press notices, which were excellent, and I remember Ivor said: "I've left it too late to get my tickets for your Thursday matinée, Cis darling. But don't worry, I'll be along on Thursday week, when I can get the seats I want all in a row." I didn't worry, for I knew Ivor would be along. He telephoned again a few days later. "I've got the seats I wanted, Cis," he said. "I'll be with you on Thursday with the usual crowd, so look out for me." That was the only promise Ivor gave which he did not keep. Those matinée tickets were never used. For, at the height of his fame and success, he died quite suddenly only a few hours after making that promise.

Some think of Ivor as the composer of great patriotic songs like 'Keep the Home Fires Burning'—others as the composer of romantic music like 'We'll Gather Lilac'. There are those who find the complete Ivor in *The Dancing Years*, while there are others who find his passion and feeling in *Glamorous Night*. But the real Ivor was more than all these things. Beverley Baxter was quite right in saying that we should have honoured him long ago for his wonderful and varied gifts. He was brilliant, quick, fantastically hard-working, kind, gentle, and he had a tremendous sense of humour.

My feelings for Ivor, through more than twenty years of close friendship, go very deep indeed. I did not love him for his brilliance as an author or composer but for all the things that women find most moving and lasting in a man—his sympathy, wisdom, gentleness, and tenderness. I am not going to talk of Ivor as though he were gone or as though he were a tragic figure in any way. Courage and laughter do not die. I am so proud and happy that Ivor really did write a play for me in the end, and I shall never forget his remark to Tom Arnold on the night he died as he was driving past the Saville Theatre: "Isn't it wonderful," he said, looking up at *Gay's the Word*. "Here is one success, and I've just come from playing in another. Two different successes running at the same time." Most of all Ivor was thrilled about Beverley Baxter's tribute to his music. When he rang me up to congratulate me on my success, I said to him, "Yes, isn't it lovely—but isn't it wonderful about you— what Beverley Baxter has said?" And he replied, "Oh, darling, I've read about these things being said so often about other people that now it has actually happened to me I can't believe it."

Ivor left no family, but a host of friends. In his will he forgave all personal debts, and apart from a small number of bequests, everything went to charity.

Not long after Ivor's funeral, Tom Arnold said to me, "I've been wondering if we couldn't do something permanent for Ivor?"

"Some memorial," I suggested, "that would remind us of his kindness to others." And we tried to imagine what Ivor himself would have liked. And then came the big idea. To buy Ivor's country house, Red Roofs, near Maidenhead, and turn it into a home for convalescent actors and actresses. It was a big house and the one in which, for more than twenty years, Ivor had written his songs and plays. It would mean buying, staffing, and supporting both house and garden, to do the thing properly as Ivor would have wished. No easy task these days. "The first thing is to think of a way to appeal to the public," said Tom. "It is no use just asking for money or beginning a fund; we must think of something individual that will touch people's hearts." "Ivor's music did that," I said. "Then I've got it," said Tom. "Ivor's shows and Ivor's music. A complete memorial show of his own work." And so it started. The idea of buying Red Roofs and turning it into the Ivor Novello Memorial Home.

How Tom Arnold worked on the project! But then, how Tom Arnold works on any project! He is one of the busiest men in show business. He stages circuses, rodeos, ice shows, pantomimes, musical comedies, plays—the lot. If you work for him, you can never be sure whether you are going to play your part on a bronco or a pair of skates. One of the few public entertainments which is not yet under his management is the Changing of the Guard, but give him time. Any moment now. He has a tremendous sense of humour, and he likes to ring me up, assuming a weird and wonderful accent over the telephone. Sometimes he is my Russian admirer calling from behind the Iron Curtain. Sometimes he is my French admirer, sometimes my Scots, sometimes my Irish, sometimes American. He is very versatile and continues to take me in. He will, so long as he continues to be my manager. Seriously, the nicest thing about Tom Arnold is the way he understands artistes. To work for him is a pleasure.

Tom formed a committee for Ivor's Memorial Home, and each one of us was given jobs to do. Jack and Robert Nesbitt to produce, famous stars to sing and appear in sketches in an All-Star Sunday Night Performance. My immediate job was to raise some money, and I did this in the same way as I had done in the war, by appealing to my audience. And to show you how generous you all are when your hearts and memories are touched, I actually collected £600 in ten days by making a short speech to the audience at the end of each performance of *Gay's the Word*, with my letters to friends which I sent all over the place I made my collection total nearly £1,200.

What a job it was behind the scenes that night at the London Coliseum! There were between 350 and 400 artistes to appear, and they all had to be brought on at exactly the right moment. Each artiste had to have not only a special pass but minute instructions as to timing his or her entrance. We rehearsed all day long on the Sunday, prior to the performance in the evening, having snacks of meals in the theatre. Many of the artistes had to come long distances from other parts of the country and the result of the show was an enormous success.

The total receipts were in the region of £17,000. But money

is still coming in, as the fund is by no means closed, and will not be closed as long as Red Roofs stays open. So it is not too late to send donations to me and address your envelopes:

> Miss Cicely Courtneidge,
> Ivor Novello Memorial Fund,
> 15 South Audley Street,
> London, W.1.

I'll repeat that:

> Miss Cicely Courtneidge,
> Ivor Novello Memorial Fund,
> 15 South Audley Street,
> London, W.1.

XXI

They Remember

★

NOEL COWARD once told me that no one should attempt to write an autobiography unless they had kept a diary, letters, and a press-cuttings book. I told him I had kept all three, and he said encouragingly, "Then all you have to do is to write," as though this was the easiest part of the job. Noel should have added to his list of sources necessary to write a book of this sort, one's friends. I admit without blushing that I have used all of mine. As soon as I began this project I wrote to them asking for their help and all of them have done so. Some of them sent me anecdotes which I have not been able to fit into any of the preceding chapters, so I am using them here on their own.

From NOEL COWARD.

"I remember I have laughed with you, on and off the stage, since we were both in our teens, but, in my experience, the joke has always been shared; I cannot remember one that was against you. So, dear Cis, here is my love to you and the memory of much laughter, the warm gaiety of a valued friendship and please believe that I would do anything in the world to please you that is in my power to do."

From SOPHIE TUCKER.

"I remember your first glimpse of me on the balcony of the Kit Kat Club. Your enthusiasm and your appreciation made it possible for me to find success in Britain. The night you joined in my song, singing, 'Soph, old top—you need a lot of new clothes', I thought you would fall out of the balcony with laughter. And I shall never forget your great faith in me when I

My only two
brother-in-laws
Peter Haddon and
Claude Hulbert

From the film
Take My Tip

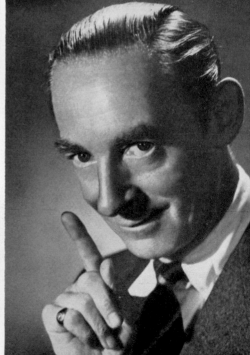

Looking ahead . . .

went into *Follow a Star* with Jack, and how you helped me to choose my costumes for the show. Such fun! I shall never forget your wonderful smile and goodness to me."

From SIR GYLES ISHAM, BART.

"I remember you in Hollywood in 1935, when I very nearly appeared in a film with you, after the usual Hollywood manner. I never thought that M.G.M. really found the vehicle worthy of your talents (I am not sure what kind of conveyance this should have been—perhaps a Rolls-Royce drawn by horses in tandem), but luckily British films supplied what Hollywood did not. I think I was the first person to greet you in Hollywood, and I think that it is rather remarkable the way the British stick together there. (Is this the cue for a song? Perhaps you can write one.)"

From JOHN MILLS.

"I remember one occasion when you were hysterically funny and didn't mean to be. You had been asked one afternoon last Summer to present some prizes at, I believe, a fête somewhere on the River Thames. You were all teed up looking as pretty as a picture, surrounded by most of the cast of *Gay's the Word*. You were on a raft which had been moored to the bank for the occasion. The raft decided suddenly to sink and you disappeared gracefully below the surface. Unfortunately, I wasn't an eye-witness of this wonderful spectacle. I came in much later in the story.

Mary and I were just finishing some cold Sunday-night mutton and salad at our home in Richmond, when the door-bell rang. We opened it to find about a dozen little Indian squaws with blankets over their heads. One of the smallest little squaws said, 'Do you think we could come in for a drink, please?' We recognized the voice (who could fail to!) and, of course, it was you. Do you remember how you all sat round and drank hot whisky and water—it had rather a lot of sugar in it!

Well, Cis dear, we rather expect you to be terribly funny on the stage now—after all, you get paid for it, don't you—but you weren't paid anything on that Sunday night at 'The Wick' and I don't think Mary and I have ever laughed so much in our lives as at your description of the prize-giving. Do please arrange

N

to fall in the river again next summer and come to supper on the way home!"

From MARIO GALLATI (the proprietor of the Caprice Restaurant).

"I remember after a first night someone remarking that you were as much a part of England as roast beef, and so long as we had you we could all afford to be merry about the short supply of butter. I also remember one day after lunch at the Ivy, as we stood with others in the entrance, a V 1 bomb came down rather too near, and we all rushed downstairs to the Gents. And I shall never forget your kindness and encouragement to me when I left the Ivy after twenty-eight years."

From ANNIE (my dresser for many years).

"I remember the smell of the greasepaint . . . the sound of you laughing and the excitement of the theatre . . . I remember you telling me that anyone who has been part of the theatre can never leave it without wanting to return. How I miss those quick changes we used to have, and all the people visiting you in your dressing-room after the show."

From LORD INVERCLYDE.

"I cannot remember any incident of general interest sufficient to print. Nor can I recall any incident unprintable. That is, perhaps, the best kind of friendship to have—don't you think?"

From GLADYS COOPER.

"I remember, three days before Ivor died, he wrote to me and said: '*Gay's the Word* is a riot, breaking every record since the Saville was built, and Cis C, is magical—wonderful Press. I am sending you two or three, but they're (for the first time) unanimous.' "

From HARTLEY POWER.

"There are a great many things I can remember like those magnificent and expensive parties I gave in Italy and North Africa when we were students together in E.N.S.A. I always tell my friends that to know Cis Courtneidge is to love her. To have her friendship is to have a gift of a treasure. The gift of her laughter, generosity, and unshakable loyalty. As an artiste of the Theatre she has no equal on the English stage. As an artiste—to work with in the theatre—I would gladly cut her throat. May I remind you that once more I am out of a job and open for invitations to parties, picnics and light entertainments."

From COLLIE KNOX.

"I have many vivid memories of Cis, but perhaps the one which most of all has forged a bond between us was the great Hulbertian Fire. The passing of time will never dim in the minds of those privileged to be present at that epoch-making occasion the sulphurous incidents of an otherwise sylvan country week-end. Whenever Cis and I meet we begin by discussing life in general, but inevitably within a matter of minutes I look at her and say, 'Do you remember?' and she replies, 'Shall I ever forget . . .' Then the famous laugh rings through the rafters, and to the accompaniment of delirious gurgles and abandoned merriment we relive our fire-fighting days. Cis and Jack owned a delightful hundred-year-old farm at Essendon, near Hatfield, to which they would invite their town-weary friends—and where Jack, clad in a rustic costume which had to be seen to be dis-believed, would farm, cultivate the soil, and develop both his muscles and the estate. It was a beautiful warm day, and I, Bobby Nesbitt, Lee Ephraim, Ivor Maclaren, Vivian Ellis and others stood, in our best Côte d'Azur attire, contemplating the peaceful scene. In front of the house stood a large pond, with water-lilies dancing thereon. Back from the pond loomed the pride and joy of both Cis and Jack, a gigantic barn of immense antiquity, full of wheelbarrows and an incredible assortment of garden implements. Cis said to me, her voice trembling with pride, 'Come and have a look at our barn.' Off she dashed. When, breathless, I had caught up with her, we stood side by side admiring the edifice. Very fine it looked in the sunlight, mellow with years, fashioned by the skill of craftsmen of another age, and solid as a rock. Cis turned towards me, and announced, "And that, my dear Collie, is—The Barn.' Upon which the said barn burst into flames. So long as I live I shall remember the expression depicted upon the features of Cis. For once at a loss, she was rooted to mother earth, her eyes nearly falling out with astonishment, her mouth wide open. And then everything happened at once. Cis returned to consciousness, and streaked up to the house to telephone for the Fire Brigade. Jack arrived at the double and sent us all flying to action stations . . . while the barn hissed and crackled. It was really rather frightening. The fire had at all costs to be stopped before it reached the house. Within three minutes the barn roof was ablaze. Shrieking defiance, I plunged into the barn, seeking to rescue some of the garden tools and the wheelbarrows so beloved by Jack. A piece of burning wood hit me on the shoulder. Ivor Maclaren followed me in, and was instantly knocked unconscious by a still larger burning beam. I dragged him out, nearly breaking my back in the process. I raced to the pond where Bobby, Vivian, Lee and Cis were standing up to their knees, filling buckets with water. We passed the filled buckets from hand to hand, and hurled the contents over the barn. Jack, entirely surrounded by hosepipe, was playing streams of water on to the blaze. Vivian is a distinguished composer, but as a fireman he is a total loss. Black with soot like the rest of us, he seized buckets of water from willing helpers, and shot them all over me. I was drenched from head to foot. Had I not neatly tripped him up, and sent him headlong into the depths of the pond, I would have drowned where I stood. Cis alternated between tears at the loss of her lovely barn and laughter at the incredible spectacle confronting her. She darted about here, there, and everywhere . . . urging us with shrill cries to greater efforts, shooting cascades of water everywhere in sight except at the barn, torn, tattered, practically coal-black from head to foot, but the life and soul of what was undoubtedly one hell of a party. We worked like avenging demons. But we could not save the barn—though we did save the house. Charred, and ruined as it was beyond recall, we gazed sadly on what had once been a barn to end all barns. We were exhausted, soaked to the skin, and extremely giddy. At that moment Cis yelled, 'Well, of all the . . .!' We turned our bloodshot eyes towards the far side of a grass verge, and beheld a figure immaculate in white flannel trousers, superb shirt, tweed jacket and snowy shoes. It leant nonchalantly on a shooting-stick. It was Peter Haddon come to have a look. Cis is devoted to her brother-in-law, but this was past all bearing. Seizing a bucket, she hurtled up to him, enquired in ringing tones, 'And what do you think you're doing?' and emptied the lot over him. I sank to the ground helpless with laughter. At that moment the local Fire Brigade arrived . . . several years late. Leaving Peter to cope with it, we trooped into the house and regarded one another. We presented a sorry spectacle. We were all too full—of water—for words. But I gasped to Cis, 'Never mind, dear. With the barn gone, you will have the most wonderful view for miles.' My prophecy was to be proved true, but only Jack's exquisite sense of duty to a guest stopped him from hitting me with an axe. . . . When I am very old, I shall fall out of my bath-chair chuckling at the happenings of that memorable day. I still consider the Hulbertian Fire would make a wonderful musical play . . . I to write it, Bobby to produce it, Vivian to write buckets of music for it, and Cis and Jack to play the leads. We would allow Peter to come on just before the final curtain. Which is exactly what he did, bless his heart.

Ah me! That was a fire indeed."

From ANTHONY HAWKE,
Chairman of the London Sessions.

"I can remember when Dar Lyon and I were sharing rooms in the Temple, and you came to tea. That was in the early 20s, and was, I think, when I first met you. But I first saw you during the holidays from Charterhouse, and you had just taken over Phyllis Dare's part in *The Arcadians*. I can see (and hear) you now in the racecourse scene, singing with Harry Welchman what was then (and possibly still is) my favourite tune, 'Oh, what very charming weather'."

From HER GRACE THE DUCHESS OF ATHOLL.

"I remember your presentation of a W.A.A.F. doing gymnastics made me laugh more than anything else I ever saw. I see it yet."

From CLAUDE HULBERT—my brother-in-law.

"Do you remember once, when you were playing on the halls, Jack and I were motoring you to the theatre on the Monday? We had a puncture and Jack had to get some man on the road to help us mend it. When he had finished, Jack did not like to tip him, as he was rather superior. As neither Jack nor I were working at the time, Jack rather diffidently asked the man 'if he would like a couple of seats for his wife's show'. The man answered, 'I'd rather have a beer if you don't mind.' When I lived with you and Jack, and always came to see your shows, my Cambridge pal, Trixie Kingdom, once said to me, 'You must be terribly proud of your family the way you always go to see them?' He says I replied. 'It isn't that. I don't have to pay to see them.' "

From CECILE COURTNEIDGE—my sister-in-law.

"I remember the first and only time, over a period of twenty years, I have ever heard you swear. It was at the beginning of the war, at the farm, the black-out restrictions had only just come into force, and you were in one of your famous sergeant-major moods! It was dark and you were marching round the buildings inspecting all the cracks and shadows and glimmers of light. The black-out precautions did *not* meet with your approval. I warned you to be careful where you were walking, but you were in no mood to listen to warnings. You fell flat into that dirty stagnant pond. You lifted yourself out, dripping with filthy green slime, saying, as you strutted up the stairs, 'Blast the bloody war!' "

From CHARLES REARDON, stage-door keeper, Palace Theatre, W.1.

"I remember you during the war in *Something in the Air*. In this show you had to sing a song called 'Home is the place where your heart is', and strangely enough as soon as you started to sing the air-raid siren would sound. Night after night it got so regular that I knew as soon as I heard the orchestra strike up for this number I must take that as my cue to black out the lights at the stage-door. While the guns were firing and the bombs dropping outside, you were on the stage singing and clowning so as not to let the audience know what was happening outside.

I remember during the run of *Full Swing* some Russian airmen (Defenders of Stalingrad) came to see the show. They occupied two boxes. After the show they came round back-stage to meet the company. No one in the company could speak Russian and none of the Russian airmen could speak English. This was rather an awkward situation, but not for long. You talked to them with your hands and your eyes and soon had our Russian allies laughing.

I remember General Montgomery visited the theatre one

night and during the interval he came back-stage to meet you. It was a wonderful sight to see this famous General bubbling over with excitement because he was going to your dressing- room.

I remember in *Under Your Hat*, Leonora Corbett had a white turban hat which she would only wear if some celebrity was in front watching the show. Whenever you saw the turban you would give a cough and say, 'There must be someone of importance in tonight, Leonora is wearing her turban.'

I remember during the song 'Home is the place where your heart is', you had some dialogue about a cat, and one night during the dialogue on walked a black cat with a pink bow round its neck. People off-stage were making all sorts of noises to get the cat off, but it wouldn't come and it strolled off in its own good time. Nobody knows where that cat came from or how it got on the stage."

From MARY MARTIN.

"I remember when you stopped the end of the world for me. It was during rehearsals of *Pacific 1860* when there arose, almost inevitably, a period of abject, unadulterated depression which made one feel it was not only the end of all my hopes and ambitions but the end of the world. I left rehearsal with my husband thinking I would never be able to eat or sleep again . . . so we decided to eat and talk. It was very late, the Grill at the Savoy was almost deserted. With heads bowed and eyes down we slipped into a remote corner table. We had been talking, almost whispering, without stopping for about half an hour when suddenly from across the room we heard the most cheerful voice calling our names. Looking up, we saw you walking towards us with a radiant smile and the most heart-warming glow seemed to be walking all around you, with you. The moment you were there, all was right and well and the world was full of fun. You chattered and chattered and made us laugh and then, as if you had a magic wand, you turned serious. What is more, as though you were a soothsayer or an awfully attractive witch, you said: 'Things aren't all that bad, you know'—and then, as though you were a part of my inner thinking and feeling, you said that watching our expressions from across the room you knew what was troubling us. And you did. No, you are not a witch, not a soothsayer, not even a lip-reader. You revealed yourself to be something much rarer that night as with patience, understanding and kindness you lifted the rehearsal problems from my shoulders. Here I saw the real Cis Courtneidge, a sensitive, astute, human being. And rarer still (unheard of in the theatre), an intelligent woman. And rarest of all, you proved that night to be a truly helpful and very dear friend."

From ARTHUR WOOD. The Musical Director and Conductor of the original production at the Shaftesbury Theatre of *The Arcadians*.

"I remember my first meeting with you on the stage of the Shaftesbury Theatre—young, charming, unaffected, and full of the joy of life. You rehearsed with me the small part of Chrysea in *The Arcadians*. Some months later your father released Phyllis Dare from her contract to join George Edwardes and you took up her part of Eileen.

How you were made to work in those days!

Lessons in riding, deportment, fencing, gymnastics, elocution, painting, singing and music. Do you remember that I came to your house twice a week to give you music lessons? I was not a very good teacher and I am afraid you did not make much progress. So I handed you over to a handsome, auburn-haired young member of my orchestra, with whom you were much more successful. His name was George Yates, and he is now one of the principal members of the London Symphony Orchestra.

I remember it was part of your father's scheme that you should study all the arts connected with the theatre and so fit yourself to become a Shakespearean actress. 'Oh, Hamlet, what a falling off was there!'

I remember the joke you played on me when you told me that I was going bald, and that from the stage the little bald patch shone brightly when the spotlight was on me. You worked up all the other artistes in the company to look at the top of my head during the performance. I spent many hours trying to find it, and you may like to know that at seventy-eight I have still got my hair.

I remember being on tour with you and Jack when you were first engaged and your father asked me to keep an eye on you, which I did, with, I hope, some success. I have often wondered whether you realized why I so often stayed at the same hotel.

I remember going to Colchester with you when you tried out your first attempt as a male impersonator. I was conducting at the Gaiety at the time, but at your father's request I got off for a week to conduct the local orchestra of six (myself at the piano)."

From DOROTHY WARD.

"Do you remember when your father would insist on you playing 'straight' in *The Light Blues*, and in a scene with Shaun (I still have a picture of this), when you are both on your knees looking for clues with a magnifying mirror, you suddenly did some business of your own and got screams of laughter from the audience—the first time I think you had ever attempted real comedy. Your father said, 'Why this strange business—you are the love interest, not the comedy woman.' And you, I also think for the first time, looked at him and smiled and said, 'Cannot I be in love and have a sense of humour too?'

Shaun and I always say this was the beginning of your career as our greatest comedienne.

Do you remember when you and Jack were first starting your romance and your father was being difficult about things and so Shaun and I asked you both to our rooms to tea? And after a hurried cup of tea Shaun and I went to the pictures, as we realized you were never left alone for a second, and we could not get a seat when we arrived at the cinema and so we had to walk around Leeds in the rain. I believe when we returned you were engaged."

From ARTHUR MACRAE.

"I remember my professional association with Cicely began in the late summer of 1938, against a background of world-shaking events. We chose to start planning the plot of what we hoped would be an entertaining musical comedy at about the same moment that Hitler was planning to spring some more of his unedifying surprises on the world, so that most of the preliminary work on *Under Your Hat* took place against a background of, 'I'm afraid I must now go to the Public Library and get my gas-mask,' or more bluntly, 'Is there or is there not going to be a war?'

Cicely and Jack were quite determined that whatever else there was going to be, there certainly was going to be a musical

comedy, and in the ensuing deep concentration that was needed
to exclude world affairs, we became great and lasting friends.

I had never before worked with two people who had such
courage, determination, and knowledge of their job, and I learned
invaluable lessons on planning for the theatre. No fault in
construction, however small, was allowed to pass. Jack would
sit and frown at it in silence. Cicely, annoyed by her inability
to pin down the fault in exact words, would walk about uttering
inarticulate noises, making gestures expressive of vast frustration,
and punching the cushions and banging the chrysanthemums
as though it were their fault that we had suddenly realized it
wouldn't suit our story if the foreign spy were a man, and that
he'd better immediately be turned into a glamorous young
girl. Alarming changes of this nature are almost a routine matter
in musical comedy construction, but they also tend to be hilarious.
Jack, whose sense of the ridiculous is just as keen as Cicely's,
but more controlled, would decide, if Cicely and I were going
to continue in gales of laughter, we had better postpone further
work until next day.

Cicely's laughter is unique; always unmalicious and infectious,
and usually uncontrollable. I remember it ringing out as, sitting
down to supper after the first night of *Under Your Hat* in Liverpool, I told her a remark I had overheard in the stalls. Jack had
taken immense time and trouble with the opening of the show.
He wanted to express the title, clearly and firmly, in ballet form,
and at the dress rehearsal it was agreed that he had been successful. The idea was completely clear. A large black velvet hat
had been constructed, and under it a girl was discovered dancing.

'How sweet,' said a lady sitting next to me, as the curtain
rose on the first night. 'How very sweet. A fairy dancing under
a mushroom.'

In 1940, a few days after we had decided to start planning
a sequel to *Under Your Hat*, the blitz on London began. Trying
to think of new and amusing situations for a musical comedy
during air-raids was a new and extraordinary experience, and I
remember feeling that if we thought of anything at all, it would
probably be something highly macabre. We did not, in fact,
produce anything very much, and the plan was shelved until
the following year, by which time I was an A.C.2 in the Royal
Air Force, fortunately posted near London. I could come up to

London on twenty-four hours' leave, confer with Jack and Cicely, then go back and volunteer continually to be Duty Clerk so that I could work at night in the Orderly Room where, muttering over a typewriter, I became an object of suspicion to the Waaf Security Officer.

On one of my trips to London to discuss some urgent point, I found Cicely alone. She gave me her views, but she felt that we must also consult Jack. He was by that time a Special Constable, and out on duty, but Cicely said she was sure I would find him directing the traffic in Bond Street, at the Grafton Street crossing. I protested that I could not possibly go there and start a discussion, but I had forgotten that with Cicely absolutely nothing is impossible where the preparation of a new show is concerned, and I was told not to be silly and to go to Bond Street immediately. I went there, and there was Jack. I crossed to the middle of Bond Street, we greeted one another, and while he continued to deal with buses and cars, I told him of my difficulties. From subsequent conversations, I know we both felt that no fantasy we might invent would be half as odd as my standing in the middle of the Bond Street traffic, dressed as an A.C.2, discussing the possible plot of a new musical comedy with Jack Hulbert dressed as a policeman.

After *Full Swing*, the show in question, I worked with Jack and Cicely on *Something in the Air*, and finally wrote *Under the Counter* for Cicely alone. We had done four shows together, and with each show my respect and affection for Cicely had grown. Over and over again she played scenes which I had thought fairly strong and amusing on paper, and she made them not only a hundred times stronger and more amusing, but added a warmth which is entirely her own, and which springs from her infinitely kind and generous heart.

She has made hundreds of thousands of people laugh, cry, and forget their troubles. One lady coming out of *Under the Counter* summed it up by saying to another, 'I feel as if I'd had a wonderful *treatment*.' I doubt if Cicely has ever given, unconsciously, a more unusual treatment than the one I was told about some time ago by a lady to whom I had been introduced at a party. 'So you wrote *Under the Counter*,' she said. 'I owe you an enormous debt of gratitude.'

I began to murmur, but she cut me short. 'Oh, but I really

couldn't be more grateful. You see, my son was expelled from his Public School.'

She stopped, and gave me a radiant smile.

'Was he?' I said. As she seemed so happy about it, I added, 'What for?'

She told me.

'Fancy,' I said.

'Yes,' she went on, 'and of course he arrived home simply dreadfully depressed. This first afternoon was *ghastly*. I simply didn't know what to do with him, and then I suddenly had a brain-wave. 'I know,' I said to myself. 'I'll take him to see *Under the Counter*, and dear Miss Courtneidge will cheer him up.'

'And did she?' I asked.

'Oh yes,' she said. 'He came out a different boy.' Which, after what she had told me of him, seemed to be a good thing.

From S. C. Dorrill, M.B.E., New Theatre, Oxford.

"I remember you coming to Oxford, soon after you started in Music Hall, in June 1918. You were a single turn on the bill and you were terribly nervous. I was not, because of the reports I had had of your début in Colchester. Your performance that week in Oxford confirmed that you had done the right thing changing from romantic leads to comedy. Recently, when you came to Oxford with *Gay's the Word*, I thought how much I would have missed, and tens of thousands of others too, if you had gone on playing romantic leads."

From Phyllis Monkman.

"I remember during the rehearsals of *Seesaw* at the Comedy Theatre, when Jack and I had just started to work together for the first time and Arthur Weigal had written an excellent sketch for me, but we were not satisfied with the ending. However, in those days you and Jack had a flat in Great Portland Street and I used to come back in between rehearsals and have food with you both. We were all nearly going mad trying so desperately hard to think of something to finish that particular sketch with, when you came into the dining-room with a jelly, far from set, and you suddenly cried out, 'I've got it!' Up went the jelly all over the place, but you gave me one of the most successful tags to a sketch I've ever had. If you want the details I can give them to you but I think it is a pity to spill the beans in case we should ever want to use the sketch again."

From HANNEN SWAFFER.

"I remember the row with Elsie Janis's mother because I said you acted her daughter off the stage in *Clowns in Clover*. 'To think that I brought my little girl thousands of miles,' she said, 'to be crucified by that man!'

Then there is our enjoyable holiday on the Lido, where Jack took a movie of you and me acting together on the sands, and Cliff Whitley's disgraceful conduct in teaching our gondolier wicked words to shout over the lagoon waters in the darkness.

A third thing is my vivid memory of your frankness over the way they used to book you when you first started, believing you only had the job because you were your father's daughter. I would like to prompt your memory, although I cannot help you much in this regard, about your father's activities in Manchester, and to tell you a few things about Alfred Lester.

You will now understand, after reading these few lines, that memories are jogged by somebody else. Most autobiographies would have been improved if friends had been consulted more. They have a way of reminding you of things that otherwise you would forget.

"There is one thing about you I would like to say—that you are the best audience I have ever known. A guy has only to say, 'It's a fine day,' in your presence, for you to burst out in appreciative merriment. If all the people in an audience were like you, plays would run for ever."

From MRS. PAT STONE.

"Do you remember one of our Continental holidays, one when we toured Italy by car? At that time Jack's hobby was *Marble*, and he had arranged that each time we stopped anywhere it would be near a quarry. When you found this out you were furious, especially as the car became more and more ladened with specimens of marble, until we began to look like a travelling Stonehenge. One day I noticed that villagers were staring at us extra hard as we drove by, and then suddenly I saw that you had been quietly dropping the specimens overboard, leaving a trail of marble for miles. Next day Jack changed his hobby.

Do you remember our cruise to Egypt? We set up a new record. We were both seasick before we left harbour. On our return we went to San Sebastian to see a bull-fight—our first. The seats cost us a fortune, but we were very bright and gay when we arrived, and extremely enthusiastic over the parade. Then the fight started and we began to feel a little sick. In those days the horses were not padded very well, and after five minutes we decided to get up and go. When we stood up the people around shouted at us to sit down but we went on pushing our way along. Then a very big man looked up at you and muttered, 'You something foreigners.' You drew yourself up to your full height and in that sergeant-major voice of yours said: 'Foreigner! Me, a foreigner! I'll have you know I'm British and proud of it!' And with that you swept out of the arena."

From VAL PARNELL, Managing Director of Moss Empires Ltd.

"I can remind you that you have played the London Palladium five times:

Two weeks commencing 20th May, 1929.
One week   ,,   29th September, 1930
Two weeks   ,,   7th December, 1931.
Four weeks   ,,   2nd May, 1932.
Two weeks   ,,   6th June, 1938.

NOTE.—It is about time I had a return date. Val."

From YVONNE ARNAUD.

"I remember that I was extremely touched when you wanted to have me among your friends in your book because I have never stopped admiring your integrity as an artiste and your tremendous vitality. Although I have not had the privilege to be in a play with you I remember that we have met at the hairdresser for many years because by some happy coincidence we have always managed to arrange our appointment on the same day and at the same hour. We always exchange affectionate greetings and as we are both such busy people, always in such a frightful hurry, we immediately plunge into writing our letters, reading a play, or, from time to time, try to carry on brief snatches of conversation when under the dryer. But as it is quite impossible to hear one's self speak, let alone hear what anyone has to say, these conversations have never been really successful and are always reduced to a sign language of our own making. However, when we emerge from 'under the furnace' we are ourselves again and we enjoy our little jokes, exchange affectionate greetings and another little kiss, and go our different ways. So you see, darling, I know we have a real affection for each other because we should both feel so lost if, by some unhappy coincidence, we did not manage to arrange our appointment at the hairdresser on the same day and at the same hour."

From RONALD JEANS, *Author of* Young Wives' Tales.

"I remember I wrote most of the sketches for the first Hulbert and Courtneidge revues and I sometimes wonder that I am alive to tell the tale. You were the most rewarding artistes that I have ever written for, but you were also the hardest taskmasters. Cis expected in others the same dynamic energy she brought to everything she did, just as producer Jack expected the thoroughness, which at times could be maddening, that he brought to the work of producing. When on tour, 'getting the show right' for London, I would be expected to sit up with the bosses until three or four every morning, discussing alterations: and I found that the only way to be able to get myself up at eight o'clock to work on the book was to go to sleep during these discussions. As far as I know I never missed anything of vital importance.

They were wonderful, happy, if harassing days. One had to be young to stand them. Eventually I gave up the crazy kind of existence of revue for the more ordered life of the 'legit', and in doing so I lost the stimulation of a great personality and a great friend—but at least I can go to bed when I want to."

From PETER RUSSELL.

"I remember a whirlwind of gaiety and friendliness unlimited swirls into my atelier, causing the very chairs and tables to dance and shiver with glee—and the staircase to bend in a curtsy as this immortal star ascends to try on 1, 2, 3, 4, 5, 6, or more dresses after a morning's rehearsal."

From HERBERT WILCOX.

"I remember when Anna and I were listening to a broadcast coming from the Albert Hall. It was a big moment in British history—the disbanding of the Home Guard. Suddenly we felt as if Cis had joined us and for our special benefit was paying her tribute to the Home Guard. It was an incredibly moving experience and I am sure that most of those who heard it will, like Anna and me, never forget it.

I remember the opening night of *Gay's the Word* at the Saville Theatre.

Ivor had returned from Jamaica and although his face was sun-tanned, it was quite evident that he was a sick man. He sat in his box and acknowledged the cheers of the audience with his usual charming self-effacing manner and pointed towards the stage and blew a kiss to Cis, who, at the first interval, had worked—or perhaps I should say overworked—the audience into a frenzy of enthusiasm whilst she sang and danced the hit number of the show, 'Vitality'. When she came out to take a call, a chair was slipped behind the tabs for her to sit on and she sat down in a way that indicated she had given all she had to give and loved every minute of it.

The producer of a new American musical turned to me and said, 'How often does she do that?' I told him eight times a week. 'They can't do that to her. They can't do it,' was all he could mutter. He was too astonished even to applaud."

From THE REVEREND ARTHUR BUXTON, late Rector of All Souls Church, Langham Place, W.1.

"I remember my first visit to you in a flat in Great Portland Street when you and Jack and Rosaline discussed the details of her wedding that I was to take at my church, All Souls, Langham Place. A year later, after Rosaline's birth, she died after a gallant fight and I took the funeral at Marylebone Cemetery. Then I conducted the christening of little Rosaline. You later offered to give something to All Souls in Rosaline's memory and my Council suggested a specially designed cover to the font with an inscription round it.

A year or two later you made another offer in her memory. I said, 'You have already given your memorial to Ros', and I well remember your reply. 'Yes. But I want to keep her memory green.' I have never known a second memorial given as you did for Rosaline. This was a very beautiful floor to the Baptistery in All Souls.

One cannot go through times of sadness as well as gladness together as we did with Rosaline without welding a friendship that goes much deeper than ordinary friendships.

I remember Jack was a sidesman at All Souls and my congregation were always on the look-out for you both in your usual place in the North gallery. I am afraid that some attended in the hope that you would be there. The collection was then a time of special interest for they would get a good near-view of Jack attending to his sidesman's duties. On one occasion they got more than they hoped. (I must explain that the sidesmen, after presenting their collections, lined the altar rail until I had put the collection plates on the altar. They then returned to their seats.) At this service, Jack duly presented his plate and took his place in the line of sidesmen along the rail. While he waited the picture, a notable feature of All Souls, over the altar caught his eye. The other sidesmen turned about and left, and Jack, still meditating on the picture, was left alone. There were many there who watched with intense interest to see what would happen.

Suddenly he came back to reality and to his sidesman's duties. He stopped examining the picture, looked right—there was no one there—looked left—not a sidesman there. He was alone. He turned about, and with complete composure and to the huge delight of the congregation walked alone and slowly down the whole length of the church.

Next a memory of a Christmas Day service at All Souls. In my sermon I asked for a bumper collection to provide funds for treats and presents for our Day School and Sunday School children. There was one little girl in a very poor home who had long hoped in vain for a bicycle. With the help of some friends I had bought a bicycle which was concealed behind the pulpit and I also made sure that the child was in church. After the sermon I told the congregation what was afoot and then called her to fetch the bicycle. This she did, and with her face aglow with delight wheeled it down the aisle. I give this story as a preface to what happened after the service, as it may well have influenced you with your ever-generous nature. I was in the vestry when I had a message. 'Will you please see Miss Courtneidge? She is in her car waiting for you.' She was indeed. You had been deeply moved by my appeal. 'Arthur,' you said, 'I want to give you something to add to the collection for the children.' You got out your cheque-book and wrote out a cheque then and there, and gave it to me. It was for £100. I tried to express what I felt, but I am afraid it was pretty feeble, and I expressed my thanks with tears of gratitude rather than words. Further comment is needless. Generosity like that speaks for itself. I wish there were more like it.

When I left All Souls the congregation made me a presentation of a very beautiful canteen of silver. You, Cicely, came to the Langham Hotel to present it. You were looking wonderful and were the life and soul of the party. I was feeling very sad but you quickly altered that."

From LEE EPHRAIM.

"I remember the only time I have ever seen you in a real temper, and it happened at the Savoy Hotel. I had asked you to be there for supper after the show to meet Lee Schubert so that we could arrange for *Under the Counter* to go to America. Just as Lee Schubert was coming over to your table Glynis Johns engaged him in conversation. At first you waited patiently, but as the conversation showed no signs of ending the impatient tapping of your foot became faster and faster, until finally you got up, your eyes narrowed with anger, and you said, 'I refuse to be kept waiting any longer.' And with that you walked out."

From MY DAUGHTER PAM.

"Do you remember, after you had received your C.B.E. at Buckingham Palace, Nannie Kennedy addressed your letter Miss Cicely Courtneidge, *O.B.E.*, and when you corrected her the next letter was addressed, Miss Cicely Courtneidge, *C.B.F.*"

From STEINER, my hairdresser.

"Do you remember when your hair turned green? It was after one of your provincial tours and you were opening in London that night, and when the Hulberts open in London— London stops. There was the usual motley of people around you, all intent upon their various endeavours, your dress, your shoes, your hats, your secretary, and the last-minute check to see what you had forgotten. The same lotions were applied as ever, but there was no doubt at all—it was green. Not even mildly green, but the green that is loved by all nature enthusiasts.

Through manicurists, pedicurists, hairdressers, fitters, and secretary, you somehow managed to catch a glimpse of it through the mirrors, and a stony silence descended upon the scene. I shall never forget your expression. It was as if you had seen the Ghost Train again.

Do you remember my composure? My air of reassurance? As if this was an everyday occurrence? Well, now I can tell you I was terrified, and in the second or so that silence ensued I worked out my plans as follows:

1. Whether I could reverse the reaction and cause the green to disappear. (But this would be a miracle.)
2. Whether I had a suitable wig for you.
3. Whether I could introduce it as my new season's colour and get away with it.
4. Whether I could hastily depart from this planet.

Whilst these thoughts were occurring, the silence was replaced by the general activity that my composure created. You set about giving your instructions with artificial confidence, while I did some considerable mental chemical research to determine the cause. I suppose that fate smiled upon me (or was it you?) and I theorized that a certain compound had been applied to your hair whilst you were on tour and it had reacted with disaster with the lotion I had used. A snip of your hair and a quick test proved that I was right. A miracle had happened and the green disappeared. To this day you have never mentioned the incident, but I have never forgotten it, and I confess that several months were removed from my life's span in those few minutes."

From NAOMI JACOB, the well-known novelist.

"I can remember you in *Princess Caprice*, and with all due respect to your father there could never have been a worse piece of casting. I saw you doing a male impersonation at— and here I may be wrong—Chatham Empire, in Air Force uniform, and even then you hadn't 'found yourself'. I didn't know you personally at that time, of course. You were still to me the elder daughter of 'The White Man of the Theatre', and I used to think what a lucky person you were.

Then in the war when I was doing Public Relations Officer

for E.N.S.A. you came out to Italy. I thought, 'More stars, more trouble, more grumbles about accommodation, about food, about every single thing,' and it just didn't happen that way at all. I have quoted this fact again and again, that the bigger and brighter the star, the fewer the grumbles and grouses. I remember how unaffectedly pleased you were because I, having been brought up with a proper respect and admiration for leading ladies, sent you flowers for your first night in Rome.

You were in my mind the perfect trouper, there to do a job and to do it just as well as it could be done. Friendly, kind, ready to smile and do everything without demanding a fanfare of trumpets to herald your arrival at the hotel—not a particularly good one either if memory serves me right—or at the theatre. Unlike Miss ——, no names no pack drill, who is a star in her own mind but never in her own 'right', who in Naples sent for me, just like that—sent for me. 'I hear,' she said, 'that you have a typewriter. Is that so?' Much in the same tone that she might have said, 'I hear that you have the Crown Jewels hidden in your baggage, is that so?' I admitted that I had and she asked if I could type. I replied that I could. 'Then I don't suppose you have much to do. You might come up for an hour every morning and help me with my mail.' I recovered from the shock, then in my best and most offensive manner told her exactly—or nearly exactly—what I thought of her and quoted *you* as what a 'star' was actually like, and how they behaved. She was very angry and when she saw my C.O. told him that I was the most unobliging person she had ever met. 'I asked her to give me a little help over a small personal matter and all she did was to talk about CICELY COURTNEIDGE. Why, she's not even a straight actress.'

So there you have it—you're not even a straight actress. I told my C.O. that the lady in question wasn't an actress at all.' "

From JOHN ROBBINS, the house-man at 15 South Audley Street.
"Madame, I remember how I lost your pound note. One morning in answer to the house telephone I came into your bedroom. You were already late for an appointment and busying yourself with endless bits of paper as you gave me instructions for the day. Your feathered hat wobbled precariously as, still talking urgently, you arranged letters for Miss Cole, notes about

an engagement, an ear-ring to be sent to Aspreys for repair, an odd piece of paper with notes for the maid, telegrams, bills, receipts, and endless other things. You continued sorting your papers as you talked without stopping, and from time to time you emphasized the importance of your instructions by tearing up a whole pile of papers and throwing the lot into the waste-paper basket. During this time the telephone rang twice and you merrily carried on two important conversations whilst you again gave me further instructions. Then, with one eye on the clock you carefully arranged your notes, telegrams, and other papers into little piles on the bed. A pound note you carefully put beside your handbag, all ready for your taxi when you left the house. The hall clock chimed and suddenly you looked at your bedroom clock. 'Is that the time?' you questioned, and without waiting for my reply you answered your question and said: 'It can't be. Get me a taxi quickly.'

I ran downstairs to find a taxi and hadn't been gone two minutes before I heard a shout: 'John! John!' I hurried back to the bedroom where all the assembled letters and notes were feverishly being sorted through again. 'I've lost a pound note,' you said. 'See if you can find it.' A moment's pause and you said, 'No, never mind. I haven't time. Have you any small change?' I gave you what small change I had and you went off in a flurry.

The bedroom was hoovered and tidied but I could not find the missing pound note. Because the waste-paper basket had been emptied by this time it occurred to me to look in the dust-bin. Fortunately the debris from the bedroom was on top of the bin and I searched through it all most carefully when, lo and behold, there was the pound note. Obviously, in a moment of fluster you had thrown it into the basket with the other papers. I rang you at the theatre during the matinée. 'I've found the pound note,' I said triumphantly. 'Oh! John, you are a good fellow,' came the reply. You were delighted. 'Where did you find it?' 'In the dustbin,' I replied. 'The dustbin!' you exclaimed. '*The Dustbin!* Oh! John, how very stupid of you. Fancy doing a thing like that. Never mind, John. It's found. That's the important thing. Good-bye.' And you rang off without another word.

That, Madame, is how I lost your pound note."

From ROBERTSON HARE.

"I remember I have never had the pleasure or the privilege of working with you. OH! CALAMITY."

From SYBIL THORNDIKE.

"I remember a whirlwind. I always say: 'Hurrah! Hurrah!' after I've come away from being with you. The other day my son went to see you to ask you a few technical questions about the production of musicals and not a question did he ask for you gave him a whirlwind talk on theatre, plays, musicals and life. He came away feeling the whole world was a musical and he had only got to look at life and humans and appreciate them, and do his best to show to the public what an entertaining lovable place the world was. For that is what you have done—made something lovable, exciting, and deeply enjoyable for us all. So here's to the whirlwind and her creations."

From SIR MICHAEL BALCON.

"I remember your good trouperishness. But why is this always considered a compliment? This is the moment for me to confess that your good-trouperishness over the years we made films together drove me to distraction. Albert de Courville, directing you in a comedy tennis sequence, decided that a close shot of a tennis ball striking you sharply on the face would achieve the desired effect. I found you on the set meekly submitting to this treatment. Heaven knows what you would look like today, had I not stepped in and called it game and set. On another film I saw you being brutally man-handled in an adagio act. Like a knight in white armour I came to rescue what I thought was a damsel in distress. 'You can't do this to her,' I protested violently to Tim Whelan, the director. 'Why not?' he said, unperturbed. 'She worked out the routine herself.' It was ever thus. There is nothing, bless your heart, literally nothing, you will not do to make us happy."

From SIR LAURENCE OLIVIER.

"I remember we called each other 'Darling' (and meant it) at first meeting, and ever since we have waved. We have had an evening or so in Australia (God help us), and whenever we do meet I feel you are my oldest friend and I am yours. (I say, I do hope this feeling is mutual), and it isn't as if it didn't feel that we knew each other inside out, it's just that too little time has been spent in company to make any history. Oh dear, I do hope you will understand and not think me horribly unco-operative and waxenly unhelpful. I adore you, darling, and know you intimately, so there. For God's sake let us fill in the rest of the things expected of friends from now on. Up to now our relationship has been uniquely beautiful, but sternly uninitiated, and at this moment, quite disastrously unproductive."

From Vivien Leigh.

"I remember that some of the happiest times I have ever had in the theatre have been spent watching you and I have thought your vitality an inspiration to the whole profession, and although I am afraid this may not be of much help for your autobiography, it is lovely to have a chance to tell you what one really feels about you."

From Clemence Dane.

"I have, except in reading, a stupid sort of memory, almost entirely visual, so that I can remember little bright pictures of scenes and people but seldom anything conversational or continuous. If I had to tell you a straight tale of our friendship, I just couldn't. All I can jot down is impressions. I have an impression, no more, that for about twenty years we looked at each other across the floor of the Ivy, and that you never wore the same hat twice. (It was always a wicked nonsensical mad hat that suited you perfectly.) And that at the end of twenty years we got as far as 'winking' at each other, and that one day you (and I) decided that it was time we talked, and that somehow we were rather suddenly sitting together at somebody else's table. Does that match up with your recollections? And wasn't the hat you were wearing on that day composed entirely of real red roses?"

From Peter Haddon, my brother-in-law.

"I remember in 1919 when we met for the first time in your dressing-room at Finsbury Park Empire you made me feel I was the one man in England you wanted to meet. The next time we met you called me John.

I remember a visit you paid to Cambridge, a May week ball, a Footlight show, your interest, your enthusiasm, your encouragement and your laugh.

I remember when I told you I was going to marry Rosaline and you said, 'I'll fix Father.'

I remember when I was in hospital and the nurse said, 'Don't make him laugh, Miss Courtneidge, otherwise he will have to go back to the operating theatre.' I went back to the operating theatre.

I remember, during an economy drive, when you rang up from Glasgow and complained bitterly on the telephone for twelve minutes about an extra tin of peas which appeared on the weekly household account. Cost of peas 1s. 6½d., cost of telephone complaint 16s.

I remember I flew to Paris because you had lost your luggage and I came back to tell you it was there.

I remember playing tennis and golf with you and how you never hit a ball, and taking you to Lord's where you never watched a ball.

I remember when I was broke and you lent me a quid and I bought you a bunch of violets for sixpence and you were more pleased than with anything I have ever given you.

I remember you have enjoyed more, felt more, suffered more, than a great many of your fellow creatures.

I remember how your heart has ached and the tears have rushed to your eyes at some touching picture or some unhappy story.

I remember how the breath of a warm, sunny day, the scent of flowers, the purple on the distant hills, the freshness of the waves breaking on the shore has filled you with a love of life.

Most of all, I remember you are in love with life."

XXII

Conclusion

★

AT THE moment of writing *Gay's the Word* is still going strong and every night when the final curtain comes down it is a bitter sweet moment. It is sweet because for a few hours, against a background of colour, music, and laughter, we on the stage have brought some happiness into the lives of people in the audience. It is bitter because the time has come for parting, and the lights will go out, and all of us who have been joined together in a common experience of escape to happiness have to go on our own separate ways.

There is a finality about a curtain coming down even when you know it is going up again on the following night. Each performance has a flavour and a subtle difference of its own. One night the curtain will come down for the last time on *Gay's the Word*, and on part of my life. That has been true of every show in which I have appeared. But I have never become used to something I love ending, and I know I never will. That is true of this book. I have been very happy writing it, meeting so many old friends; and although there have been times when I have wished I had never begun, I am sorry now that the time has come to say good-bye.

I began this book in my dressing-room at the Saville Theatre, looking at the photographs which prompted my memory. At the inadequate jottings in my diary, and at letters and press-cuttings. All these reminders have taken me back through my life, to my childhood, to my family, to old friends, old triumphs and some failures. My! How the world has changed since I began.

Gone are the proud days of Empire, but gone also are the squalor and poverty which lurked in the shadows of the Victorian

era when I was born. There have been so many changes during
the past five decades that I wonder if anything has remained the
same. Is there one thing in the new Elizabethan age—an age just
starting with a young Queen—an age whose life is threatened,
as well as nurtured, by the advances of science—is there anything
which remains the same? Yes, I think there is.

I have been a comedienne long enough to know that your
laughter is the same. Outwardly, you may laugh at different
jokes now than you did then. But basically your humour is
unchanged and certainly the quality of your laughter. The laughter
of the British people is kindly and warm and never so loud as
when laughing at itself. But that is not all that remains unchanged.
The British people are the most loyal public in the world. That
sense of loyalty is the finest thread in the pattern of our lives.
So there are two things which I have found constant through
the years. Laughter and Loyalty.

I would not be a comedienne in any other country for all
the tea in China. Of course I might change my mind, but not for
at least another fifty years, and, oh, before I say good-bye, I
should tell you that Jack was on the telephone to me this morning
and he has an idea for our new show. It is a wonderful idea and I
would tell you all about it but there is not time. They have
called 'Overture and Beginners, please,' and I cannot be late
for curtain up.

P.S. I have just thought that the final chapter of a book is
not so final after all. You can always start at the beginning and
read all the way through again.

Index

Unless another town is mentioned all the theatres refer to London.